"In an age of increased digital and virtual possibilities, Cockayne and Salter offer a powerful argument for why physically gathering together to worship remains essential for churches. A uniquely rich and deep interweaving of theology and psychology, *Why We Gather* is interdisciplinary work at its very finest."

—**JOANNA LEIDENHAG**, *Associate Professor of Theology and Philosophy, University of Leeds*

"I have eagerly anticipated the arrival of *Why We Gather*, in which a theologian/pastor and psychologist working in tandem offer outstanding and friendly critique of popular ritual and liturgy scholarship. Their employment of the psychology of 'joint attention' appears to me a better lens through which to assess what liturgies can actually do. With lucid writing and a pastor's deference to the biblical literature, they draw us away from the individual into the helpful details of why corporate worship works humanely. Highest recommendations!"

—**DRU JOHNSON**, *Templeton Senior Research Fellow & Director of the Abrahamic Theistic Origins Project, Wycliff Hall, University of Oxford*

"In *Why We Gather*, a theologian and an empirical psychologist explore the nature and significance of the fact that, in liturgical enactments, the participants act jointly and have a sense of doing so. What is novel and distinctive about their exploration is that they do not write separate chapters, each from their own professional standpoint and expertise, but that the entire book is a dialogue in which the two disciplines complement and inform each other. Emerging from this dialogue is a probing, multi-faceted, deeply informed way of understanding what they call 'liturgical jointness.'"

—**NICHOLAS WOLTERSTORFF**, *Noah Porter Professor Emeritus of Philosophical Theology, Yale University*

"Emerging from an interdisciplinary collaboration between psychology and theology, this book offers an original exploration of joint attention and the communal actualization of memory in liturgical practice. It illuminates the social and formative power of worship, bridging academic research and church life while broadening the scope of liturgical studies."

—**HWARANG MOON**, *Professor of Worship, Korea Theological Seminary*

JOSHUA COCKAYNE
GIDEON SALTER

WHY WE GATHER

PSYCHOLOGY, THEOLOGY, AND LITURGICAL PRACTICE

BAYLOR UNIVERSITY PRESS

© 2025 by Baylor University Press
Waco, Texas 76798

All Rights Reserved. No part of this publication may be reproduced, stored in a retrieval system, or transmitted, in any form or by any means, electronic, mechanical, photocopying, recording, or otherwise, without the prior permission in writing of Baylor University Press.

Cover and book design by Elyxandra Encarnación
Cover image: Luis Quintero/Pexels

The Library of Congress has cataloged this book under ISBN 978-1-4813-2291-1.
Library of Congress Control Number: 2024055254

CONTENTS

ACKNOWLEDGMENTS

Those who are familiar with the geography of the University of St Andrews in Scotland will know that within St Mary's College, either side of a four-hundred-year-old oak tree, lie two university departments: the School of Divinity and the School of Psychology and Neuroscience. This project has its origins in the crossing across the St Mary's quad, meeting in the middle, and asking what we might learn from one another. After (quite literally) crossing over the quad, a seemingly innocuous cup of coffee shared by a theologian and a psychologist led to half a decade of collaboration, discussion, and friendship, which has culminated in the writing of this book.

It seems right, given the origins of the project, to begin by acknowledging those departments which made such collaboration possible. The Logos Institute in the School of Divinity fostered an environment of deep interdisciplinary engagement and constructive dialogue with those who think differently, using different methodology and terminology. Without the leadership of Alan Torrance, Andrew Torrance, and Oliver Crisp, this project would not have been possible. Likewise, the School of Psychology and Neuroscience was and is a department in which interdisciplinary thinking is valued. A particular thank-you goes to Malinda Carpenter for supporting Gideon to pursue this collaboration alongside his doctoral research.

This collaboration which has led to the writing of this book started first as a handful of research papers and eventually led to a number of research grant projects, which provided resources to explore new areas of interest. First, through the TheoPsych program (hosted initially at Fuller Seminary, Pasadena, and lately with Blueprint 1543) and through the encouragement of Justin Barrett and Rebecca Dorsey, we were able to explore new areas of dialogue between theology and the psychological sciences. We received grant funding to run a short project on liturgy and infancy, including a one-day workshop at the University of St Andrews on this theme, as well as writing retreats to create space for further collaboration. Chapter 1 and chapter 6 of this book emerged from our conversations around infancy and liturgy, and we are grateful to the Blueprint 1543 team for making this possible.

Second, the Gratitude to God Project hosted at Biola University and headed up by Bob Emmons and Peter Hill provided opportunities to learn more about the world of positive psychology, as well as providing funding to host a workshop on liturgical gratitude in St Andrews. Two research papers were published as a result of this funding, and these are developed further in chapter 4 of this book. Thanks especially to Phil Watkins and Jo-Ann Tsang for their helpful feedback on draft material, and to other members of the GTG cohort for their input on psychological and theological perspectives on gratitude.

Third, the New Insights in Theological Anthropology Project (NViTA) at the University of St Andrews, led by John Perry, provided a further context to explore new areas of research. In particular, the grant funding made possible a number of workshops and external consultants to give feedback on early draft material of the book. Thank you to those who gathered in St Andrews while the book was in its very early stages: Andrew Torrance, Roger Bretherton, Liz Gulliford, Jason Stigall, and Joanna Leidenhag. These comments allowed us to develop a set of unrelated ideas into a coherent book. Thanks also to the external consultants who provided invaluable feedback on later versions of the book: Malinda Carpenter, Adam Green, Dru Johnson, Emily Burdett, and Eve Ridgeway.

There have been a number of supportive colleagues and friends who have provided input (both formal and informal) while we were finishing the project. Special thanks are due to the group of MA students at the University of York who devoted a whole term to studying a draft manuscript of the book and providing feedback under the leadership of David Worsley. Thanks to Ryan Winterbottom, Genevieve Mynott, Allen Zhang, Joseph Forrester, Heather Perfect, Imad Khan, and Daoyuan Zhang.

Our thanks go to our current and former institutions: Cranmer Hall, St John's College, University of Durham, the Department of Psychology at the University of Sheffield, and the Department of Psychology at the University of York. They have allowed for space and encouragement to explore an area of research that lies outside of our central responsibilities in each institution. We are grateful for their ongoing support.

To those church communities which have provided (often unbeknown to them) contexts to think through the ideas of this book and to see the practical implications of this research, we are thankful. It is a testament to the support and friendship we have found in these places of worship that we are able to write a project like this.

Finally, to our families, who have provided unending support and love. Thank you.

Josh: Eleanor, Judah, Emmeline, and Zac.

Gideon: Becky, Ava, and Eli.

INTRODUCTION
Why Do We Gather?

THE SIGNIFICANCE OF GATHERING

Gathering with other people matters.[1] If there were previously any doubts about this, then the events of the COVID-19 pandemic demonstrated that our engagement with other people (or the lack of such engagement) radically shapes how we relate to the world. For nearly two years, we were forced to redefine what it meant to gather. Visits to loved ones were strictly virtual, Friday-night drinks were mediated through laptop screens, and corporate worship featured a tapestry of faces wrangling cameras into their most flattering position. For many, the novelty of gathering online quickly wore thin, and with time the restrictions on gathering took a huge toll on our mental health.[2] In experiencing its lack, we came to see the importance of in-person gathering in a new light. Recognizing the importance of gathering also brought with it many questions: What does it mean to gather? When is an experience shared, and when is it something that we are doing on our own? These are questions we grappled with throughout the pandemic as we confronted the difference between virtual and in-person interaction.

But in many respects these questions are not new. Understanding the nature and limits of shared experience has long been of interest to psychologists and philosophers. A large body of research in developmental psychology has explored the role of social interaction and shared experience in human development, highlighting the capacity for *joint attention* that emerges during infants' first year of life. Joint attention is the ability to attend to some feature of the world with another person, with the awareness that this attention is shared. This ability is not only of profound importance during early development but continues to play a key role in human social life across the lifespan.

In this book, we focus on gathering in the context of Christian worship. Whether reciting words of formal liturgy, participating in extemporary prayer, or simply sitting in silence with others, we are being asked to attend to something with someone. This is the basis of all liturgy. This emphasis on the shared nature of worship is an important part of the Christian tradition.[3] For example, we are told that the early church "devoted themselves to the apostles' teaching and the fellowship, to the breaking of bread and the prayers" (Acts 2:42).[4] This sharedness is crucial for worship; the author of the Epistle to the Hebrews insists on the importance of "not neglecting to meet together, as is the habit of some, but encouraging one another, and all the more as you see the Day approaching" (Heb 10:25).

In an age in which digital and online modes of worship are increasingly common, questions about the nature and purpose of in-person gathering are all the more significant. Many church leaders are forced to ask why people would come to their services if the preaching and music are inferior to the thousands of podcasts and live stream worship events available online. This book seeks to provide an account of what it means to think of worship as shared. We do so in dialogue, with insights from theology and psychological science. In seeking to explore the nature of gathered worship from a psychological and theological perspective, we seek to show why gathering is so important and to highlight what is lacking from virtual acts of worship.

One obvious answer to the question of what is lacking is: our bodies! There are many works exploring this theme from different perspectives, particularly exploring the role of embodiment in the liturgical act of gathering together.[5] As W. David O. Taylor writes in his excellent book *A Body of Praise*, "Our physical bodies powerfully shape our experience of the world around us. Our bodies are not a bonus, and they are never neutral. They are a gift."[6] Relatedly, another answer might be: our relationships! As Warren Brown and Brad Strawn describe in their work on the extended cognition of worship, "Christian faith and life exist primarily (but not exclusively) within a network of relationships that serve to enhance the Christian life by extending us beyond what we are capable of as independent, private, solo individuals."[7] These two focuses—embodiment and relationality—provide a helpful starting point for thinking about the shared nature of Christian worship. This book takes much of this prior work for granted and draws on the importance of embodiment and relationality at various points. But it provides a different focus from these two themes. In focusing on the mechanisms of how our world is shared with others, particularly the role of jointly attending to the world, it seeks to ask the psychological question of how liturgy might allow participants to share the act of worship, and the theological question of why this is important for the life of faith.

Who is the target audience of this book? The aim of this book is primarily theoretical (i.e., to offer a conceptual account of what it means to think of liturgy as shared). In this sense, it is intended to be a scholarly book that will contribute to the ongoing discussion of worship in theology and psychology. But one intended implication of this theoretical and scholarly focus is to encourage those leading acts of gathered public worship to reflect more deeply on the nature of the practice, thereby understanding how vital it is *not to give up meeting together*, as the author of Hebrews is keen to stress. And so, it is best thought of as a scholarly work with important practical implications.

THE MOVE TO SPECIFICITY IN "SCIENCE AND RELIGION"

Before we outline the main claims made in the book, it will be helpful to pause to consider our method. We think that novel insights on the nature of gathering for liturgy can be gained from a constructive dialogue between theology and psychological science. But what does a dialogue between theology and psychology look like, and why is it helpful? In the remainder of this introduction, we aim to address these questions before outlining how this book will go about drawing upon the resources of theology and psychology to address questions of liturgy, community, and the significance of gathering together.

Much work in the field of "Science and Religion" has been concerned with addressing the big-picture question of the relation between these domains. Various options have been suggested and critiqued—that science and religion are in conflict, that they are separate, that they can be integrated, or that they ought to be put in dialogue.[8] Much ink has been spilled in seeking to mediate this conflict, and adherents on both sides remain entrenched in their views. But in recent discussions of science and religion, a more radical approach has emerged that has questioned the taxonomy and challenged traditional conceptualizations of the relation between these domains.

The key challenge, put forward forcefully by historians of science such as Peter Harrison,[9] is that these grand questions reify science and religion, treating them as coherent historical entities that have essential features. In other words, they assume that it is possible to give singular definitions of both science and religion that can be applied consistently to all domains of science or forms of religion, both as they are currently practiced and throughout history. Against this view, arguments have been made that highlight that both *science* and *religion* are complex, multifaceted terms that cover a wide range of practices, views, and methods.[10] This critique applies to the various domains of the sciences, and the psychological sciences[11]—understood as the scientific study of human thought and behavior[12]—are no exception.

Compared to many other domains of scientific study, psychological science is a young field. There is no "mature science" of the mind and behavior (human or otherwise);[13] that is, there is no agreed-upon set of theoretical frameworks, methods, and findings that are the hallmarks of a mature field of scientific study. Furthermore, because psychological science is an immature field, it is one that is rapidly growing and changing, with the often rapid shifting of consensus making engagement with it a challenging task.[14]

Seeking to avoid the problems that arise with reified notions of science and religion, a recent strategy in discussions has been to move toward increased *specificity* or *particularity*. Rather than seeking to resolve issues of methodological tension from a top-down perspective, this approach takes a ground-up approach, characterized by a focus on particular subdisciplines of both theological and scientific inquiry, and on specific, constrained questions. Andrew Davison describes this movement as a shift towards "thinking *with* science" rather than "thinking *about* science."[15] A clear expression of this approach is that of science-engaged theology. John Perry and Joanna Leidenhag, leading proponents of science-engaged theology, highlight that theologians often make claims with implicit assumptions that are "already entangled with scientific theories and findings."[16] The goal of science-engaged theology is to address narrowly focused theological questions that are, thus, entangled, which Perry and Leidenhag label "theological puzzles." In doing so, the focus moves away from "grand methodological questions" of "science and religion" that risk continuing to reify these categories.[17] In a similar vein, Alister McGrath argues for a move "towards a plurality of cultural and domain-specific methodologies and rationalities"[18] in order to reject a monolithic view of science and religion.

This approach has also been endorsed by psychologists interested in the relation between theology and psychology. Malcolm Jeeves and Thomas Ludwig, in their discussion of different ways of understanding the relation between Christian theology and psychology, favor a "perspectivalist" position, which they characterize as

> focusing less on attempts to build a complete, integrated system of "psychology-theology" or "Christian psychology" and more on looking for points of contact between the two disciplines that can provide mutual insights and enrichments from these different perspectives.[19]

Both the resistance to building a "complete, integrated system" and the notion of "points of contact" align well with the domain-specific approach advocated by those engaging in *bottom-up* dialogue between science and religion.

Also addressing this issue from the perspective of a psychologist, Justin Barrett, in his recent psychological science primer for theologians, encourages a focus on "specific problems"[20] for which psychological science offers helpful tools. Barrett's use of the word "tools" is part of an extended metaphor that presents the theologian's task as the construction of a building—a task that requires a range of tools and varieties of expertise that are highly specialized, from plumbers to stonemasons. As Barrett highlights, theologians are no strangers to drawing upon, for example, particular facets of history, philosophy, and linguistics. He suggests that, in a similar vein, psychological science (and the "human sciences" more broadly) can provide specific tools that serve theological "construction projects." Barrett also emphasizes a practical benefit of this approach: it renders the task of engaging with the sciences more tractable for the nonexpert by constraining the range of theories, methods, and findings with which one attempts to engage.

It is worth stressing that if there are to be genuinely *mutual* insights and enrichments,[21] it is necessary that the engagement across disciplines is genuinely dialogical—not, for example, requiring theology to submit to the expertise of psychology. Take the example of *actualization*, which we discuss in chapter 5. Theologians have been keen to emphasize that remembrance in the Judeo-Christian tradition is not merely a case of recalling facts about the past but requires somehow participating in the life of the past, feeling the emotions of the past, and allowing the past to shape the present. This theological notion of actualization helps to frame how we understand what is happening psychologically when one participates in rites of remembrance. Theological discussions of remembrance can thus promote novel applications of philosophical and psychological concepts, ones that would be unlikely without the "view from within" that theological reflections provide.

OUR STRATEGY

The approach taken in this book is aligned with the broader trend of domain-specific engagement that seeks to offer a ground-up dialogue between theology and the psychological sciences. Throughout the book, we will be drawing upon specific areas of theology and psychology, depending on the questions under consideration.

There are primary subdisciplines that provide a focus to our discussion of liturgical gathering. On the theological side, we seek to contribute to the "liturgical turn"[22] in recent philosophical theology. This turn is characterized by an emphasis on the practices of worshiping communities rather than a focus on doctrine or belief. Work on the philosophical theology of liturgy is an emerging and important area of study. The liturgical turn has generated work on liturgical action, liturgical epistemology, ethics, sacramental metaphysics, and more.[23] It is important to qualify here that by "liturgy," we do not mean to talk only of traditional worship with formal scripts (although we will discuss such cases); any religious community that gathers to enact rituals and actions together is liturgical. Every religious tradition, no matter how "traditional," can only act together by agreeing on prescribed expectations about how to act (e.g., standing up to sing, and to listen if someone is talking from the front). In other words, all religious traditions have liturgies. This book seeks to contribute to the liturgical turn in philosophical theology and to advance the conversation in new directions by drawing insights from the psychological sciences.

On the psychological side, this book draws heavily from research on joint attention, which we will define as the ability to attend to some feature of the world with another person, with the awareness that this attention is shared.[24] The concept was first used in the context of caregiver-infant interactions, highlighting the capacity of infants to share experiences of the world with their caregivers by following their gaze.[25] The concept was subsequently elaborated, with later psychological research examining the ways in which infants and caregivers coordinate attention through facial expressions, vocalizations, gestures, and eventually words.[26] More recently, psychologists and philosophers have together examined the conceptual issues that arise when attempting to understand and define joint attention.[27]

As the significance of joint attention to human social development has become more widely recognized, it has started to play a role in discussions beyond infant-caregiver interactions. Recent work has drawn upon the concept in discussions of humans' distinctive social and cultural capacities.[28] Others have sought to expand and extend the concept, highlighting the complex, multifaceted nature of humans' capacity for shared experiences, from participating in direct social interactions, to being sensitive to minimal cues that others are attending with oneself.[29] Indeed, a key theoretical issue is how to make sense of the "jointness" of joint attention,[30] with recent work arguing that shared experiences lie on a scale of jointness (i.e., from minimally joint to truly joint).[31] These expansions and diversifications of the concept of joint attention, and the attendant notion of jointness, provide a valuable set of resources for understanding the shared nature of liturgical practices.

These subdisciplines of theology and psychology serve as a potentially fertile point of contact for interdisciplinary engagement. It has been highlighted that the practices and behaviors of religious communities have often been neglected in discussions of "Science and Religion."[32] It has also been suggested that the effects of texts, rituals, and practices on participants are an area in which psychological research is well positioned to contribute.[33] This book therefore comes at a timely point in the trajectories of three domains of inquiry: an increasing emphasis on rituals, liturgies, and practices in theological discussions; growing exploration of the role of joint attention in human social activity; and the need for further consideration of the role of the practices and behaviors of religious communities in interdisciplinary discussions of theology and psychology. This is not to say that other areas of psychology might not have important contributions to this conversation (such as the focus on embodiment of relationality, as discussed above) but that this book seeks to offer a focused approach to the topic rather than offering a general theological psychology (psychological theology) of liturgy.

However, it is also important to highlight that the particularized nature of our collaboration goes beyond engagement between specific subdisciplines. Our work has arisen as a dialogue not solely between abstract ideas but also between two persons, with all the unique interests, history, and expertise that this entails. One of us (Cockayne) is a philosophical theologian and Anglican priest with an interest in Christian spirituality, worship, and ecclesiology. The other (Salter) is a developmental psychologist with an interest in joint attention, communication, and language in infancy and early childhood, using empirical methods to investigate these topics. The collaboration arose while we were engaged in postdoctoral (Cockayne) and doctoral (Salter) research at the University of St Andrews and has continued through moves in and out of full-time ministry, as well as a number of institutional moves.

We highlight these details because to completely abstract away from this particularity would present a view of the process of engagement far neater than the practical reality of trying to develop ideas in collaboration. Thus, as much as the approach taken in this book is aligned with the aforementioned arguments for the value of a domain-specific approach and is influenced by various projects that exemplify this approach, this book primarily emerged out of an extended dialogue between two particular people, rather than attempting to be the application of a framework. We thus cannot label this book as straightforwardly or consistently psychology-engaged theology, theology-engaged psychology, or psychology of religion: it combines elements of each, but ought to be viewed as the working-out of a particular theologian and a particular psychologist exploring a set of questions in a constructive and imaginative manner.[34]

Indeed, this introduction began with a set of questions, and it is this focus on questions that best characterizes our approach. In doing so, we can seek to avoid getting overly bogged down in issues about the precise interdisciplinary framework we have adopted and get our hands dirty with the practical challenge of engaging our respective subdisciplines of theology and psychology. McGrath, reflecting on the possibility of mutual understanding between scholars in the sciences and humanities, makes the following argument:

> The best answer, in my view, lies in recognizing the need for epistemological pluralism to engage our complex world, and then having to confront the somewhat troubling challenge of weaving the multiple outcomes of such methods together in a coherent whole.[35]

This book is our attempt to confront this challenge. The process of weaving together two areas of investigation takes seriously the possibility of genuinely mutual enrichment. The issues we explore have been chosen because we think they are issues that matter, and because we think that drawing upon theology and psychology will help us respond to them, or at least make some progress towards doing so. It is our hope that our exploration of these questions might be a source of enrichment for theologians and psychologists alike and may offer directions for future theological and psychological inquiry.

Before summarizing the argument of the book, it will be important to first define some key concepts. Throughout this book, we use the terms *practice*, *ritual*, and *liturgy*. There is no uncontentious way to use these terms, particularly when attempting interdisciplinary engagement. We opt to use them, broadly following their usage in the psychological sciences, as increasingly specific terms capturing related concepts. "Practices" are any kind of repeated, defined sequences of bodily activity,[36] while "rituals" are practices as used in symbolic, culturally meaningful ways that are at least partly noninstrumental; either the ritual has no apparent practical effect, or it is not clear how the ritual achieves its stated aim.[37] Rituals are also conducted with the goal of generating various cognitive and affective responses in participants.[38] Finally, we use "liturgy" to refer to the format of specifically religious rituals, with liturgies in the Christian tradition being the primary focus.[39] However, the work with which we engage will not always use these terms in the same manner, and thus we will try to be clear on the sense in which each term is used.

THE ARGUMENT IN BRIEF

Before proceeding it will help to see the contours of the argument developed in this book. In a nutshell, the account offered seeks to emphasize the importance of joint attention in the practices of liturgy. Our central thesis is that a fundamental feature of liturgical practices is that they allow participants to share attention with other people, and thereby create rich and varied experiences of jointness with others.

We begin in chapter 1 by considering the underlying anthropology behind our account of liturgy. Certain claims about what kind of creatures human beings are and how they are formed underlie much of what we go on to say about the nature of liturgical practices. While we are primarily concerned with liturgical practices within religious worship, we agree with the philosopher James K. A. Smith in maintaining that our practices and habits are fundamental to our being human. The practices in which individuals participate each day radically shape the kinds of people they are. We contrast two approaches to thinking about ritual formation. The first approach (which we dub the "brains-on-sticks" model) thinks that cognition is primary to human beings and that ritual seeks to shape the beliefs of its participants. As a number of scholars have highlighted, the brains-on-sticks approach to ritual formation fails to see that human beings are embodied creatures who are more often shaped by their desires than their beliefs. Contrastingly, the "hearts-on-legs" model, exemplified by Smith (and others), seeks to emphasize the primary role of affect in ritual formation. For instance, practices of consumerism (such as the worship of the shopping mall, or the endless scroll through Amazon) instill certain desires that aim at a goal that someone else has prescribed for us. For the proponent of this model, it is not that a person believes a new espresso machine will bring fulfillment but that consumerist practices have shaped our desires to be aimed at a certain way of life; they want to be the kind of person who pulls exceptional espresso shots each morning.

While we agree with many of the critiques of the brains-on-sticks approach to liturgical formation, we wish to nuance the sharp divide between affect and cognition that is implied by this work. As work in developmental psychology shows, these two ways of relating to the world are interconnected from the earliest stages of development. In other words, from a psychological perspective, it is problematic to think of either desire or belief as the primary mode of relating to the world. Instead, we offer a holistic view of liturgical formation that focuses instead on the social role of liturgies. Put simply, liturgies are formative because they create shared experiences that simultaneously form both beliefs and desires.

Building on this anthropology, in chapter 2 we give an account of what it means for liturgical practices to be shared. We argue that liturgical practices allow participants to jointly attend to a common object with a group of individuals. Like many other social gatherings—watching football matches, attending the theater, listening to piano recitals—liturgy involves a gathered group attending together to objects or events. Where liturgical practices differ is in the object of attention. While it might be tempting to think that the object of attention in liturgy is the liturgical script (the hymns, the prayer, the readings), instead we argue that the theological motive of liturgy is to create experiences of joint attention to the presence of God, and in some sense *with* God. We then go on to consider the limits of this jointness in liturgical practices—for the sense of jointness that is gained from gathering appears to extend beyond cases of embodied copresence. "Gathering" for worship online seems to be one such case, and we might also think about the ways in which those who are housebound or otherwise unable to attend worship can share in the practices of liturgy. Drawing upon a range of theological sources, we highlight that for the Christian, liturgy is shared because it is embedded within the community of the mystical body of Christ—the Church. And thus, we need an account of jointness that can explain how these different levels might be enabled through liturgical participation. Drawing on psychological work on joint attention and the concept of "shared situations," we offer an account of jointness that comes in degrees—from acts of embodied copresence in which participants jointly attend to a liturgical script, to the broad sense of communal identity that derives from a sense of belonging to the Church.

In expanding this thesis, we seek to show how it can help shape our understanding of some key liturgical practices, namely prayer, gratitude, and the Eucharist. In each of these chapters, we consider a different benefit of engaging in practices of attention. First, in chapter 3 we explore the nature of communal petitionary prayer and the notion that communal petitionary prayer has a greater "efficacy" than individual prayer. Using our account of jointness, we explore the diverse ways in which practices of petitionary prayer enable joint attention with others. In doing so, communal petitionary prayer results in an increased sense of social bonding, common knowledge, and mutual commitment that motivates and enables the community to address the targets of its petitionary prayers. However, we also stress that communal prayer differs from other collective acts that may have similar benefits, because the experience of prayer is one of joint attention with God, not just with others. Understanding this theological dimension is key for understanding prayer as a communal practice. Focusing on the specific case of confession, we will also explore the ways in which prayers of confession allow for a vulnerability and openness and help to show the ways in which joint attention, by itself, might not always lead to a greater depth of community.

Second, in chapter 4 we explore the importance of gratitude for liturgical practices. Many of the hymns and songs of the Christian tradition provide an opportunity to thank God for who he is and for his good gifts. There is an extensive literature in psychological sciences on gratitude, yet, we argue, this literature pays insufficient attention to the shared nature of gratitude. Applying our account of jointness to gratitude, we show the ways in which gratitude might be an action performed by a community. The benefit of thinking of gratitude practices in this way, we argue, is that liturgy allows participants to carry the voices of those who cannot be grateful (because of their suffering or their doubt, for example) to be part of a united voice praising God in gratitude. Moreover, this allows us to explore the significance of sharing emotions and attitudes in the context of liturgy.

Third, in chapter 5 we argue that practices of remembrance—specifically the Eucharist and the Jewish Seder meal—are practices which extend this sense of jointness to the past. Drawing on psychological work on "mental time travel," we show that practices of remembrance allow for a kind of *actualization* in which individuals can experience events of the past in a way that unites the community throughout history. The benefit of applying the concept of joint attention to the issue of remembrance lies in its ability to provide perspective and unity across disparate traditions and cultures.

Finally, in chapter 6 we consider the limits of jointness, asking: Who do these practices of joint attention include, and who do they exclude? What role might children and young infants play in a community that gathers to shape and direct one another's attention? To answer these questions, we consider the role of baptism in marking the boundaries of liturgical communities. We argue that baptism serves as an explicit marker of who is included in the life of the community and who is not. However, while baptism may tell us something important about the boundaries of a community, it is not the only relevant factor. Many churches baptize children yet continue to exclude children from their liturgical practices. We outline existing work on the place of children in the liturgical life of the Church and the importance of engaging in play and imagination for liturgy. However, we argue that these approaches stop short of being fully inclusive—they do not make space for the very young or those with the most severe cognitive impairments. Instead, the approach we defend is pluralistic; there is more than one way to participate in joint experiences.

1

THE FORMATIONAL POWER OF LITURGY

RITUAL, LITURGY, AND ANTHROPOLOGY

Human beings are ritual creatures.[1] Looking back through human history, across the diverse societies found around the world, we see humans engaging in conventionalized forms of behavior that structure our social world and play a foundational role in our systems of meaning. From different expressions of dance and movement (such as the Maasai Adumu dance or the Maori Haka) that strongly shape the perceptions of a culture and people group over time, to the more mundane rituals that structure individual daily lives—what we eat for breakfast, when we exercise, or how we prepare for sleep—these rituals shape our attention, making people, objects, and events more salient in our daily experiences. Our development is influenced by ritual participation, enabling each person to connect with and learn from others in our social groups, as well as to identify who might be trustworthy.[2]

The importance of ritual for understanding human nature has not gone unnoticed by theologians or psychologists.[3] Much theological work has been devoted to showing the importance of the embodied, social, and ritual nature of the religious life. Rituals, and liturgies more specifically (by which we mean rituals of a religious nature), play a crucial role in the development of the self. It has long been recognized that patterns of ritual and liturgy shape religious ideas and worldviews, captured well by the oft-quoted idiom "lex orandi, lex credendi" (the law of prayer is the law of belief). Recent work has attempted to ground this important formational aspect of liturgy in our understanding of anthropology. Rituals shape human beings in ways that are social and embodied because human beings are social, embodied creatures. Thus, there are clearly points of contact between the psychological sciences and the topics of theological anthropology. Yet, we think that the discussion stands to benefit from a more in-depth dialogue between aspects of these two disciplines. For, as we show, presuppositions made by some theological approaches to ritual oversimplify, and sometimes contradict, the insights found in psychological sciences.

In this chapter, we offer a vision of liturgical anthropology which can hold the complexity of psychological and theological insights on ritual formation. As we show, focusing on the role of joint attention is central to this account. First, we begin by outlining some recent approaches to liturgical anthropology in order to properly locate our own account within the broader discussion.

BRAINS ON STICKS OR HEARTS ON LEGS?

Recent theological discussions of liturgy and anthropology have sometimes been premised on a set of related psychological questions: What is the primary mode of engaging with liturgy: cognitive or affective? What role does the body play in formation? And how do cognition, affect, and bodily movement interact? Put simply: Are human beings *brains on sticks*? Or *hearts on legs*?

The brains-on-sticks model of liturgical formation thinks that one's understanding of liturgy must start by focusing on its cognitive role. For surely liturgies teach participants to believe something; in the Christian tradition, the hymns and said liturgies are filled with propositional content. What is communicated, and how, is of crucial importance for those involved in leading and writing liturgies. For instance, in a recent book exploring the role of liturgy in forming communities of those who work, Matthew Kaemingk and Corey Willson reflect that

> poorly worded songs, prayers, and sermons can all divide a worker's life into a series of compartments and competitions: church versus world, private versus public, spiritual versus material, faith versus work. Congregations will never develop vocationally conversant worship until they take a hard and honest look at the ways in which their existing forms of worship actively inhibit and obstruct conversations between workers and their God.[4]

To be clear, Kaemingk and Willson are not defending a brains-on-sticks approach to liturgical formation here. But what they show is the importance of attending to what is communicated and how this shapes the beliefs of those who participate, for liturgies clearly shape how and what communities believe. Taken to its extreme, this observation about the importance of belief formation can make the formation of cognition the central role of liturgy. Consider contexts in which the sermon is the center of the liturgical life of the church; for forty-five minutes a week, congregation members are given a set of ideas or beliefs to reflect on and discuss together. The goal is that these ideas shape and form the rest of their lives. It is these ideas exposited from the scriptures that form the basis of the rest of formation—in being convinced by a compelling sermon about generosity, for example, one comes to believe that giving money to the Church is important, and one's change in behavior naturally follows after.

The brains-on-sticks approach to liturgical formation is limited in many ways, not least because (as its name suggests), it has little to say about the role of the body in liturgy. As Warren S. Brown and Brad D. Strawn observe,

> in the predominant modern view of spirituality, neither one's physical body, nor other persons, nor church communities, are relevant. Spirituality is both disembodied (that is, manifest in the inner state of the soul, which we experience as emotions and feelings) and disembedded (an entirely individual state not directly relevant to any other person). Spirituality is an inner reality—one that is only distantly related to ourselves as physical/social beings, or to the nature of our relationships with other people or communities.[5]

According to Brown and Strawn, this view of spirituality as disembodied and atomistic is neither psychologically nor theologically adequate. This has important implications for thinking about the liturgical life of the Church; if human beings are fundamentally social, bodily creatures (and not merely souls *with* bodies), then worship is not about reaching a disembodied state of divine consciousness.[6] Rather, liturgy involves engagement with emotions and bodies. Liturgy might involve the use of the body in physical gestures (such as making the sign of the cross or raising one's hand in musical worship), it might involve the physical acts of listening and speaking (such as in the hearing of a sermon or the reading of the Creed), and it may also involve the bodily engagement with emotions, as well as with ideas and beliefs. As W. David O. Taylor describes, it is not just that bodies provide a means of engaging liturgically; rather, "our physical bodies powerfully shape our experience of the world around us. Our bodies are not a bonus, and they are never neutral. They are a gift."[7] For Taylor, and Brown and Strawn, liturgy forms those who engage with it through the body, because human beings are fundamentally bodily creatures. In other words, their understanding of what role liturgy plays in formation is bound up in questions about the kind of creatures human beings are.

This focus on the relationship between embodiment and the formational work of liturgy is explored at length by James K. A. Smith. As Smith summarizes his position,

> the way we inhabit the world is not primarily as thinkers, or even believers, but as more affective, embodied creatures who make our way in the world more by feeling our way around it. . . . One might say that in our everyday, mundane being-in-the-world, we don't lead with our head, so to speak; we lead out with our heart and our hands.[8]

For Smith, one of the results of emphasizing the bodily nature of human beings is the centering of affect in our understanding of formation. And this focus on the body leads us to see another inadequacy with a brains-on-sticks model, namely that a focus only on cognitive formation fails to capture the affective dimension of how liturgy shapes us. This alternative model, which emphasizes the body and the emotions, we call the hearts-on-legs model of liturgical formation.

In contrast to what he takes to be a dominant view in Western philosophy and theology, Smith argues that human beings are not fundamentally thinkers but lovers. Human desires, he thinks, are shaped by the practices one participates in, whether that be one's shopping habits or the liturgies of religious worship. Hence, Smith thinks, human beings are *Homo liturgicus*: creatures shaped by desire-oriented practices, which aim to inculcate competing visions of the good life. The problem, Smith argues, is not that cognition is unimportant, but that views which emphasize cognition over and above emotion or affect "are focused on only a slice of being human and so tend to be blind to other, more significant factors that constitute human identity. Instead, they take the slice to be the whole and thus absolutize just one aspect of the human person."[9]

This desire-oriented account is supposed to emphasize the importance of intentionality in all ritualized behavior. This is not to suggest that human beings always consciously intend an aim of some sort; rather, Smith has in mind a kind of "noncognitive and prereflective" intentionality.[10] What this amounts to, it would appear, is a kind of teleological claim: human action is always directed towards some good or goods. The implications of this account are far-reaching. Indeed, Smith thinks that his model provides an account of what a human being *is*, namely "a lover—a creature whose orientation and form of life is most primordially shaped by what one loves as ultimate, which constitutes an affective, gut-like orientation to the world that is prior to reflection and even eludes conceptual articulation."[11]

The telos of human desire is, unsurprisingly, something which is decided not intellectually through conscious reflection but through "rituals, routines, and exercises . . . [which] train your adaptive unconscious."[12] If human beings are primarily desire-oriented, ritual creatures—*Homo liturgicus*—then religious practices must reflect this.[13] Liturgy that aims only at changing the mind, but which does not engage the body or the unconscious—for instance, through ritualized movement and repetition—will not engage the fundamental part of the person but only the cognitive slice of that person. Those engaged in Christian formation must wrestle with the fact that Christian liturgy competes for a person's telos with the liturgies of culture, whether they be goals of nationalism, capitalism, or any other ideology. Thus, we should pay attention to not just *what* people say they worship but *how* they worship. The clothes they wear, the buildings they worship in, the bodily gestures involved in liturgy—these all influence how one's desires are shaped.

BRAINS OR HEARTS? COMPLICATING THE PICTURE

We have seen two approaches to thinking about liturgical formation that prioritize the cognitive and the affective aspects of anthropology. Given that we attempt to present a psychological and theological account, it seems pertinent to ask what the relationship is between cognition and affect.

One answer to this question, exemplified by the hearts-on-legs model, is to claim that affect is fundamental to human beings. Smith repeatedly claims that affective processes are more fundamental to human functioning than cognitive processes, which have a secondary role. But given the repeated insistence that this model is "non-reductive," it is difficult to establish what the precise relationship is between human cognition, affect, and ritual on Smith's account. Instead, we are offered suggestive language—his model "shifts the center of gravity of human identity away from a fixation on thinking, ideas, and doctrines and locates it lower, a[s] it were, in the region of our affective, nonconscious operations."[14] Such claims, while evocative, are hard to unravel from a psychological perspective, even though psychologically loaded terminology (e.g., "nonconscious") is employed. What seems clear—especially given Smith's claims about the fundamentality of desire rather than cognition—is that the account thinks of human beings as necessarily (or fundamentally) affective creatures, and cognition merely provides an input to this affective, noncognitive core of a human person.

Proponents of the hearts-on-legs model wish to make an anthropological claim about what is fundamental to the identity of human beings; all knowledge, desire, and motivation are rooted in an affective core. It is not that cognition drops out entirely but that it must be grounded in affect, or else we end up with the Cartesian "thinking I" at the center of anthropology. Consider an example to help show why. In a revealing passage, Smith considers how engaging with liturgy alongside young children and the cognitively differently abled might tell us about the way it shapes human beings:

> As I've been articulating this, I have had two special cases in my mind: children and mentally challenged adults. Both have limited capacities for grasping theological concepts or the sorts of theoretical formulations that characterize even worldview-talk. Their ability to process the sorts of abstractions that characterize even beliefs is limited, either temporarily (in the case of children) or chronically (in the case of the mentally handicapped). Does that mean that they cannot achieve fullness in Christ? Do the limits of their cognitive abilities impair the hope of their "growing up" into Christ (Eph. 4:15)? Does their inability to traffic in concepts preclude them from being educated? Not according to the anthropology I have sketched above; rather, because we are more fundamentally creatures of love and desire than knowledge.[15]

An appeal to those with different cognitive capacities is supposed to show that we cannot be content with a brains-on-sticks model and we must move toward a model that sees the role of affect and embodiment at the center of anthropology. But why suppose that the relationship between cognition and affect operates as such? As we argue shortly, it is not so easy to simplify the relationship between cognition and affect from a psychological perspective such that we can neatly point to the operations of these parts of the human person.[16] In other words, neither brains nor hearts are primary in our understanding of liturgical anthropology. Indeed, as we look at how cognition and affect develop in early infancy, we will present a mutually reinforcing relationship rather than one taking priority over the other. We do not need to think that affect is fundamental or primary in order to show that liturgy forms its participants in ways that do not involve learning facts and doctrines. As we will go on to show, human cognition is shaped implicitly and subconsciously through ritual participation, just as affect is. Even in the very early days of infancy, cognitive development is occurring. And so, a simplistic picture in which liturgy is said to shape its participants only, or primarily, as creatures of desire will not suffice.

Perhaps, it will be argued, we are merely splitting hairs, and that Smith is using "noncognitive" in a loose and nonscientific sense. While it is true that there may be good reasons to oversimplify psychological frameworks to enforce a conclusion, the effects of this oversimplification downstream, so to speak, are significant. If liturgical practices are seen to be primarily desire-shaping and only ever secondarily belief-shaping, then Smith's account of liturgical anthropology is potentially as problematic as the position he critiques. In the final two sections, we will show that a holistic approach is needed to explain the formative effects of liturgy. It is important to see here that while Smith is *not* offering a psychologically informed account of anthropology, he is using psychologically charged vocabulary such as "affect" and "cognition." And so, a nuanced discussion about liturgy and formation cannot proceed without consideration of the psychological literature.[17]

DEVELOPMENT AND PSYCHOLOGICAL HOLISM

Moving beyond the false dichotomy presented by the brains-on-sticks versus hearts-on-legs approaches to liturgical formation, let us provide a more detailed account of a holistic picture of liturgical formation. The right starting point for thinking about liturgical anthropology from a psychological perspective, we think, is to examine the critical role of *development* in the process of ritual learning. Looking at the development of cognition and affect in infancy can help shed light on how ritual participation shapes the way one thinks and feels in adulthood. We explore three insights that can help provide what we call a "psychologically holistic" account of liturgy and formation, which we summarize in the next section.

First, developmental psychology underscores the unity of affect, cognition, and action in human experience; while each can be contemplated in abstraction from the other, in lived experience they are always aspects of an interdependent whole.[18] The question of which aspect is primary or fundamental is not a well-formed question from a psychological perspective. Second, a developmental perspective highlights the need for a nuanced approach to "cognition," which recognizes that cognition involves processes that are implicit (nonpropositional) as well as explicit (propositional).[19] Finally, we argue that an appreciation of development provides insight into the developmental and evolutionary origins of explicit cognition. It has been widely argued, even from divergent theoretical perspectives, that explicit cognitive processes find their origin in social engagement.[20] And thus, we have a helpful paradigm for thinking about how liturgical practices shape minds (i.e., cognitively and affectively, implicitly and explicitly), the contexts and situations in which this development takes place (i.e., in social interaction and shared practices), and indeed the central place of development in providing an understanding of human psychology and behavior. In what follows, we unpack these insights in more detail.

THE UNITY OF COGNITION, AFFECT, AND ACTION

The first issue we address is the relation between cognition and affect. These terms are notoriously difficult to define and are used inconsistently in the psychology literature.[21] However, for our purposes, it suffices to use a broad definition to allow us to highlight the salient issues we are aiming to address.[22] Cognition is classically defined as those processes used by an agent to organize incoming information and to use this information to plan and direct behavior.[23] We are employing cognitive resources when we compare multiple streams of incoming information, suppress unneeded information, switch between tasks, and draw upon previously stored information.[24] For example, to cook a meal, one may need to remember the recipe, plan in what order to prepare the ingredients, and track the temperature of the pan while chopping the onions, all while ignoring the phone ringing. Behavior controlled by cognitive processes is considered intelligent in that it involves planned and coordinated action as opposed to reflexive, automatic responses.[25]

In defining affect, we follow a broadly constructionist approach in treating affect (or "core affect"),[26] as the feelings arising in the body that are consistently present to us. They can be felt more or less strongly, and more or less positively. When one tries to understand or communicate about specific episodes involving these feelings, they conceptualize them in the form of emotions.[27] For example, if one has a conversation, our inner affective state will constantly fluctuate, remaining low-level and slightly positive as one engages in small talk, being experienced as strongly negative as someone says something rude. These fluctuations may need to be conceptualized in order to be articulated, leading one to interpret these feelings as "I am *angry* she said that" or "I am *worried* by that statement."[28]

It has been argued that cognition and affect only make sense in relation to some kind of situated action involving sensorimotor (bodily) activity; cognition is primarily a means of deciding how to act using the body, and affective patterns arise in response to the environment and the need to act within that environment.[29] Critiquing approaches that split cognition, affect, and sensorimotor activity,[30] Jerome Bruner coined the label "tripartism."[31] He cautioned that

> it seems far more useful to recognize at the start that all three terms represent abstractions, abstractions that have a high theoretical cost. The price we pay for such abstractions in the end is to lose sight of their structural interdependence. At whatever level we look, however detailed the analysis, the three are constituents of a unified whole. To isolate each is like studying the planes of a crystal separately, losing sight of the crystal that gives them being.[32]

While Bruner elsewhere accepts that it can be useful to study each in isolation (and that it may be practically expedient to do so), his core claim is that, however we conceive of cognition, affect, and sensorimotor activity, we must recognize that they are fundamentally interdependent.[33] What Bruner offers is a psychologically holistic approach. This approach emphasizes that the three are only separable when considered in the abstract. Treating each independently, and only building theoretical bridges between them after constructing domain-specific theories, will create insoluble theoretical issues.[34]

Bruner's claim is explicitly developmental. He highlights that the tendency to split the three domains has a chronological dimension, with cognition purportedly emerging later in ontogeny than affect and action. However (as we explore in more detail below), cognition is not the "late bloomer" of the three. In fact, the importance of recognizing the unity of cognition, affect, and sensorimotor activity is strikingly apparent in the study of infant development.

Infant social development is one domain that helpfully illustrates the importance of Bruner's thesis. First, starting early in the first year, we see that infants engage in responsive, reciprocal "proto-conversations,"[35] in which attention and positive affect are shared between infant and caregiver.[36] These engagements are so named as they exhibit features of timing, coordination, and contingency that are characteristic of a conversation and have been shown to be the basis of later, more complex communicative exchanges.[37] When a caregiver completely ceases to respond (as in the "Still Face" paradigm[38]), infants will employ a range of methods in order to resume the interaction, such as breaking attention away and back, and vocalizing loudly.[39] These behaviors are not only involved in developing socio-cognitive understanding, but also are implicated in the development of socio-emotional attachments.[40] To understand these early engagements, both the cognitive (control and timing and coordination) and affective (motivation to seek interaction, pleasure gained from interacting) each need to be appreciated.

Second, toward the end of the first year, infants go beyond "dyadic" engagement involving engagement solely between persons and begin to engage in what have been termed "triadic" engagements, involving two persons attending to some object or event of interest.[41] For example, an infant may point at an interesting sight, smiling and vocalizing toward their caregiver. If the caregiver responds with smiles and vocalizations to acknowledge this act of communication, this situation can be described as one of triadic engagement or joint attention.[42] It has been repeatedly argued that such engagements cannot be understood in solely informational terms, whereby this change is purely a shift in cognitive resources such that infants can process objects and persons simultaneously. Rather, infants' attention sharing is an experience charged with positive affect for infant and caregiver alike.[43] Infants share attention and interest at least in part because of the pleasure it brings them to do so. Efforts to distinguish "mere" looking from looking to communicate about some target frequently involve a concurrent behavior such as a smile or vocalization.[44] Put simply, to make sense of early attention sharing, it is necessary to recognize the role of both the cognitive dimension (namely the attentional and memory resources to keep track of both a person and an object) as well as the affective dimension (evidenced by a smiling expression, for instance).

Third, while we have focused so far on cognitive and affective processes, research on the impact of sensorimotor developments in infancy also reveals that, as one recent review put it, "motor development and psychological development are fundamentally related."[45] In other words, the seemingly straightforward theoretical divide between mental and bodily development is more complex from a developmental perspective. For example, the onset of self-locomotion towards the end of the first year has cascading developmental consequences for infants, with some researchers going so far as to claim it heralds the "psychological birth" of the infant.[46] Self-locomotion has been linked to shifts in cognitive abilities such as understanding of causal relations, working memory, and intention understanding.[47] The ability to move oneself also changes the kinds of social situations that infants encounter. Some have argued that it increases the number of situations in which caregiver and infant will be required to communicate at a distance.[48] This sort of communication may be positive, but it may be in response to the new kinds of potentially dangerous situations encountered by a locomoting infant, such as encountering a high cliff edge or steep slope.[49] These new and uncertain situations require the infant to apply their cognitive, affective, and sensorimotor resources in new ways, whether by assessing whether they are capable of descending alone,[50] or seeking information or emotional support from a caregiver.[51]

The findings of research into infant development are undoubtedly complex but demonstrate that cognition, affect, and action are intertwined and interdependent domains. Early social interactions involve an interplay of cognitive and affective processes, while sensorimotor developments have cascading consequences on infant social and psychological development.

IMPLICIT AND EXPLICIT COGNITION

The second issue highlighted by a developmental perspective is the nature of cognitive processes. In a nutshell, the point is this: even if we artificially restrict our focus only to the role of cognition in liturgical development, this does not mean we can only talk of conscious or explicit cognitive processes.

Recall that on our broad definition, cognition refers to processes involved in processing and organizing information and using this information to plan and direct behavior. What is not part of this definition is any requirement that cognitive processes need to have propositional content, of the kind enabled by language. The work of developmental and comparative (across species) psychologists has shown that pre- and nonlinguistic beings behave in ways that indicate that there are coordinating and planning processes involved.[52]

Developmental psychologists have long recognized that prelinguistic infants behave in intelligent, purposive ways. Perhaps the most famous exponent of this view is Jean Piaget, whose account of "sensorimotor intelligence" has been enormously influential in helping psychologists appreciate that infants' behavior is not random and disorganized but controlled and intentional.[53] Even simple behaviors like reaching towards an object or turning and visually attending to a target involve intentional, goal-directed coordination of multiple movements, with careful timing and responsive corrective maneuvers.[54]

Recently, new experimental methods have found ways to assess implicit forms of understanding demonstrated by infants in their first year. Novel methodologies have identified that infants reliably look longer at surprising or unexpected events and will look to locations where they predict an expected event.[55] These methods have subsequently been leveraged to identify that infants have an implicit, "naïve" grasp of physics and psychology. In the physical domain, infants expect inanimate objects to behave in consistent ways, such as being solid[56] and being affected by gravity.[57] In the social domain, there is evidence suggesting that infants understand agents' goal-directed and referential actions[58] and may prefer agents that are helpful over those that hinder others.[59]

Similarly, comparative psychologists have provided overwhelming evidence that, despite lacking language, animals behave in intelligent ways that indicate a capacity for cognition. There is evidence that chimpanzees act according to others' knowledge and beliefs[60] and fashion tools that they can use to solve tasks.[61] Likewise, evidence suggests that corvids understand causality, manufacture tools, and engage in prospective behaviors.[62] Further work in animal cognition has looked at the cognitive abilities of a range of taxonomically diverse creatures, from cetaceans,[63] to elephants,[64] to bees.[65]

As a consequence of such research, it is common to draw a distinction between implicit and explicit cognitive processes.[66] Broadly speaking, explicit cognitive processes are of the kind that have propositional content and can be expressed using language. In contrast, implicit cognitive processes are those that cannot be expressed in propositional terms.[67] There is an important theoretical role for processes that are genuinely "thinking" processes yet are not explicit, or forms of knowledge that are implicit.

It is important to see that implicit and explicit processes differ in the manner in which they operate. Implicit processes are typically rapid and automatic, in comparison to slower, reflective explicit processes. While some have argued for distinct cognitive systems, such as in Kahneman's "two-system" account,[68] others have argued that implicit and explicit processes are instead aspects of a unitary system.[69] Regardless, there is broad agreement that the different kinds of cognitive processes allow for flexible ways of dealing with different challenges that arise in complex environments. Furthermore, there is agreement that implicit cognitive processes are not in any sense replaced by explicit cognitive processes; explicit processes build on and supplement implicit processes.

Theorists have also tried to understand the process of change between implicit and explicit cognitive processes. On Karmiloff-Smith's "representational redescription" account,[70] learning involves the transformation of representations from implicit to explicit and vice versa. Being able to do so allows for great flexibility in learning, whether over the course of development or in skill learning in adults. For example, a violinist may have developed a technique that contains flaws on the implicit level. She will have acquired implicit-level knowledge of how to angle the bow or where to put her grip on the violin's neck, knowledge which she cannot propositionally express. To unlearn this implicit technical flaw, it can be helpful to have a skilled teacher who can identify and articulate the issue in an explicit manner (e.g., "Try gripping higher up on the neck"). The reverse process is also important; it would be dangerous to learn to swim just by acquiring knowledge of facts about the bodily movements involved in swimming.[71] One must also build up the requisite implicit forms of knowledge regarding how these movements are to be performed.

Bringing these ideas together, we can see how the account of cognition that we have articulated understands a simple case that is provided by Smith, that of driving a car:

> Most of the day, we are simply involved in the world. We navigate our way and orient ourselves in the driveway unable to remember driving home. Our default mode of intending the world is noncognitive and pre reflective: it is an affective mode of "feeling our way around the world."[72]

On our account, driving a car involves a range of cognitive processes at both implicit and explicit levels. When driving home along familiar roads with predictable levels of traffic, one can rely on implicit cognitive processes. These are not solely affective, as they still involve processes of memory, inhibition, and prediction in the service of behavioral control. While driving a familiar route may be experienced in a nonconscious, "felt" sort of way, there are many cognitive processes that continue to occur to facilitate this activity. Furthermore, we can see how a range of cognitive processes are involved in learning to drive. One must develop the forms of implicit knowledge and memory that allow one to have a sense of the biting point of the clutch or how early to brake. But this will involve both explicit instruction in addition to the accrual of experience. In fact, following Karmiloff-Smith's insights, we can see the situation of learning to drive as involving a complex integration of a range of implicit and explicit processes, with explicit knowledge being redescribed into implicit knowledge (e.g., being explicitly told the process of checking one's mirror and signals versus having an implicit grasp of when to do so) and vice versa (struggling with reversing and trying to articulate explicitly why one is struggling to do so).

What this example also nicely highlights is the relation between explicit thought and communication. Implicit forms of knowledge or belief are difficult (if not impossible) to articulate, whereas explicit knowledge or beliefs can be shared, discussed, and debated. And as we highlight in the next section, there is a close relationship between explicit cognitive processes and social engagement.

THE SOCIAL ORIGINS OF EXPLICIT COGNITIVE PROCESSES

Writing on the development of "higher cognitive function"—what we are labeling explicit cognitive processes—the pioneering developmental psychologist Lev Vygotsky made a striking claim:

> Every function in the child's cultural development appears twice: first, on the social level, and later, on the individual level; first, between people (interpsychological) and then inside the child (intrapsychological). . . . All the higher functions originate as actual relationships between individuals.[73]

Vygotsky's claim was that to understand the developmental emergence of any explicit process, one must first examine the developmental precursors of that process within social engagement. While Vygotsky's approach has been refined and critiqued, recent research has vindicated many aspects of his approach to the development of explicit cognitive processes. It is now widely argued, from a range of theoretical standpoints, that explicit cognitive processes are both ontogenetically and phylogenetically dependent on social engagement.[74]

Recent work in developmental psychology has provided evidence that explicit cognitive processes emerge out of early social experiences. Before explicit reasoning is used to solve abstract problems or make sophisticated future plans, it is used to interpret and understand the behavior of others in social contexts. There is evidence that sophisticated understanding of others' perspectives can be traced back to early shared engagements.[75] Through engaging in joint attention, children can begin to differentiate perspectives, leading to an understanding that others have their own perspectives on the world that are distinct from one's own. This in turn allows children to understand that what another believes about the world might not only be different but in competition with what they know about the world, an ability known as "false-belief understanding."[76] Research has supported the view that successful explicit understanding of others' beliefs relies on the ability to manage conflicting perspectives on the world,[77] combined with developing linguistic capabilities for talking about others' minds.[78] By engaging in social interactions, children are introduced to the world of reasons and beliefs. They can then apply these abilities to plan and problem-solve in other domains and to assess and update their own beliefs.[79]

Similarly, it has been argued that reasoning emerged phylogenetically as a result of the selection pressures of complex social living.[80] While some have suggested that reasoning is adaptive, as it helps with planning and dealing with novel challenges,[81] it is not clear why such an issue cannot be overcome through learning and other forms of cognitive adaptation, as it is in other species. Clearly, reasoning can be useful in planning and dealing with novelty, but it does not follow that this is why it evolved. Mercier and Sperber argue that complex social groups create challenges such as determining trustworthiness and being able to convince others.[82] Their "argumentative" account of reasoning explains humans' tendency to favor information that supports already-held conclusions by proposing that this is a symptom of a system that has arisen to deal with social conflict, not abstract truth. Thus, "errors" such as confirmation bias (preferring information that fits with one's preexisting beliefs) are in fact features of a system that has evolved for argumentation.

Overall, a developmental and evolutionary perspective on explicit cognition understands it as emerging as a result of social processes.

Developmentally, explicit cognitive processes are hypothesized to emerge in the context of social engagements, as children start to talk about reasons and beliefs. Evolutionarily, explicit cognitive processes are hypothesized to have arisen primarily as a means of dealing with cooperation and conflict in social groups. Taken together, the picture is clear: to understand human thinking, we need to understand human sociality.

LITURGICAL ANTHROPOLOGY: A PSYCHOLOGICALLY HOLISTIC APPROACH

Where can these insights from psychological sciences take us in thinking about the relationship between liturgy and theological anthropology? Drawing the above discussion together, in this section we offer three insights we think can move us toward a holistic liturgical anthropology. Then, in the next section, we argue that these insights build towards an overarching conclusion that a liturgical anthropology requires a recognition of the centrality of humans' social nature.[83] Finally, we propose that these insights suggest that understanding the role of joint attention in liturgy is crucial for understanding liturgical formation and anthropology, something which will provide focus for what we argue in the remainder of this book.

First, it seems clear that affect and cognition are present from the very earliest stages of development. The attempt to artificially separate these categories simply does not reflect the way psychologists think human beings learn to navigate the world. A liturgical anthropology that takes this insight seriously will resist thinking of liturgy as shaping its participants as creatures that are primarily either cognitive or affective. Instead, it will affirm that in all ritual behavior, cognitive and affective states are intertwined in ways difficult to disentangle. While there may be polemical value in opposing a dominant trend to think of worship and formation in only cognitive terms, overemphasizing the role of affect is equally detrimental to the extent that it implies that one can be affectively transformed with only incidental effects on explicit cognitive processes such as reasons or beliefs. On a holistic account, there is a dynamic interplay between (explicit) cognitive transformation and affective transformation, and liturgy involves psychologically holistic changes.

Thus, it is clear that beliefs about God are shaped by the practices of liturgy in significant ways. Take the example of the "early high Christology" movement in New Testament studies. As Larry Hurtado has argued at length, understanding the practices of the early Church in worshiping Christ as God is key to understanding the doctrinal commitments of the early Church. "The devotional life of early Christianity involved the hymnic celebration of the risen Christ in the corporate worship setting."[84] Hurtado argues that this led to a "redefinition of Jewish monotheistic devotion,"[85] in which "the risen Christ came to share in some of the devotional and cultic attention normally reserved for God: the early Christian mutation in Jewish monotheism was a religious devotion, in which Christ shared in the worship of the one God."[86]

Sidestepping the issue of whether Hurtado is right to affirm the early origins of Christological doctrine, it seems plausible to think that we need a liturgical anthropology that affirms both affect and cognition to make sense of claims like these. If we assume that worship requires some level of affect (i.e., of devotion or desire for God), we might ask the following: Did the early Christians worship Jesus because they believed he was divine? Or, did they believe he was divine because they worshiped him? We think there is little value to answering these questions.

Similarly, in Chris Seglenieks' recent work, the relationship between devotion and belief is explored in the context of John's gospel.[87] As Seglenieks argues at length, there are strong similarities between the *pistis* word group used by John (e.g., "For God so loved the world that he gave his only Son, so that everyone who believes [pisteuōn] in him may not perish but may have eternal life" [John 3:16]) and ancient Greco-Roman devotional practices which focus on the affective, relational response of the participants. Seglenieks argues that for John,

> the ideal response to Jesus entails cognitive, relational, ethical, ongoing, and public aspects. The ideal response to Jesus, the genuine belief that leads to life (20:31) requires: (1) knowing and accepting that Jesus is the Messiah, the divine Son of God, and the one who is risen, along with belief in the Father who sent Jesus; (2) a close interpersonal relationship with Jesus, characterised by trust and love, and extending out to fellow believers; (3) a life of obedience to Jesus, living in imitation of him, particularly in imitation of his visible love for others; (4) an ongoing allegiance to Jesus, expressed through continuing in the cognitive, relational, and ethical aspects of belief; and (5) a public witness that acknowledges one's own faith, as well as presenting Jesus in order that others might believe.[88]

As Seglenieks shows, the relationship between the cognitive and affective dimensions of faith is complex; Johannine views of faith are not primarily cognitive or affective. Rather, they emphasize the insight offered from the psychological sciences, which suggests that questions about belief and desire in liturgy are not in conflict; the relationship between affect and cognition in this case is instead irreducibly complex.

The point is also important for the use of liturgy with children. For if we assume that liturgy as an activity is primarily either desire-shaping or belief-shaping, then we will not realize the formative power of liturgical action for the development of faith in children. In her discussion of childhood spirituality, Rebecca Nye argues that the "core" of children's spirituality is what she calls "relational consciousness." As she summarizes her studies: "Children's spirituality was recognized by a distinctive property of mental activity, profound and intricate enough to be termed 'consciousness', and remarkable for its confinement to a broadly relational, inter- and intra-personal domain."[89] As Nye goes on to clarify, what she means by "consciousness" is close to what psychologists have called "meta-cognition," that is, the capacity to reflect on one's own mental states (both cognitive and affective). In a revealing example, Nye writes,

> Six-year-old Ruth's conversation included a sensual description of heaven. She referred to the key elements in her spiritual response as "waking up" and "noticing," both of which suggest that a different quality of consciousness was crucial to her experience. The relational component in this was a strong feeling of connection to the natural world as something that was full of gifts for her and deserved her love and respect in return. This sense of intimacy also had reverberations in her relationship with herself, as seen in her self-conscious perception of a symmetry between her own joy and the joyful leaping of lambs.[90]

Is Ruth's religious understanding best understood as cognitive or affective? It seems to us that this is a question that we cannot answer easily. Indeed, in listing the different dimensions of religious consciousness, Nye includes both typically cognitive activities such as "reasoning" and "searching for meaning," alongside typically affective activities such as "staying with a mood" and "stimulation."[91] In discussing these dimensions she notes, "It is unlikely that light will be shed on spirituality of a child by considering these dimensions in isolation."[92] Thus, in nurturing childhood spirituality, David Hay goes on to argue, it is important to use "rituals, stories, music, poetry, art and architecture . . . [which] articulate the inexpressible."[93] Citing Vygotsky, Hay suggests that these mediums can help provide a "scaffolding of language" in which children can "come to grips with their spirituality."[94] The developmental insights considered previously suggest that Nye and Hay are right to emphasize both the affective and cognitive dimensions of childhood spirituality. To understand how liturgy shapes children, we must avoid overly simplistic accounts of liturgical anthropology.

Second, even if we artificially restrict our focus only to the cognitive effects of liturgy, the overall evidence suggests that cognition is not a monolithic category. It is more helpfully considered as involving a range of processes, both fast, nonreflective processes and slow, deliberative processes.[95] These processes are important and useful in their own right, as is the ability to transform our representations of the world between different formats. This ability is bidirectional; we can both come to articulate implicit knowledge in explicit ways but also understand explicit knowledge on an implicit level. Implicit thought is also not something that is left behind over the course of development; while implicit cognitive processes appear prior to explicit processes, this amounts more to an enriching of the available cognitive resources than the addition of cognition. On this approach, humans are not fundamentally nonthinkers who come to think; they are thinkers through and through, even though the kinds of thought processes they bring to bear differ depending on the activity at hand and the stage of their development. Furthermore, humans are not unique in their status as thinkers, even if their cognition is distinctive in its complexity.[96]

Consider a recent account of liturgical epistemology from Nicholas Wolterstorff that helps press the complexity of cognitive formation through liturgy. Wolterstorff argues that what is taken for granted about God in liturgy shapes the way individuals relate to God, even if they do not directly attend to the propositional content of a liturgical script. For instance, consider the American Episcopal liturgy that Wolterstorff cites:

> Eternal God, heavenly Father,
> *you* have graciously accepted us as living members
> of *your* Son our Savior Jesus Christ,
> and *you* have fed us with spiritual food
> and the Sacrament of his Body and Blood.[97]

According to Wolterstorff, addressing God using these words allows participants to gain knowledge in virtue of the things one takes for granted. Just as in taking for granted that the world existed before one was born, it is possible for one to know that the world existed before they were born, in taking for granted certain things about God through the use of liturgy, they can come to know that God is a certain way. Repetition of certain content shapes one's understanding of who God is in ways that are not purely explicit. One can come to know, for example, that God is worthy of praise and adoration and that he is capable of listening. Wolterstorff argues that:

> To participate in engaging God liturgically in the form of addressing God is to take God to be a "thou" whom it is appropriate to address, to take God to be capable of listening, to take God to be worthy of praise and adoration, to take God to be capable of listening, to take God to be worthy of praise and adoration.[98]

It is not that one solely comes to know propositions about God in this way, for Wolterstorff. Rather, repeated exposure to these words, which one begins to take for granted, provides a kind of knowledge of God akin to phenomenal knowledge; one knows what God is like by repeatedly engaging God in a certain way and not another. Just as repeated exposure to a biography might provide one with a thick nonpropositional knowledge of the author, engagement with the liturgy can shape one's perception of God, Wolterstorff thinks.[99] The temptation is to think of Wolterstorff's insight purely in explicitly cognitive terms, namely that the kind of formation that occurs in taking for granted certain things about God is shaping one's explicit beliefs about God. We think this is mistaken. For if the psychological insights above are correct, the process Wolterstorff describes involves shaping of both explicit and implicit beliefs. A child might implicitly believe "God listens to my prayers," and only later in development be able to articulate explicit reasons for this belief. Or, following Nye, explicit beliefs can serve as "scaffolding" that provides a framework that is later complemented by implicit beliefs and desires. We take this scaffolding to be the purpose of practices like catechesis.

We do not see these routes to psychological change as competing; rather, liturgies can potentially create a positive "feedback loop" between explicit and implicit forms of knowledge; repeated exposure to forms of explicit knowledge about God can start to gradually shape one's implicit beliefs, which in turn make one more likely to accept further explicit beliefs and more open to a greater range of affective experiences. Whatever one concludes about these issues, the terminology of implicit and explicit cognition provides a means of developing more nuanced accounts of liturgy and its formative effects.

Third, this body of work has built a compelling case from early ontogeny to adulthood that provides convincing evidence that explicit reasoning processes emerge out of the needs of negotiating complex social worlds, not primarily for discerning abstract logical truths. It is important to note that we are not claiming that humans cannot think in such abstract, logical ways. Rather, it is to argue that explicit cognitive processes have evolved and developed to deal with issues that arise in complex social groups; making sense of what others know and believe, discerning plausible reasons for others' behavior, convincing others of one's views, and discerning others' deception.[100] As such, those that hold to the primacy of belief formation not only are mistaken regarding humans as fundamentally *Homo cogitans* but also miss the fact that explicit cognitive processes are themselves a consequence of humanity's social nature.

Nye's notion of "relational consciousness" in childhood spirituality helps show the theological import of the social origins of development. She writes,

> the child's awareness of being in relationship with someone or something was demonstrated by what they said and, crucially, this was a special sense that added value to their ordinary and everyday perspective. . . . In this "relational consciousness" seems to lie the rudimentary core of children's spirituality, out of which can arise meaningful aesthetic experience, religious experience, personal and traditional responses to mystery and being, and mystical and moral insight.[101]

Nye's claim that relationality is at the core of children's spirituality fits much more comfortably with the psychological literature we have been considering than the attempt to place either affect or cognition at the core of liturgical anthropology. Moreover, this emphasis on sociality or relationality as a fundamental quality to being human fits with a number of recent discussions in theological anthropology. For instance, in Susan Eastman's recent book, *Paul and the Person*, she argues that there are some parallels between developmental psychological views on the nature of persons, and Paul's anthropology in the New Testament. After summarizing the psychological discussion on the importance of relationality for human thought, she argues that something similar can be found in Paul's thought:

> communion is the presupposition for a self that is capable of self-knowledge and action—and even for believers in Christ, such

> capacities are always limited under threat short of the final consummation. This is "relationism about persons" in which individuality presupposes relationality . . . There is no possibility of existence outside such other-relation. The determining factor in whether such other-relation is for good or for ill depends on the relational partner. Apart from Christ, humanity is so enslaved and deluded by sin that there is no individual at all; agency is, as it were, swallowed up by the powers of sin and death.[102]

In congruence with developmental psychology, Eastman claims that, for Paul, the human self cannot be understood in isolation but only in relationship. Thus, she thinks, human beings are fundamentally relational beings, defined either in their relationship to sin or, ideally, in right relationship with Jesus Christ. According to a recent article by Simeon Zahl, even individualistic soteriological language must be understood in its social context: "To feel guilt towards God and to experience it being resolved, or to feel gratitude toward God, is always 'social' experience, cognitively speaking, in that such feelings depend upon a mental representation of God as an 'other' to whom the subject stands in a social relation."[103] As Zahl shows, existing tensions in theological anthropology and soteriology between "individualism" and "communalism" can be alleviated by engaging with psychological sciences. He argues that a psychologically engaged anthropology will emphasize both the importance of the individual person and the relational nature of the person. As both Eastman and Zahl show, there is much in common between psychological sciences and theology on the issue of whether the human self is relational in nature. What remains to be seen is where the issue of liturgy comes into play.

LITURGY, DEVELOPMENT, AND THE IMPORTANCE OF JOINT ATTENTION

We began our discussion with the claim that ritual behavior plays a formative role in the development of human thinking and feeling. Our intention has been to build on those who have rightly pushed back against a brains-on-sticks approach to liturgical formation, in which liturgy primarily shapes the beliefs of participants. But we have also resisted the hearts-on-legs approach advocated by some of those skeptical of overly cognitive approaches to formation. Our contention has been that any attempt to prioritize either cognition or affect risks oversimplifying what is happening in liturgical formation.

Throughout, we have considered examples in which liturgy and ritualized behavior shapes us. Having presented an account of human development as deeply social and psychologically holistic, we can now conclude by considering the place of liturgy as an important part of this development. In this section we argue that crucial to our understanding of how liturgy shapes individuals is understanding how liturgy is shared between persons. This will help us to see the crucial role of joint attention in thinking about liturgy, which is fundamental to the account of liturgy developed in the rest of the book.

In keeping with our approach, developmental psychology has found that infants do not employ their cognitive, affective, and sensorimotor capacities in isolation. Rather, the three are unified in the "narrative envelopes" of structured activities.[104] In other words, developmental psychology repeatedly attests to the importance of repetitive, structured activities (games, routines, liturgies) in the development of these interrelated capacities. Structured activities of various kinds provide a foundational structure of repeated, predictable experiences but also provide a backdrop against which changes can take place.[105] The practices considered by developmental psychologists are overwhelmingly social, whether they be simple routines such as being picked up,[106] shared games like peekaboo,[107] singing songs with actions,[108] or shared activities like reading a story.[109] Since these practices begin while the infant is unable to self-locomote and dependent on others for their basic needs, it is no surprise that the practices of infants' lives are intrinsically social. However, social practices and activities continue to play a central role throughout early ontogeny and indeed across the human lifespan.[110]

What makes humans capable of forming and participating in such structured shared activities? One key aspect is the capacity to engage in joint attention. As we will see, through joint attention, humans can establish some part of the world as shared with others, what some have termed "shared situations."[111] By establishing such shared situations, humans can fluidly coordinate their attention, communicate, and act with others on the understanding that those others are sharing the same experiences. Shared practices can thus be understood as involving the creation of a predictably structured shared situation, through which attention and activity are coordinated.[112] Thus, the ability to engage in joint attention enables shared practices to be developed, and in turn practices can be a means of shaping the joint attention of practitioners.[113] For example, through repeatedly engaging in shared book reading, a child becomes aware of the importance of attending to the words on the page, which are likely not to be the focus of attention prior to the more engaging images or textures that are present. In light of the relation between social practices and joint attention, we suggest that viewing liturgy through the lens of joint attention is a promising line of investigation. In the upcoming chapter we will focus in greater detail on how the concept of joint attention can contribute to discussions of liturgy. For now, we will draw together the argument of this chapter.

SUMMARY

Human beings are ritualized creatures, who are shaped by participation in various practices and liturgies. We are now in a position to see the psychological and theological significance of the observation that we began by noting. It seems clear to us that it is right to push back against an overly cognitive understanding of this claim exemplified by the brains-on-sticks approach, namely that rituals shape human beings because they are rational, thinking creatures who are influenced by exposure to the propositional content of liturgy. However, it should be clear now why the alternative hearts-on-legs model is false. This alternative model runs something like the following: rituals shape human beings because they are affective, desiring creatures who are influenced by the telos of rituals.

And here is the view we have been developing, in a nutshell: rituals shape human beings because they are social creatures, whose minds and bodies are shaped through engagement with others. Rituals are fundamentally shared activities that facilitate diverse experiences of jointness with others. Moreover, as we shall see in the next chapter, an important aspect of this shared nature of liturgical formation is the experience of jointness not only with others but with God.

2
THE SHARED NATURE OF LITURGY

THE VALUE OF JOINTNESS

We have now seen the crucial way in which liturgies help to shape the beliefs and desires of participants in the context of community, and the way in which joint attention plays a key role.[1] It should not be surprising, then, given the power of these practices, that jointness between persons is increasingly valuable in our culture, especially at a time in the West in which communities are increasingly fragmented and decentralized. On the launch of their new product, Quest, Meta (formerly known as Facebook) claimed that their virtual reality headset will revolutionize our working practices:

> Imagine if you could feel truly present with your teammates, no matter where you are. With virtual and mixed reality, you can work together like never before.[2]

Mark Zuckerberg and colleagues clearly see the financial potential in creating a medium through which people can feel present to one another even if they cannot gather in the same physical space. They are happy to use the word *together* to describe working with others in a virtual reality. But many of us would have the intuition that no matter how realistic virtual reality becomes, there will always be something missing from online interactions. The jointness of such situations seems different to the jointness of a physically copresent gathering.[3] This is not to say that there is no value in virtual connection, or that virtual spaces are simply incapable of creating a sense of personal presence or jointness. Rather, it is simply to notice that jointness comes in degrees.

This chapter seeks to provide a framework that can help us to make sense of the notion that jointness comes in degrees. This framework can provide a helpful way of understanding how liturgical practices—both in-person and not—facilitate different sorts of shared experiences. We argue that there are degrees of jointness for liturgical practices, from embodied copresent acts that depend on jointly attending with others, to those that are more difficult to characterize, such as the jointness of a large gathering, of virtual worship, or even of synchronous practices conducted in the total absence of others, like praying at the same time as others but in a different space. In many respects, liturgical practices are like other practices, such as sports matches or concerts, that create a sense of jointness amongst a gathered group. A football match creates a situation for those gathered, in which features of the game itself are shared—the players, the score, and so on. Similarly, in liturgical practices, the forms contained with the liturgy (whether these are music, reading, or some kind of liturgical script) facilitate a sense of jointness amongst those who are gathered. However, liturgical practices have a further purpose. These forms have a theological function: to point towards the presence and attention of God. Making things more complex still, God is understood not as a mere object of attention between two people but as another co-attender. We thus argue that understanding the theological significance of liturgical practices requires addressing the question of how a community might experience God's presence together—and delving into the many and complex ways that *together* might be understood.

PHYSICAL COPRESENCE AND JOINT ATTENTION

As we have claimed in chapter 1, humans are an immensely social species, and our experience of the world involves many varied shared experiences. We watch football matches together, we go to parties together, we sit on public transport together. Moreover, sharing these experiences plays an important role in how we relate to one another—our relationships depend on, and are deepened by, the extent of our shared experience with one another. Liturgical practices are one such instance of shared experience. They can therefore be understood, to some extent, by considering the cognitive mechanisms that underpin such shared experiences.

An influential hypothesis advanced by Michael Tomasello and his colleagues is that this capacity for shared experience stems from what he and others have termed "shared intentionality."[4] Shared intentionality refers to the ability and motivation to engage in cooperative activities that involve the sharing of intentions and goals (as well as other psychological states such as shared emotions and shared beliefs)—to act as a "We." Typically, examples that are given of shared intentionality refer to two or more individuals coordinating in some task such as performing a dance routine[5] or playing a musical duet.[6] These cases all involve individuals not merely acting as individuals but also intending that their actions form part of a wider "We" (something we explore in more detail in chapter 4). While how we should analyze the nature of these *we*-intentions is hotly contested,[7] there is widespread agreement that there is *some* difference between individual and collectively intended action.

Notably, it has been observed that our first shared experiences of the world, and the earliest expression of shared intentionality, are found in the primordial sharing situation of joint attention.[8] In its broadest sense, joint attention describes a situation in which two or more individuals attend to something together. The canonical example is a situation in which an infant playing with a toy looks up to his mother, smiles, and holds the toy up to her, thereby "triangulating" their attention onto the toy. Gaze, gesture, facial expressions, vocalizations (including words), and touch all play a role in coordinating joint attention.[9]

However, it is important to note that simply orienting to a common focus is not joint attention in a strict sense.[10] Consider, for example, the situation in which a number of passengers at a train station attend to the screen displaying information about train times. Even though the passengers attend to the same target, it seems intuitive to say that this experience is not joint in a strong sense. Even in cases where an attender causes another to attend to a common target (e.g., in following another's gaze to a target), there might still be a critical absence of interpersonal connectedness that provides the crucial ingredient of jointness.

So, to give an account of jointness, more detail is needed than simply noting the importance of simultaneous object attention. Following a number of researchers,[11] we suggest that joint attention should be understood through the lens of the "second-person perspective." Broadly conceived, the second-person perspective highlights that human social understanding is different in important ways when people are engaged communicatively as a "You" ("second-personally") as opposed to viewing others as a "He," "She," or "It" (i.e., third-personally).[12] This claim has a developmental dimension; second-person engagements in early infancy (see chapter 1) are the foundation on which later forms of social understanding and shared experience are built.[13]

Take the following scenario. Suppose John and Mary are reading separately in a library at the same time for a while and then become aware of one another by, say, sharing an irritated look concerning a disturbance from a group of noisy students. The look provides an interactive, communicative connection that makes the experience of the noisy students shared between John and Mary.[14] Prior to the knowing look, we would say that the experience of the students was *common* between John and Mary but is only *shared* once the second-person connection is established.[15] Interactive engagements are inherently other-involving and reciprocal in a way that is not possible from simply observing another's behavior.[16] John might intently study Mary's behavior and carefully consider her perspective, but no amount of individual thinking can make an experience truly mutual or shared. Mary must be both aware of John's attention towards her and indicate her attention to John for true mutuality to be present. In other words, there must be a sense of "bi-directionality."[17] In second-person interactions, both participants contribute to the structure of the interaction; timing and responsiveness become key.[18]

This mutual involvement means that the experiences that arise through joint attention are the kind that are only possible with another's involvement. As John Campbell argues,

> the individual experiential state you are in, when you and another are jointly attending to something, is an experiential state that you could not be in were it not for the other person attending to the object. The other person enters into your experience as a constituent of it, as co-attender, and the other person could not play that role in your experience except by being co-attender.[19]

Similarly, Axel Seemann notes that joint attention requires "each involved creature to be causally sensitive to the thing in his or her own focus of attention and behavior, and second, for each creature to be casually sensitive in this way to the other's focus of attention and behavior."[20] Joint attention is not something one can do alone, and in joint attention one is allowing others to influence one's experience of the world.

A final important feature of the psychological discussion is the potential targets of joint attention. So far, we have focused on joint attention to material objects like toys and books, or other perceptible events (e.g., noisy students). However, humans can jointly attend to aspects of the world that are not straightforwardly perceptual features, even in infancy. At twelve months of age, infants can point to absent referents such as the location in space where a puppet had previously appeared but is no longer present.[21] In later stages of development, the targets of joint attention can also be mental contents[22] or amodal properties of objects, such as weight.[23] This psychological work on joint attention has much promise to help us think about the shared nature of liturgies.

LITURGY AND JOINT ATTENTION

Practices and rituals provide many opportunities to attend to features of the world with others. For example, when a family watches television together, or a group of medical students observes an operation, they depend on joint attention in order to participate in the activity. What we see from the psychological sciences is that these instances of attending to objects together (whether TV shows or body parts) are importantly different from doing these things alone. The co-attenders have the capacity to shape and direct one another's attention and, thus, the experience of that feature of the world. These instances of joint attention in groups need not be focused only on perceptual objects either. Consider, for instance, a lecturer who gets a room full of students to think about an abstract idea such as "beauty" or "transcendence." In using certain words, or perhaps visual aids, the lecturer encourages the students to think together about these abstract concepts.[24]

So, what is the focus of attention in liturgical practices? As already noted, at least part of our answer must be the forms of liturgy themselves: pieces of music, readings, sermons, lines of spoken liturgy, and so on. As the Anglican theologian Evelyn Underhill writes,

> In every human society which has reached even a rudimentary religious consciousness, worship is given its concrete expression in institutions and in ritual acts: and these institutions and acts become in their turn powerful instruments . . . The painted cave of those prehistoric worshippers of an unknown God who were "simple minded enough to give of their best to the supra-sensible powers," the Pagan temple, the Christian cathedral, are all expressions of the same fundamental human need to incorporate, make visible, the spirit of worship.[25]

As Underhill shows, visible mediums and forms are fundamental to human expressions of worship. In a certain sense, then, the acts themselves (along with the bodily movements and physical mediums which are used in the acts) are an object of joint attention in liturgy. Underhill stresses (in agreement with Smith, Brown, Strawn, and Taylor, whose work we considered in chapter 1) that worship cannot be disconnected from human embodiment; there must always be a visible, incorporate medium through which worship is expressed. But it is also important to note that these ritual forms themselves are not the primary focus of liturgy, or at least they are not supposed to be. Underhill continues to note that the "liturgical life" of the Church "is not merely a collective of services, offices, and sacraments."[26] While these are important ways of participating in the life of the Church, she writes,

> the corporate worship of the Church is not simply that of an assembly of individuals who believe the same things, and therefore unite in doing the same things. It is real in its own right; an action transcending and embracing all the separate souls taking part in it. The individual as such dies to his separate selfhood—even his spiritual selfhood—on entering the Divine Society: is "buried in baptism" and reborn as a living cell of the Mystical Body of Christ.[27]

In other words, unless worship is animated by God and focused on drawing the community into closer relationship with God, it is not meaningfully different from a football match or any other form of social entertainment. To talk about jointly attending only to the ritual forms themselves is not sufficient for thinking about the shared nature of liturgy. Liturgy is not merely an opportunity to enact a ritual with a group of like-minded people. As Underhill emphasizes, these rituals must be understood theologically and not just psychologically or sociologically. We must not mistake the means for the ends, nor lose sight of liturgy as an act of worship. If we are to understand liturgical practices in their fullness, we must not only ask how liturgy allows for joint attention to liturgical forms but also take seriously the experience of joint attention to and with God.

How can liturgical practices allow for experiences of joint attention to God's presence? One way of answering this question is to maintain that liturgy allows participants to mutually attend to God in concrete, bodily ways. For example, to take a case from the Roman Catholic tradition, in using the words of the Agnus Dei ("Behold the Lamb of God, behold him who takes away the sins of the world"), the priest lifts the consecrated elements, and, using verbal cues, invites the congregants to attend to the bread and wine. In some Christian traditions, it is believed that (in some sense) these elements of bread and wine are physically the body and blood of Christ. In such cases, then, it is true that in jointly attending to the consecrated elements, one is jointly attending to the body of Christ. On this view, the priest's use of the Agnus Dei in liturgy is literally true. It seems straightforward to think that if Christ's presence is thought of in these bodily terms, then co-attending to the eucharistic elements gets to count as an instance of co-attending to the presence of God. Note that this view is straightforward in thinking about God's presence as an object of attention, but its application is fairly narrow. While many Christian traditions defend some version of a bodily account of Christ's presence in the Eucharist, there are reasons to seek an alternative approach. For even in traditions which emphasize the importance of eucharistic presence, very few would think that this is all we mean in talking about God's presence.

Another sense in which we might think liturgy can allow a congregation to jointly attend to God's presence requires thinking about presence not in bodily terms (i.e., not that God is somehow physically located in the Church) but in second-personal terms. That is, we might think that the eucharistic liturgy allows one to jointly attend to God as not only an inert object (i.e., when a congregation jointly attends to Christ's flesh in the elements) but another person to attend to. To take a more mundane example: suppose a family is having a meal, and Grandma is asleep in the corner. Sleeping Grandma is an object of joint attention to the other members of the family (she is snoring very loudly). But when Grandma suddenly wakes up, the object of their attention changes in an important way. It is not just Grandma's body that is an object of their joint perceptual field, but Grandma herself—her presence—becomes the object of joint attention for the other members of the family.

A helpful way of understanding what is going on in cases like these is in terms of being present *to*. Eleonore Stump, in her discussion of omnipresence, draws from much of the psychological literature above to explain the kind of second-personal presence that exists between persons. For instance, we might say, "She read the paper all through dinner and was never present to any of the rest of us."[28] Stump argues,

> In these examples, there is presence at a time and in a place; but some kind of presence, characterized by one or another kind of

> second-personal psychological connection, is missing. Typically, this kind of presence is characterized as presence with or presence to another person. I will call this kind of presence "personal presence."[29]

Just as Grandma might enter into our attention as an object of our joint attention, we might think liturgy aims at achieving something similar with respect to God. In gathering together, the congregation is seeking to attend together to God's presence with them. The Danish theologian Søren Kierkegaard argues that this is precisely how we should think of the task of preaching, for example. Preaching is not primarily about acting as a wise and learned performer on a stage, but more like serving as a stage prompter who stands at the side of the stage to remind the actor of their lines. The preacher's primary role, as stage prompter, is to make the listeners aware of God's presence. Kierkegaard writes that the sermon

> is not spoken for the sake of the speaker, so that he may be praised or criticized . . . at the religious address God himself is present; in the most earnest sense he is the critical spectator who is checking on how it is being spoken and on how it is being heard, and for that very reason there are no spectators.[30]

Thus, Kierkegaard thinks, the preacher should be more like a stage prompter than a performer; their job is to whisper "the words to the listener," so that the listener becomes aware that they are "standing before God."[31] For Kierkegaard, to truly engage with preaching the listener must become aware of God's presence. He writes,

> As soon as the religious address is viewed from the secular point of view . . . the speaker becomes an actor and the listeners become critical spectators; in that case the religious address is performed secularly before some people who are present, but God is not present any more than he is in the theater. The presence of God is the decisive element that changes everything. As soon as God is present, everyone has the task before God of paying attention to himself.[32]

In other words, preaching in particular, and liturgy more generally, provides a medium by which participants become aware of God's presence with them. In the Church of England, a greeting that is sometimes used at the beginning of the eucharistic liturgy begins with the priest stating, "The

Lord is here!" and the congregation are invited to respond: "His Spirit is with us." At the beginning of the liturgy, the congregation is reminded that they gather not just to become aware of one another but to make themselves aware that the Spirit of God is present.

What it means to think of God as present in this way has received some attention in philosophical theology. Drawing from the discussion of joint attention in the psychological literature, Adam Green argues that the objects of our environment might be used as mediums by which individuals come to be aware of God's presence. As Green puts it, "one is engaged in . . . [joint] attention with God" if "one is aware of God as exhibiting some mental state which is directed towards oneself and the mental state which God exhibits involves an awareness of the co-operative nature of the present attention."[33] Thus, to experience God, on this model, is to experience God through some medium in which God's intentionality is communicated to the individual. Thus, for Green, what is directly perceived by a subject is some internal sensation or some ordinary perceptual experience, but the individual experiences these ordinary sensations as experiences of God's presence. As he describes it, "the pattern of one's experience appears to manifest a shared awareness between the divine and oneself within which affect and information can be communicated. . . . Using the shared-attention account, we can claim that sound, light, and affect are all mediums that can be manipulated by God in such a way as to reveal the mind of God toward the subject of the experience."[34] In other words, Green claims that ordinary perception of the world can provide an opportunity for individuals to jointly attend to God and to become aware of God as another "you." While the mechanisms for joint attention might be different (i.e., we do not share eye contact with God), the psychological concept of becoming aware of God second-personally provides a fruitful way of understanding encounter with God's presence.

Building on this notion of joint attention with God, we can see how liturgy might provide a medium through which to jointly attend to God's presence. Consider some recent discussions of this idea. First, according to Green and Quan, "the Scriptures [might] direct one's attention to one's pride. . . . God might elect for the contents of Scripture to shape [an] . . . experience of the divine. [Joint] attention requires that the agent one is sharing attention with be experienced as present, even if implicitly."[35] Here, the act of reading Scriptures provides a means of becoming aware of God's presence to and with the individual.

Similarly to Kierkegaard's notion of the preacher as a stage prompter, the texts themselves provide a means of becoming aware of God's presence. Take another example, this time of eucharistic liturgy. According to Cockayne and coauthors, a person and Christ might "share attention by focusing on the Eucharistic meal, which is able to bring about reconciliation between them . . . [for] participation in the Eucharist to count as an experience of Christ as present . . . [one] must be aware that Christ is present and that Christ is attending to [them]."[36] Just as Scripture might prompt an awareness of God's presence, the Eucharistic meal might prompt this second-personal encounter with God as present in the liturgy.[37]

Thus, in liturgy, we might think, the object of attention is not ideally the liturgical forms themselves but the presence of God, which the forms seek to mediate. In this respect, then, the object of attention is not a perceptible object, but nor is it a mere abstract concept either. Rather, liturgy allows participants to focus their attention on God. To think about how this might be so, consider another mundane example from George Orwell's novel *1984*:

> there seemed to be no colour in anything, except the posters that were plastered everywhere. The blackmoustachio'd face gazed down from every commanding corner. There was one on the house-front immediately opposite. BIG BROTHER IS WATCHING YOU, the caption said, while the dark eyes looked deep into Winston's own. . . . In the far distance a helicopter skimmed down between the roofs, hovered for an instant like a bluebottle, and darted away again with a curving flight. It was the police patrol, snooping into people's windows. The patrols did not matter, however. Only the Thought Police mattered.[38]

If we grant that Winston can be aware that Big Brother is aware of him, and that Winston can be aware that Julia is aware that Big Brother is aware of her, we might ask: How is it that Big Brother's awareness can be an object of joint attention between Winston and Julia? At least one answer to this question is that environmental cues enable Winston and Julia to become aware of Big Brother's attention. From the more overt "BIG BROTHER IS WATCHING YOU," to the more subtle sight of a snooping helicopter, these cues serve to activate beliefs about attention. Winston and Julia can use these cues as means to share attention to Big Brother's attention.

Something comparable is happening in liturgy. The comparison between God and Big Brother may be unpalatable to some, but our comparison is not to suggest that God's character ought to be viewed in similar terms to Big Brother's but instead solely to make the point that material objects can be used as cues to the attention of an immaterial other. These may involve the words used ("Let's take a moment to make ourselves aware of God's presence"), the use of environmental cues (such as lighting or architecture that emphasizes divine glory and transcendence), or even the layout and arrangement of the room (such as a focus on the communion table or the pulpit). In the context of liturgical practice, many of the symbols and actions that participants share with others allow them to jointly attend to God's presence by serving as representational vehicles that remind participants that God is attending to them. It is important to see that the above examples are of physically copresent individuals jointly attending to God's presence; it would require a further step to also describe individuals jointly attending to God's attention.

As Cockayne and Efird have argued, in jointly attending to God's presence in liturgy, participants are able to shape and guide one another's direction and awareness of God's presence. Building on the observations from Campbell and Seemann (about the shaping function of joint attention), they write that

> when alone, we might have the tendency to focus on certain aspects of God's character, and thereby build up a biased picture of God, in worship, it is possible to be guided by the focus of another's attention. This change in our focus might simply be by means of the emphasis another person places on certain words, the shape and posture of their body, or even the focus of their gaze (on, say, the altar, or the cross, for example). All these ways might serve as pointers to redirect our own attention and thereby to experience some different aspect of God, thereby removing our biases in important ways.[39]

Thus, jointly attending to God together through liturgy means not only that God's presence is the focus of gathered worship but also that who one worships with impacts the way in which one pays attention to some things and not others. Certain communities may serve only to mirror or echo one's own biases and conceptions (or misconceptions) of God. Others will provide a different point of focus. Consider the way in which a TV show you might previously have found amusing (despite a few crass jokes) becomes an excruciating experience when watched with your prudish relative; you suddenly become aware how bad the language is. The presence of another impacts your experience of the same event in profound ways. And thus, in jointly attending to God's presence with others, liturgy has immense power to shift and direct beliefs and desires about God, as explored in chapter 1.

SHARED SITUATIONS AND GROUPS: MOVING BEYOND PHYSICAL COPRESENCE

So far, we have described the importance of joint attention in understanding shared experience, and the necessarily interactive, engaged character of joint attention. We have also suggested that understanding liturgy in terms of joint attention provides a helpful starting point for understanding the jointness of liturgical practices. This analysis fits cleanly within small-scale cases of gathered worship, where participants can interactively respond to each other's actions. But humans are capable of collective intentional acts that go beyond the here and now and create richly complex cultural activities and institutions.[40]

In this section, we consider how broader claims about the nature of praying as part of a larger community can have implications for what gives certain kinds of prayer their sense of jointness. We seek to broaden our understanding of what it means to share attention beyond the kind of attention sharing that occurs in an embodied, second-personal interaction. Consider the following three cases to see how such an account might be developed in more general terms:

1. *Taxi*: John drives his taxi with Mary riding in the back.
2. *Cocktail party*: John and Mary have a conversation while standing in a circle of friends at a cocktail party.
3. *Cup final*: John and Mary watch the World Cup final together in a large public football match screening.[41]

While these cases have important differences, we could describe them all, following Jon Barwise, as "shared situations."[42] Our use of the phrase "shared situation" aims to capture two key points. First, joint attention occurs in temporally extended episodes or activities (such as in the taxi example), and within these activities there is a continual sense of jointness that persists even in the absence of direct second-person engagement with some of the people involved. This sense of jointness is weaker than that which emerges from engagement, but is nonetheless important.

Second, we use the language of "shared situations" to emphasize the significance of being embedded in spatial, social, and historical settings that shape cognition, and social cognition in particular.[43]

What do we mean by "a continual sense of jointness"? Let us return to cases 1–3 to explore this concept more carefully. In the taxi example, there may be true moments of joint attention between John and Mary, where they lock on to the same feature of the world (e.g., when Mary points out the right street for John to turn into). But even when they do not (e.g., when Mary is on her phone and John watches the road), there is the sense that there is still something shared about their situation. By participating in the shared activity of the taxi ride, they both inhabit a shared situation, with particular spatial and temporal boundaries; spatially they are constrained by the taxi and its environs, and the temporal limits are set by the length of the shared activity of the taxi ride. They also inhabit a shared culture of norms and information that they can draw upon if need be. This sense of jointness provides contextual framing by which individuals' actions, communicative or otherwise, can be interpreted.

It is important to note that this embeddedness occurs on multiple scales.[44] In the example of the cocktail party, while there is the situation of the conversation between John and Mary, the situation also involves a wider sense of jointness in virtue of the circle of friends, which contains the situations involving John and Mary. Each of these layers can be viewed as a shared situation, that is, a context in which there is a sense of common participation and jointness and which individuals can attend to as it is relevant to them. In the example of a cup final, just as in the cocktail party, John and Mary's jointness extends to those who are also gathered at the public screening, but it also seems to extend wider than this—to the other millions of viewers of the television broadcast of the match, alongside those watching in the stadium. National events such as football matches, royal weddings, and national prayer rallies foster a sense of jointness that extends much more broadly than those in which one is directly engaged in joint attention with physically present others.

What does it mean to say that jointness can be experienced even in the absence of others? We have so far considered various conceptual components of joint attention. One is that it requires the motivation to share experiences and attention with others.[45] Another is that it is, in many cases, an activity or action,[46] something that is enacted with others in embodied, second-personal interactions, by directing each other's attention using a point of the index finger, a shift of gaze, or a touch on the arm. The third, and most pertinent here, is that it involves the joint attention *state*, in which one believes oneself to be sharing an experience with others.[47] Early in development, this arises primarily (arguably, exclusively) through second-personal engagement. But adults simply need the appropriate beliefs to achieve this state. For instance, a number of inventive studies demonstrate that human behavior is guided by cues to others' attention. For example, Risko and Kingstone found that participants behaved differently when wearing an eye-tracking headset that they thought was inactive versus an eye-tracking headset that they thought was active.[48] They were less likely to attend to a potentially embarrassing stimulus (a swimwear calendar hanging nearby) when they believed the headset was active. It is plausible that individuals can experience not only a sense of being a target of attention but a sense of shared attention with a nonpresent agent.

Going beyond the inferred attention of a particular other, Shteynberg and colleagues have explored the idea of a "shared attention state," in which an agent believes that others in their social group are attending with them.[49] Rather than believing another agent to be co-attending with oneself, individuals can enter a cognitive state such that they are aware in a more diffuse sense that others are concurrently attending to the same feature of the world as them, even if these others are not physically present to them or if this does not involve a defined set of individuals. As the work of Shteynberg and others shows, agents in this cognitive state show measurable differences in affect and behavior compared to those who do not believe others to be attending with them, such as experiencing emotional stimuli with more intensity[50] or being more likely to pursue a goal.[51] Jointness can thus arise from entering this "situationally-informed mental state"[52] and can be influenced by a range of factors, from spatial properties of an environment to cultural knowledge.

LITURGICAL PRACTICES AS SHARED SITUATIONS

Now that we have a fuller sense of the range of possible experiences of jointness, we can move beyond thinking about liturgical practices only in terms of joint attention with physically present others. Returning to our opening discussion of virtual reality, we can again ask how online liturgy allows participants to experience jointness with others. We might also consider cases in which joint attention fails to explain cases of in-person worship. For example, if Mary is distracted by how the light is shining through the stained-glass window for a moment while most other members of the congregation are listening to the service, we might wonder whether her experience is really shared with others.

First, if we understand jointness as lying on a continuum from minimal to maximal cases, even without being in person, online services still have ways of facilitating jointness. Details like arraying participants on a single screen foster a sense of participating together. While synchrony is not possible with the same fidelity as when in person, participants can still perform the same acts or sing the same songs. In the case of hybrid services, the virtual presence of those who are watching can be acknowledged as part of a service, and those watching online can be invited to take part in the prayers and readings. These efforts do not bridge the gap to the experience of physical participation but help remind participants that their attention is shared. Online services offer a means of creating a sense of jointness, however minimal.

Similarly, consider the following kind of case: the Church has been running a forty-day community prayer event over Lent, with materials for the congregation to take home, giving them short passages with brief prayers to use during private devotion. One woman in the community is particularly thankful for the event, as she is unable to regularly attend Sunday worship due to working away from the area. She describes the comfort that comes from praying with an awareness that others are praying alongside her. On our account, this is a liturgical practice which allows for a sense of jointness. The woman described here embeds her experience of engaging in prayer within a broader community. While the mechanism underlying this sense of jointness does not involve joint attention, there is a sense in which the woman's experience is shaped by others, even though they are not present—she takes comfort from the belief that other members of her community are joining with her in prayer (the implications of which we will explore in more detail in chapter 3).

A similar phenomenon might underlie the notion of "sacred spaces." As one author puts it, "sacred places and churches have an aroma of prayer; it's almost as if the prayers and holiness of countless faithful over generations are clinging to the walls and columns."[53] One way of understanding this notion of sacred spaces is to embrace historical and cultural influences on one's sense of jointness. By entering an ancient house of prayer, one might experience a sense of connection not only to those who might be present now but to those who were there before. In a similar vein, the French historian Pierre Nora coined the term "lieux de mèmoire" to describe "the embodiment of memory in certain sites where a sense of historical continuity persists."[54] As we will explore in more detail in chapter 5, this sense of embedding worship within the history of the community of faith is an important part of what it means to think of liturgy as shared. Moreover, physical locations play a role in shaping what is shared amongst groups, not only through cultural knowledge (e.g., "people have worshiped here for generations") but also by virtue of particular perception-shaping properties (e.g., having all seats facing a central location).[55]

Finally, in the Christian tradition, there is a sense in which all liturgical practice has a sense of jointness if properly conceived. As Underhill puts it, no worship is a "solitary undertaking,"[56] but rather it always plays a role in the wider community of the Church. She continues by writing that

> both on its visible and invisible side . . . [Christian worship] has a thoroughly social and organic character. The worshipper, however lonely in appearance, comes before God as a member of a great family; part of the Communion of Saints, living and dead. His own small effort of adoration is offered "in and for all." . . . He shares the great life and action of the Church . . . He is immersed in that life, nourished by its traditions, taught, humbled, and upheld by its saints.[57]

How might reflecting on this theological claim that worship is bound in the life of community shape the sense of jointness in liturgy? While Underhill is making a metaphysical argument here,[58] we can also think phenomenologically about these cases. For instance, one might participate in an act of worship alone while bringing to mind that one is part of the Church as a corporate whole.[59] We think such an experience involves a sense of jointness—that is, the notion that one is not worshiping alone plays an important role in shaping the experience of how one worships. This phenomenology seems to be rooted in the belief that others are worshiping alongside the Church. As we have suggested above, while the jointness of a situation ordinarily involves at least some interactive embodied engagement with others, there are cases in which jointness is grounded purely in a belief about others rather than in direct engagement with them.

This capacity to experience jointness even in the absence of others can be applied to examples such as praying in sacred spaces or singing alone with an awareness of the corporate nature of the Church. Beliefs about jointness can be triggered by entering environments that have a particular significance to individuals or communities. We have suggested that the spatial setting is important for facilitating a sense of jointness through both historical-cultural knowledge and the physical layout. Similarly, reflecting on the theological truth that one's prayers are part of a wider corporate body may achieve a felt sense of jointness.

Our claim throughout this book is that all liturgy fits somewhere on this scale of jointness—from instances of copresent acts of gathered worship in the same building, to those in which the sense of jointness derives from one's beliefs or certain environmental cues. Often, multiple levels of jointness are operative in a liturgical practice. This has a theological and psychological component. In a psychological sense, the experience of worship is nested in multiple layers of community—from those, one is physically proximate to the wider sense of direct community (i.e., this congregation) and to one's broader conception of community (i.e., the whole church, distributed over time and space). Theologically, we might put it like this: all worship, however individual it may seem, is bound up in the mystical and corporate life of Christ, and so, gathered worship is significant because it speaks of a theological reality. As Stanley Hauerwas puts it, the act of gathering for worship "indicates that Christians are called from the world, from their homes, from their families, to be constituted into a community capable of praising God."[60] This simple act of forming a community capable of participating in the worship of God (Father, Son, and Holy Spirit) provides what Underhill calls a "here-and-now embodiment" of the deeper theological reality that Christians are members of Christ's body, forming part of a social organism composed of many diverse parts. Thus, it is important to see that the liturgical act of gathering together as members of the Church is not a mere tool to further one's "personal walk with Jesus," akin to a self-help group or an exercise class. The Church does not gather just because it is good to do so, good as it may be. It gathers to express the conviction that the whole Church is united.

SUMMARY

In summary, our argument is that jointness comes in degrees. We have provided a conceptual framework for thinking about different kinds of shared situations, ranging from cases of physically present joint attention with two agents, to group cases of joint attention, to situations in which an individual's beliefs create the experience of jointness. Focusing on liturgy, we have argued that liturgies facilitate the experience of jointness with a variety of others, both those participating alongside oneself but also, arguably, with the wider Church. This framework is helpful not only for reflecting on the kinds of shared situations in which we participate with other people, but with trying to understand the ways in which liturgies facilitate the experience of jointness with God. Moreover, focusing on the shared nature of liturgy can give us a way of thinking about the value of gathering together. As we will see, in reflecting on the ways in which liturgy can exhibit jointness in different ways (specifically through petition, confession, gratitude, and remembrance), we can more clearly articulate the ways in which gathered worship is valuable and important for the life of communities.

3
PETITION AND CONFESSION
The Value of Praying Together

PRAYING TOGETHER

On May 26, 1940, Britain was at a point of crisis. Locked in war with Nazi Germany, British troops were stranded on the beach at Dunkirk. King George VI called for the nation to turn to God in prayer and plead for his assistance. Millions of individuals flocked to churches and queued for hours outside Westminster Abbey to pray *together* for God's assistance. While undoubtedly many of these individuals were already active in praying regularly for God's protection of their country and troops, there was something importantly different about the mass-scaled coordination of prayer that happened on this day. What followed was the "Miracle of Dunkirk"—a violent storm over the beaches of Dunkirk grounded many of the Luftwaffe, followed by a period of calm in which British civilians united to rescue the troops, using fishing boats and small leisure boats. Many of those who joined in these prayers saw these events as a direct answer to prayer and a work of God.

While these circumstances were extraordinary, the practice of praying together in this way is something that happens on a regular basis across churches all over the world. Praying together takes many different forms—from small prayer groups in houses, to intercessory prayer in formal church liturgies, to mass-scale prayer gatherings. Prayer comes in many forms, such as petition (requests), praise, and confession, and each of these can be expressed in community as well as by individuals. The focus of this chapter is to understand what makes communal prayer distinctive. The account of liturgy and jointness we have been arguing for so far in the book can help us to further our understanding of praying together.

JOINTNESS AND COMMUNAL PRAYER

The practice of prayer has been the subject of countless academic books and journal articles in psychology and theology.[1] Despite recent work in sociology,[2] anthropology,[3] and ethnography[4] on the social dimensions of prayer, much of the theological and philosophical literature focuses only on acts of private communication between individuals and God. Yet, we know that communal prayer is one of the central practices of the Church. The foundational prayers of the Judeo-Christian tradition—the Shema and the Lord's Prayer—are first and foremost to be expressed as a community. From the early church (Acts 1:14, 4:23–32) to the present day, almost every Christian tradition and denomination practices some form of praying *together*. Many of the Epistles encourage the practice of praying together; Paul tells Timothy that "the men should pray, lifting up holy hands without anger or argument" (1 Tim 2:8). The early Church was also clearly committed to communal prayer as part of their regular practice; Luke writes that "they devoted themselves to the apostles' teaching and the fellowship, to the breaking of bread and the prayers" (Acts 2:42).[5]

Given this emphasis on praying together, we might ask: What is the difference between communal and individual prayer? To begin to answer this question, consider two examples of communal prayer from more contemporary contexts, an American Evangelical congregation (Vineyard) and a South Korean congregation:

> People pray for each other in many different ways. In "prayer ministry," the person for whom one is praying is physically present. One stands before the person and puts one's hand on their arm or shoulder, or—if praying in a large group—on the arm or shoulder of someone who is touching them, or at least with one one's hands out facing them.[6]

> A unique and special Korean prayer style is called Tongsung Kido. Tongsung means, "cry out together loudly," and Kido means, "pray." . . . during worship, usually at the time of special prayer request, the minister or the worship leader will call the congregation to pray in unison. The whole congregation joins together to pray aloud, individually at the same time. Sometimes, in the beginning of prayer, the congregation may shout, "Lord! Lord! Lord!" in unison, as a cooperative sign of engaging in prayer. Usually the congregation is given a specific amount of time to pray, with

a common theme of petition. At the end of the time allotted, the minister's closing prayer finishes.[7]

The discussion of joint attention in the previous chapters contributes to understanding the common features of communal prayer. As we argued there, liturgical forms can provide a mutual object around which the congregation can focus and guide one another's attention to in order to experience God's presence and attention. In the first example above, the words of the person praying become a focus of joint attention between the two, and the use of nonverbal communication (e.g., placing a hand on someone's shoulder) contributes to shaping the focus of attention. Yet, the prayer is not a mere communication between two people, as in a phone conversation or a chat over a cup of coffee: What is distinctive about communal prayer is that the pray-er addresses *God*; through the mediums of speech and touch, those participating in the prayer focus their attention together on God and experience God as co-attending with them.

However, as we saw in chapter 2, while an appeal to interactive joint attention has some application, it also has its limits. These limits surely apply to communal prayer too; in instances of communal prayer, most of the congregation close their eyes and are perhaps only directly aware of the individual they can audibly hear. It is not obviously the case that the congregation actively attends to all other members of the congregation. Cases can also vary in the kind of jointness experienced. In cases of Tongsung Kido, the act is necessarily shared yet also highly individualistic in the sense that the content of each prayer is known only to the individual pray-er. It is here that a broader sense of jointness provides a helpful framework for understanding how prayer is still communal. In chapter 2, we outlined an account of "shared situations," in which there is a continued sense of jointness that continues beyond active engagement. For example, we discussed the case of a taxi ride in which the passenger stops actively engaging with the driver midway through the journey. Just as the passenger in a taxi may retain a sense of jointness through the taxi ride despite a lack of active engagement with the driver, we think that many instances of communal prayer will have a similar phenomenology of being shared with others, regardless of how often moments of interactive engagement occur. That is, even when active joint attention is not occurring, it seems reasonable to think that the context of communal worship will evoke a sense of jointness in the participants. This may provide a much better sense of why communal prayer is joint than does appealing only to active joint attention.

In the case of the taxi ride, and of communal prayer in a church building, there is a material context that sets the boundaries for whom prayer is shared with. But many instances of communal prayer lack this material dimension yet still retain a sense of jointness. For example, the case of the National Day of Prayer appears to be one such case in which the sense of jointness extends beyond those who were in the same room. In recent times, many churches have adapted their regular services so they can be attended online. Through online mediums (such as Zoom), churches hold prayer meetings and services with two-way engagement between participants. In such contexts, prayer requests can be shared and responded to, and petitionary prayer can occur in group settings, much like an in-person gathering. Other churches choose instead to worship and pray through live streaming services, such as YouTube. Those participating in streamed services are not able to engage directly with each other (except through written comments), yet they can still engage with a sense of participating at the same time as the rest of the community. Streamed services can create a sense of jointness, such as when the minister says, "now, we're all going to pray for the community project for two minutes," or encourages online participants that "even if you can't be heard in the building, God can hear your prayers."

This broader sense of jointness that can occur through streamed prayer services also points to an even broader context in which communal prayer is situated. Consider the way the Anglican Daily Offices (Morning Prayer, Evening Prayer, etc.) are described: "Praying the Daily Office as a small group, a couple, or a church tangibly realizes this promise for Christians, and as many Anglicans throughout the world will be praying these exact same prayers, so does praying the office on your own!"[8]

The examples above (National Day of Prayer, online worship, Daily Offices) are very different in kind but share a common feature, namely that they do not derive their sense of jointness from interactive joint attention. Furthermore, they are shared situations that do not involve physical copresence. Some degree of interactively grounded jointness is present in the case of Zoom prayer; despite not occupying the same physical space, participants are able to interact with one another. In the case of streaming a service or saying the Daily Offices each day, the sense of jointness does not derive from any kind of direct engagement; rather, it is the belief that other Christians are sharing in these same prayers. The sense of jointness is prompted by the use of a common liturgical script or a video that others are watching, thereby helping to contextualize the prayer in a broader community. Much like the example of praying in sacred spaces, discussed in chapter 2, the sense of jointness present in this case is not caused by interaction but by a belief in the reality of the Church.

Thus, we have seen that the scale of jointness depicted in chapter 2 helps to show what unites the different forms of communal prayer. They range from the cases that involve active joint attention (such as the prayer ministry in the Vineyard church), to those that take place in the same place without active joint attention (such as listening to prayers of intercession in formal worship), to those that have a sense of jointness with no active or embodied features (such as streaming a service on YouTube). All these cases fit under the umbrella of joint liturgical acts but differ significantly from one another. We can thereby see the practical importance of the account outlined previously. This is not to say that these forms of prayer are equivalent or equally important, but it is to resist placing a strong binary between in-person and online acts of prayer. Our account emphasizes that jointness lies on a spectrum and that prayer can have a sense of jointness in many different ways. Of course, it is likely that physically copresent forms of prayer will foster stronger experiences of jointness (for example, many of the bodily effects of joint attention we will discuss shortly will be much more pronounced in interactive, embodied cases). But by seeing the ways in which jointness comes in degrees, we can understand in-person prayer as nested in a much broader sense of jointness.

THE VALUE OF COMMUNAL PETITIONARY PRAYER

We have seen that the psychological and philosophical concepts of joint attention and shared situations offer a fruitful way of thinking about the different ways in which prayer can be shared, as well as the scales of jointness offered by different kinds of prayer. But our hope is that this discussion offers more than mere conceptual clarity about the *nature* of prayer, that it also helps us to explore something of the *value* of praying together. Put simply, our question is this: Why pray together if you can pray alone?

Many responses have been offered to this question about the value of praying together. For example, consider a description of prayer in the Quaker community:

> In the quiet we look for a sense of connection. This might be a connection with those around us, with our deepest selves, or perhaps with God. As we feel this sense of encounter grow stronger,

> we may begin to see the world and our relationships in a new way. Our worship may take us beyond our own thoughts and ideas to help us respond more creatively to the world around us . . . Anyone can contribute to a Quaker meeting for worship—there is no leader . . . You can sit anywhere you want. No seats are special or reserved. Chairs or benches are usually arranged in a circle or a square. This helps us connect with each [other] and reminds us that we are worshipping as equals. The meeting starts as soon as the first person enters the room.[9]

Here, prayer is described not only as having value in communicating with God but also as having value for strengthening relationships with other people. This value is not unique to the Quaker tradition either. While the details of specific practices in various Christian traditions might be different, a generalized point can be drawn: in communal prayer, one's engagement with God is mediated by one's engagement with other people.

The sense of connection made between those who are praying is not unique to the Quaker tradition. Reflecting on this aspect of prayer has led some theologians to posit that communal petitionary prayer has the potential to be more "effective" than private prayer in certain respects.[10] Let us consider two such claims. First, the twentieth-century Presbyterian minister and theologian H. H. Farmer claims that communal prayer has the potential to influence pray-ers in ways that individual prayer often cannot. This starts with a particular understanding of prayer and its purpose. Writing on the relationship between God's providence and the practice of prayer, Farmer writes that

> reconciled man . . . becomes a co-operator with God, so that through him God gets a purchase on the human scene not otherwise possible. The new life of co-operation with God is manifested in prayer, and in a daily activity increasingly informed and guided by the divine Spirit.[11]

For Farmer, prayer involves the individual's "awareness" of "having been sought and found and reconciled by . . . [the] love of God."[12] That is, one of prayer's primary values is its capacity to align the will of those who pray with the will of God. But it is important to see that thinking of prayer as cooperative means that mere repetition of some set of words is not sufficient for prayer to be effective; one must also enter into the situation of those they pray for, in "a deliberate act to enter into the needs of others."[13] In other words, the value of prayer is not magic! It is not the use of the right words per se, but the ways in which these words form the will of those who are praying.

Building on this understanding of prayer, Farmer stresses that an implication of thinking of prayer as a cooperation with the will of God is that we can see a particular value in praying communally. He writes that seeing prayer as a cooperative venture with God

> indicates the value of corporate prayer, on which the Christian consciousness has always insisted. If there is an added effectiveness in prayers which, without ceasing to be the expression of the individual's own heart, are also corporate, it is because such prayers are prayers of fellowship, prayers of the Church. They rest on, and carry the power of, at least a partial realisation of that to which all true prayer is directed, namely that membership of one another in the love of God, which is the kingdom. To regard corporate prayer as though it were an addition sum, so that the more people there are praying for anything the more certain is the result, merely because there are, so to say, more units of prayer-pressure per square-inch being exercised, is, of course, shallow and absurd. More people at prayer means more effectiveness in prayer only if it represents an extension and a deepening of fellowship, a passing of more personalities out of the lower and sinful status of isolation into the higher and redeemed status of loving co-operation in God for the high ends of His kingdom.[14]

It is important to stress that, for Farmer, claims about the effectiveness of prayer are not merely psychological or sociological. That is, prayer's efficacy cannot be explained only by appealing to the natural effects of doing things together. Farmer insists that "it is because such prayers are prayers of fellowship, prayers of the Church" that we can speak of their effectiveness. In other words, corporate prayer reflects something of the essentially corporate identity of the Christian life, which cannot be conceived of in isolation from the community of the Church. But in reflecting this deeper reality, we can also see a certain kind of efficacy in aligning the wills of the community with the will of God. This efficacy is defined in terms not of a capacity to exert greater influence on God but of drawing participants into a deeper understanding that they are participating with each other in the communal life of God, and thus strengthening their connectedness with each other. This claim need not diminish the value of private prayer (this would be strange, considering Farmer spends much longer discussing the value of prayer in noncommunal contexts), but, rather, it stresses the difference between the two kinds of prayer and the potential value which might arise because of their difference in nature.

Farmer's discussion of corporate prayer has led to wider discussion about the effectiveness of corporate prayer. In his influential work on the philosophy of prayer, the South African philosopher and theologian Vincent Brümmer claims that "corporate prayer is more effective than individual prayer, not because it brings more pressure to bear on God but because it enlists more people in the realization of God's will."[15] Brümmer is directly building on Farmer's remarks here, but the context of his discussions is much narrower than Farmer's. Brümmer is primarily concerned with the philosophical question (sometimes dubbed "the problem of petitionary prayer") of why a perfectly good God would listen and respond to the petitions of finite, imperfect creatures. His conception of intercessory prayer emphasizes the "double agency" of prayer, namely that "the person who prays both asks God to act on behalf of the person or cause for whom he intercedes, *and also* makes himself available as a secondary cause through whom God could act in answering prayer."[16] Like Farmer, Brümmer stresses that praying together provides a context where the telos of prayer (i.e., to fulfill this double agency) can sometimes be achieved more effectively than in the context of private prayer. The reason for this, Brümmer writes, is that

> corporate prayer not only enlists more people to become secondary causes through whom God can realize his benevolent aims in the world but also creates a bond of fellowship between those who pray. They become one body united in seeking the will of God in the world. Those who pray together, stay together.[17]

Echoing Farmer's emphasis on the shaping of the wills of the community, Brümmer stresses that one of the reasons that God asks for people to petition him in interceding for others is so that they might cooperate with God's will more fully. Adding to Brümmer's account is this emphasis on social bonds that corporate prayers establish, which he thinks will allow the community of faith to be enlisted into the double agency of responding to the needs prayed for.

Thus, as we see in both Farmer's and Brümmer's works, the claim that communal prayer is more effective in certain contexts is the implication of a cooperative view of petitionary prayer. That is, they argue that praying together allows for a kind of double agency in which those who pray become more aware of God's will and are enlisted into becoming agents of God's purposes in the world, reflecting their reality as members of the social reality of God. We are not concerned here with defending this view of petitionary or intercessory prayer but rather with exploring what makes communal prayer distinctive or valuable. We think there is much promise in these remarks about the value of praying together, which the psychological sciences can help us to explore in more detail. In the remainder of this chapter, we seek to offer psychological and theological perspectives on this question of the value of praying together.

Note that the particular "effectiveness" of communal prayer is not equivalent to saying that communal prayer is more valuable. For this would assume that the only aim of prayer is efficiency of ends—indeed, it seems obvious that private prayer serves much better as a means of developing personal closeness in relationship with God. Another way of putting this same point is to note that different forms or contexts of prayer are geared towards different kinds of outcomes, such as differential effects on mental or spiritual health.[18] As Bernard Spilka and Kevin Ladd note in their comprehensive overview of the psychology of prayer, in praying in a group situation, "the prayer is typically conceived as an occasion when one is connected not only with a singular object (i.e., one's Deity) but also is simultaneously in the presence of other believers."[19] As they go on to argue, this sense of connection with other believers can create social bonds, as well as influence and enhance individuals' own experiences of prayer.[20] It is this sense of connection as a means of influence that we explore in more detail in the remainder of this chapter.

PSYCHOLOGICAL AND THEOLOGICAL PERSPECTIVES ON THE VALUE OF COMMUNAL PRAYER

A key value of communal prayer, as Brümmer and Farmer describe it, is that it allows pray-ers to be influenced by one another so that they might enlist one another into enacting God's will in ways that private prayer cannot. As we have suggested in the first section of this chapter, all communal prayer has a sense of jointness. This can be established by means of interactive joint attention experiences, by certain material environments which enable a sense of jointness, or even by scenarios that prompt individuals to form relevant beliefs relating to the jointness of their situation, like live streaming. This can help us to think more carefully about the value of communal prayer. In what follows, we seek to offer two psychologically informed discussions of two of Brümmer's and Farmer's claims: (1) that communal prayer is effective because it enlists more people into God's will, and (2) that communal prayer is effective because it creates opportunities for social bonding within community. And last, we consider an important theological foundation to these claims, namely (3) that communal prayer is rooted in the communal life of God.

Common Knowledge and Coordination Problems

First, thinking of communal prayer with a broader concept of jointness can help us to expand the claims made in the previous section about the efficacy and distinctiveness of communal prayer. For instance, one distinctive aspect of communal prayer is its ability to facilitate "common knowledge."[21] That is, shared situations enable individuals not only to have knowledge (e.g., of some object, event, or fact) but also to infer that each other person with whom the situation is shared knows the fact, and that they each know that each other person knows that they know. As Michael Chwe describes it, common knowledge that occurs in shared situations allows one to get over "coordination problems," in which

> each person wants to participate in a joint action only if others participate also. One way to coordinate is simply to communicate a message, such as "Let's all participate." But because each person will participate only if others do, for the message to be successful, each person must not only know about it, each person must know that each other person knows about it.[22]

Chwe thinks that common knowledge allows one to overcome coordination problems in a variety of shared situations. For instance, suppose a group of friends are holidaying together and get separated in a busy street. Because each member of the group knows that the ice cream parlor is the agreed rendezvous point, as well as knowing that each of the other members knows this and that each member knows that each other member knows, group members are able to find one another when separated and thereby to overcome coordination problems. This kind of coordination can also occur in wider-scale contexts, as Chwe points out. For example, Chwe notes, when the Apple Macintosh computer was first introduced to the market, its products were incompatible with other computer devices, and its users would only be able to share data with fellow Macintosh users. This posed a kind of coordination problem—"a potential buyer would be more likely to buy if others bought them also."[23] Apple overcame this coordination problem by presenting a short, stimulating commercial and screening it during the Super Bowl, an event that viewers would know was being viewed by many others across the United States. In doing so, they aimed to create not only awareness but also common knowledge about the Macintosh.

Chwe's discussion of common knowledge points to a helpful way of thinking about communal prayer and jointness—certain goals or aims can become common knowledge between participants in a way that would be impossible with private prayer. Because prayer is necessarily an activity in which God is understood to be a participant, it provides a unique context in which to share common knowledge within a community. For example, in cases of what we could call "holy gossip," prayers can be used to make facts common knowledge that would otherwise be difficult or even socially unacceptable to introduce in a communal context, such as "God, please help David with his gambling problem." While, if misused, this has the potential to cause intra-communal strife, it could also, in line with Brümmer's argument, help achieve "an extension and a deepening of fellowship," to the extent that individual burdens can be shared and greater support provided. Such cases bring out the complexity of the interaction between context and content; such a prayer would carry a different significance if said between a married couple as opposed to in a church-wide prayer meeting.

The advantage of the approach we have taken is that it emphasizes how the situation provides contextual framing that, for those praying, shapes the significance of what is prayed. This offers one motivating factor for engaging in activities that would otherwise be overly risky, whether that is purchasing a new computer that is incompatible with other brands (which was true of the Macintosh) or launching out to sea in a sailing boat to rescue stranded soldiers. Indeed, this seems to capture what goes on in many cases of prayer, particularly communal prayer, which is supposedly more effective in enlisting others in the will of God. A part of what happens when individuals join together to pray is that some ideal becomes common knowledge between them, or at least that this common knowledge gets reinforced, making it more salient in their memories. Thus, as in the example of praying along with a live-streamed service on YouTube, which gives a sense of praying alongside the church, the pray-er might be spurred on to pray more fervently because she knows the community is praying alongside her. The jointness of the situation no doubt proved invaluable in creating this knowledge.

Moreover, it seems plausible that this sense of jointness plays an important role in overcoming coordination problems in religious communities more generally—the knowledge that I am not the only person who is aware of the needs in the community, or the world, surely plays an important role in overcoming the feeling that "I am just one person who cannot change the world." What the jointness of communal prayer reiterates is that the values and goals of a particular religious tradition are common knowledge, thereby undermining the feeling of inadequacy against the daunting task of transforming the world. This argument aligns with psychological research that has found that joint attention to a goal increases individuals' motivation to complete that task, even with unseen others.[24]

Overcoming coordination problems is more likely when participants can have confidence that others are committed to pursuing the common goal. A further influence of communal prayer may therefore be the way in which it reinforces participants' commitment to act upon this knowledge, or creates a joint commitment to act. Psychologists, medical researchers, and behavioral economists recognize the role of "commitment devices"[25] in supporting behavioral change towards valued outcomes (e.g., weight loss,[26] environmentally friendly behaviors[27]), with public commitments being one effective strategy for behavior change. Consider the individual who prays for help to overcome addiction. Making this statement in front of others, in a context of prayer, imbues this statement with a social, normative, and spiritual significance that would not be possible if made alone.

In the above example, one has an individual commitment in a joint context, but communal prayer can also involve formation of joint commitments, that is, those that require multiple agents to make a commitment together.[28] Psychological research suggests that it is typical to expect agents who cooperate on a task to be more strongly committed to their goal (e.g., less likely to abandon the task) than agents with the same goal but who are working independently.[29] Communal prayer, with its varying forms of interpersonal coordination, may serve to bolster participants' sense that others have committed to pursuing the goal that has been made common knowledge. Thus, when members of a community join together to pray about a need (e.g., greater support for elderly members of the congregation), they publicly signal that they are jointly committing to address that need. Even minimal cues like communicative eye contact[30] and the use of *we*-pronouns[31] can foster a sense of commitment between agents, and it is plausible that a sense of commitment may arise in communal prayer even without every participant verbally and explicitly articulating their commitment, but rather through being present in the gathered praying community.

One might think this dimension is concerning—that the key mechanisms at work in communal prayer are in fact obligation and guilt. It could certainly be misappropriated in this way, and commitments can indeed serve to create a sense of obligation.[32] However, commitments are vehicles that individuals and communities can choose to help them pursue a valued goal. In a wedding ceremony, part of the purpose of the commitments made is to promote valued outcomes such as loyalty and mutual service, regardless of fluctuating circumstances or mood. When these commitments are made before one's community and before God, they take on an additional normative and spiritual force. Some kinds of communal acts of prayer serve a similar function; participants need not be coerced into committing, but choose to participate out of a conviction that the praying will support them to act in a faithful manner.

The above observations are true of cases which include copresent joint attention (such as in the cases from the Quakers, Vineyard, and the Tongsung Kido prayers). They may involve particularly strong common knowledge and communal commitments to act. But it is also plausible that there are cases in which all that exists is a belief in some kind of jointness (such as Zoom prayer, YouTube service, praying the Daily Offices), which results from a particular environment or state of mind. The knowledge that one is not alone in, say, building the kingdom of God, or caring for the poor, or preaching the gospel, allows prayer to be more effective in overcoming problems of coordination. Committing to this in the presence of others and the presence of God will provide an even stronger impetus to act in accordance with one's prayers.

Alignment and Communal Bonding

The second factor of Brümmer's and Farmer's reflections on communal prayer is the emphasis on the development of community amongst those who pray: praying together is valuable because it promotes affiliation between pray-ers. In his book on coordinated movement, William H. McNeill describes how certain rituals such as dancing and military marching provide a kind of unity of feeling and consciousness between participants.[33] Writing about the example of group dancing, McNeill describes a kind of "boundary loss" occurring in which the individual feels they are one with the group because of a "blurring of self-awareness and the heightening of fellow-feeling with all who share in the dance."[34] He argues that a similar phenomenon can be found in the use of military drills—acting together in unison with others can "create and sustain group cohesion; and the creation and maintenance of social groups."[35] McNeill claims that acting together in dance and ritual fosters this sense of group cohesion, thereby achieving a kind of "practical efficiency"[36] regarding the group's aims and causes.

Numerous studies have vindicated aspects of McNeill's arguments, showing that synchronous muscular coordination produces affiliation in both pairs and groups.[37] Similarly important is the role of imitation and mimicry. Following others such as Chartrand and van Baaren,[38] we use *imitation* to refer to intentional acts of reproducing another's action, and *mimicry* to refer to spontaneous and nonconscious forms of action reproduction. Both forms have related but distinct effects. Research on imitation and mimicry has considered their role in understanding others as "like me";[39] both as thinking agents experiencing the world in a similar way and as those with whom one is (or can be) affiliated.[40] Given the critical role of imitation in the development of understanding other minds and identifying with others, it is plausible that large-scale activities involving imitation and mimicry support the process of aligning with others, increasing relational closeness and shared attitudes.[41] Communal prayer, which frequently involves both intentionally imitating a leader's or each others' actions and words, is therefore a context that is ideal for increasing affiliation between the community of pray-ers.

While not all communal prayer includes muscular bonding and the kind of physicality of acting together that dance and military drill allow for, the sense of togetherness that shared situations can foster seems more generally applicable. Evidence from social psychology suggests that it is not just muscular coordination that can produce affiliation, but also sharing experiences in general. There is evidence that sharing an experience boosts the emotional valence of that experience. Boothby and colleagues have demonstrated that sharing the experience of eating caused participants to enjoy the experience of eating chocolate more than when eating it alone.[42] This was felt even more strongly by friends who completed the task.[43] Such effects are also found in cases of negatively valenced shared experiences. Bastian and colleagues found that strangers who experienced pain together felt closer than controls who experienced a nonpainful shared experience, and were more cooperative when later asked to take part in an economic game.[44]

These findings suggest that sharing the experience of communal prayer may be both an intrinsically unifying activity but also something that increases the strength of emotions towards the target of attention (which may be a theological truth or a practical problem that needs to be overcome), thereby increasing the strength of shared belief and likelihood of action. This line of thinking follows the arguments made in chapter 1 regarding the holistic and deeply social view of ritual formation. Furthermore, it dovetails with psychological and anthropological research on ritual, which emphasizes the varied ways in which rituals foster close social bonds between participants.[45]

Communal Prayer and Joint Attention to God

Finally, it is important to note the theological reality that is expressed in praying together. As we saw in Farmer's discussion, the value of praying together is not merely psychological or sociological. Much of what we will argue about the psychological benefits of prayer could surely be said of any communal event with a cause, such as a political rally or a union strike. In both the liturgical and nonliturgical cases of communal ritual, the psychological alignment and sense of jointness create an efficiency deriving from a united community. But to understand prayer in particular, it is necessary to understand its theological rationale. As we argued in chapter 2, what distinguishes liturgy from other communal practices is that it allows for a sense of jointness not only with each other but also with God. This dimension of prayer is key to understanding its distinctiveness, regardless of one's theological commitments (or lack thereof). So, what does this sense of jointness with God achieve for participants in communal prayer?

In his book *Worship, Community, and the Triune God of Grace*, James B. Torrance recalls an incident of meeting a Presbyterian minister on a beach in California. The minister tells Torrance that his wife is dying of cancer, that he does not know how to pray for her, and that he struggles to have faith in the midst of this situation. Torrance's reply is to remind the minister that he has a great high priest in Christ who prays on his behalf (Heb 7:25). He also tells the minister that the Holy Spirit intercedes for him when he cannot pray himself (Rom

8:26). As Torrance writes, "Our first task is not to throw people back on themselves with exhortations and instructions . . . but to direct people to the gospel of grace."[46] In other words, for Torrance, prayer is not primarily an act of communal or individual response to God but one of participating in the life of prayer that is already present in the life of the Trinity. In this way, Torrance's theology of prayer aligns with the emphasis seen in Farmer's work on the social reality of prayer. Praying involves joining the constant and ongoing activity of God through the Church, rather than relying solely on the initiative of any particular individual.

In the previous chapter, we wrote of the mystical jointness that is present in liturgy being situated in the broader context of the Church. Torrance's story helps to press the case that this makes a significant difference to how prayer is approached. For the minister in Torrance's story, there was relief to be found in the knowledge that his struggle to pray was not condemned, but that his concerns were being held by the prayers of Christ and the Holy Spirit. We think that a reorientation in perspective of this kind can lead to a different kind of efficacy. As we have argued above, the sense of knowing that one's prayers are joined with other people's can help to overcome the belief that "I am just one person who cannot change the world." If this is the case for one's relationship with other praying humans, what effect might we expect for those who believe they are joining their prayers with the prayers of the Triune God? Rather than thinking of prayer as solely or even primarily coming *to* God, Torrance helps to rethink prayer in terms of joining *with* God in the renewal of the world.

This theological claim about prayer's embeddedness in the life of God is important for shaping the perspectives of those who participate in liturgy. John D. Witvliet, reflecting more generally on a Trinitarian approach to liturgy, writes,

> At their best, these trinitarian practices and ways of speaking are not merely rhapsodic remnants of past spiritual experience, but are deeply intertwined with lived trinitarian spirituality, in which believers today, without fear or bewilderment, enter into liturgical participation with a profound sense of privilege, gratitude, and holy astonishment that God has called and invited them, that Jesus is praying for and with them, that the Holy Spirit is at work crying

> "Abba" in their hearts . . . This kind of trinitarian spirituality . . . is expectant, hopeful, and patient, aware that God's Spirit works in a myriad of contexts and circumstances to bring about redemptive experiences of communion with God, including ones that we recognize only retrospectively, and others that we may never fully recognize.[47]

This point is crucial for a theology of jointness. Unlike other kinds of gathering, even those which aim at enacting change (e.g., political rallies or town hall meetings), the liturgy of the Church derives its perspective of hope from its location in the life of God, not from merely joining in with other participants. This point helpfully articulates the double agency of prayer articulated by Brümmer; praying together is not just about enlisting more people in a common cause or achieving an abstract goal. This much would be to emphasize only the human aspect of double agency; communal prayer in its ideal form draws the community together so that they can become more aware of the will of God and be formed together around a joint sense of God's will for the world.

CONFESSION AND THE ACT OF AUTHENTIC COMMUNAL PRAYER

This chapter has reflected on the ways in which communal prayer might differ from individual prayer, leading to a greater community cohesion and a greater effectiveness in seeing prayer answered. Before concluding, we will focus on another kind of communal prayer that can help provide a helpful caveat to some of these claims. For we wish to avoid the superficial conclusion that praying together through acts of joint attention always leads to a greater social cohesion. As Sipsova and Carpenter describe, joint attention is important for creating relationships characterized by "trust, openness, and intimacy." Yet, they also acknowledge that the same mechanisms can be misused to have the opposite effect. They observe that "skilled deceivers can exploit this to create an illusion of openness and use shared attention behaviors for deception in competitive or deceptive situations (e.g., being sure to make eye contact when lying)."[48] While this is not an area that has been explored at length by psychologists, these observations show the ways in which the same mechanisms might have quite different effects.

One feature of communal prayer that we think can provide a helpful context for trust, openness, and intimacy to be developed is in the use of prayers of confession. Consider the use of general confession, which in many traditions is used regularly in liturgy as a communal prayer said together, such as the following prayer from the *Book of Common Prayer*:

> ALMIGHTY God, Father of our Lord Jesus Christ, Maker of all things, Judge of all men: We acknowledge and bewail our manifold sins and wickedness, Which we from time to time most grievously have committed, By thought, word, and deed, Against thy Divine Majesty, Provoking most justly thy wrath and indignation against us. We do earnestly repent, And are heartily sorry for these our misdoings; The remembrance of them is grievous unto us; The burden of them is intolerable. Have mercy upon us, Have mercy upon us, most merciful Father; For thy Son our Lord Jesus Christ's sake, Forgive us all that is past; And grant that we may ever hereafter Serve and please thee In newness of life, To the honour and glory of thy Name; Through Jesus Christ our Lord. Amen.[49]

The words of the general confession, penned by Thomas Cranmer, provide a means by which the whole community engages in the practice of confession. As it is noted in the minister's invitation to confession, confession is especially important in the context of gathering; "although we ought, at all times, humbly to acknowledge our sins before God; yet ought we most chiefly so to do, when we assemble and *meet together*."[50]

These words are first and foremost to be used not by individuals to make their own confession to God but by communities to confess together. Echoing Underhill's claims about the corporate reality reflected in liturgy, W. S. T. Wright notes that "the Church is the sphere in which the Divine forgiveness is both proclaimed and appropriated, because it is the Body of Christ. No man sins to himself: the Body of Christ is broken by the sins of all its members. Restoration of fellowship with God must also mean the renewal of fellowship with the Family of God. Confession again bears witness to the corporate nature of sin and forgiveness."[51] In jointly attending to the words of the confession liturgy and speaking them together, the congregation expresses this reality of the Church and addresses God together in prayer. In acts of general confession, the community is given the opportunity to express its shortcomings and to receive pardon and mercy from God.

As Annemari S. Kidder has explored at length, the use of confession is in significant decline amongst churches. She attributes this to a more clinical approach to spiritual development, characterized by pastoral counseling, social work, and spiritual direction becoming more widespread features of churches.[52] However, one result of this decline in confession is an increasingly individualized sense of spiritual development. Kidder writes that spiritual development is increasingly focused on "the aim of evading or circumventing Christ and sustaining a personal level of comfort." What is lacking, Kidder thinks, in the omission of confession from liturgy is the "nudge to reveal one's ugly and sin-tainted self and to overcome personal pride in the company of another, rather than premature assurances of personal wholeness; and a glimpse of interconnectedness within the body of Christ, the church rather than a focus on sin's individuality and the exceptionality of the person's spiritual experiences."[53] In other words, Kidder thinks, confession in the context of community is vital for engaging properly with one's sin, in part by shifting the emphasis away from individual failings alone and towards a recognition of shared capacity for failure. Engaging in shared forms of confession thus has a distinctive capacity to form deeper and more sincere forms of community, which in turn liberates individuals from becoming overwhelmed and isolated by guilt.

This claim concerning the relationship between confession and depth of community is explored by the German theologian Dietrich Bonhoeffer, who writes that

> it is possible that Christians may remain lonely in spite of daily worship together, prayer together, and all their community through service—that the final breakthrough to community does not occur precisely because they enjoy community with one another as pious believers, but not with one another as those lacking piety, as sinners . . . all have to conceal their sins from themselves and from the community. We are not allowed to be sinners. So we remain alone with our sin, trapped in lies and hypocrisy, for we are in fact sinners.[54]

Bonhoeffer stresses that there is a kind of false piety that occurs when communities lack corporate confession; even if individuals confess before God individually, the lack of corporate confessions creates a community in which members of the community lack the common knowledge of one another as sinners. It is quite obvious the problems this poses for social bonding; a community that only prays superficially together, with this premise of false piety, does not create the context for true and deep social bonding. It is like the community of parents who all wrongly assume that their most favored topic of conversation is their children's routine because each makes an assumption about the other. Secretly, each parent wishes their gatherings could actually focus on something more interesting than the mundanity of when their children each eat, sleep, and defecate, but no one of them is brave enough to explore new conversational ground. As such, the lack of common knowledge prohibits their capacity for social bonding beyond sharing their desire for more consistent sleep.

Moreover, this lack of social bonding might also lead to a coordination problem of sorts. Those parents who look to signal their proficient parenting skills, rather than sharing their limitations and anxieties, will never be able to coordinate to form a community that can actually be of mutual help. Even if these parents have parenting questions or concerns where they need support, they will only be able to receive useful input through admitting that they would benefit from help.[55] Similarly, if communal prayer is about the enlisting of people into the work of God to bring about change through the power of the community, then prayers of confession play a crucial role in the forming of communities that can overcome problems of coordination in a deep and meaningful way.

Thus, it is important to recognize that the act of jointly attending to liturgy together is not itself sufficient for the kinds of value we have been exploring in this chapter. Indeed, even if one used Cranmer's words of confession each week, it would still be possible to engage in a way that is superficial and lacking in depth. Bonhoeffer writes that "in confession there takes place a *breakthrough to community*. Sin wants to be alone with people. It takes them away from the community. The more lonely people become, the more destructive the power of sin over them . . . sins that were acknowledged helped the sinner to find true community with other believers in Jesus Christ."[56] For Bonhoeffer, the key is not just the use of general confession, which itself can become a means of superficial engagement, but the admitting of "concrete" sins to others in the community (he also suggests that everyone avoids confessing to the same person, to avoid an imbalance of power). The presence of joint attention, even when the object of attention is God, is not sufficient for relational depth; joint attention must also be entered into with vulnerability for social bonding to occur.

SUMMARY

We have been considering the nature and value of communal prayer. As we have seen, while some theologians are keen to stress that communal prayer and private prayer are importantly different, it is not always clear what this difference amounts to. We have offered an analysis of communal prayer as facilitating diverse experiences of jointness. As we have suggested, this feeling of jointness has a scale of intensity and can be elicited in a variety of ways. Embodied, interactive joint attention is central to experiences of jointness, but we have highlighted other means of creating and maintaining the sense of jointness that is vital to communal prayer, such as by means of certain environmental or epistemic stimuli like praying in a sacred space or with an awareness that the whole Church is joined together in prayer. Moreover, we have given two possible explanations for why communal prayer might be more effective than private prayer in certain respects. First, it enables common knowledge and commitments to act upon that knowledge, thereby overcoming coordination problems and defeating the belief that "one person cannot change the world." Second, because communal prayer involves aligning with others, it fosters and encourages social bonding within a community, which can thereby spur individuals to engage in maintaining and pursuing ideals and goals. Finally, we have seen the ways in which jointly attending to God might fail to lead to a depth of community and explored the ways in which communal prayers of confession might provide a context for vulnerability in the act of praying together.

4
GIVING THANKS TOGETHER
Group Gratitude and Liturgical Loafing

LITURGICAL GRATITUDE

One of the central features of Christian liturgy is the expression of gratitude.[1] The Apostle Paul tells the church in Colossae to "teach and admonish one another in all wisdom; and with gratitude in your hearts sing psalms, hymns, and spiritual songs to God" (Col 3:16). Gratitude can be expressed in spoken liturgy: for example, in reciting the words of a Psalm:

> Praise the LORD!
> Praise God in his sanctuary;
> praise him in his mighty firmament!
> Praise him for his mighty deeds;
> praise him according to his surpassing greatness! (Ps 150:1–2)

As the Psalmist expresses, the praise of God expresses something of God's nature ("according to his surpassing greatness"), as well as focuses on the work that God has done ("praise him for his mighty deeds"). Or, gratitude to God may be expressed in song, in singing one of the thousands of hymns of gratitude that have been written across the full spectrum of Christian traditions, whether accompanied by rock guitars or by choir and organ. Relatedly, gratitude might be expressed in the bodily movements of eating and drinking in the Eucharist ("Eucharist" literally means "thanksgiving"), in which remembrance of God's mighty deeds (which we explore in chapter 5) provides an expression of gratitude. Along with confession and petition, gratitude is arguably one of the key attitudes expressed in Christian liturgy.

There has been an explosion of work on gratitude in the past two decades. Much of this work, led by Robert Emmons and colleagues, has focused on the therapeutic benefits of gratitude, providing evidence of the impact of gratitude interventions on psychosocial well-being.[2] In parallel with this growing interest in the practical benefits of encouraging gratitude has been an increase in conceptual work exploring what exactly gratitude is.[3] However, one frequent omission from conceptual work on gratitude is the focus on gratitude in groups rather than merely individuals. As Jo-Ann Tsang has recently observed, "the majority of research on gratitude focuses on single recipients of gratitude . . . The prototypical situation is one benefactor providing a benefit to one recipient."[4] But as Tsang continues: "Humans are social creatures. We experience benefits on a group level, as well," leading her to ask, "Do people still experience gratitude, even if the intended recipient is broader than themselves?"[5]

Tsang is surely right. If we are to understand the nature of gratitude in the context of liturgy, it will not suffice to simply understand how individuals might be said to have the virtue of gratitude or to feel emotions of gratitude. For it is typical for liturgical gratitude to be expressed by a group. As Nicholas Wolterstorff puts it, "The church blesses God, praises God, thanks God, confesses her sins to God, petitions God, listens to God's Word, celebrates the Eucharist. It's not the individual members who do these things simultaneously; it's the assembled body that does these things."[6] Thus, unlike many of the acts of practices recommended in the gratitude literature—gratitude journaling, spiritual disciplines, letter writing, et cetera—liturgical gratitude takes place in the context of a group. Many lines of liturgy use the pronoun "we" (e.g., "we thank you for feeding us with the body and blood of your Son Jesus Christ"[7] or "We thank Thee each morning for a newborn day").[8] How should we understand the meaning of these expressions of gratitude expressed as "we"? Are they a shorthand way of saying "John and Mary and Sam thank you"? That is, are they expressions of simultaneous individual gratitude? Or, can groups—couples, communities, institutions—be grateful? These questions will be the focus of this chapter.

We begin by exploring the role of attention in acts of gratitude generally and acts of liturgical gratitude more specifically. Then, drawing from work in psychology and philosophy, we offer a taxonomy of different kinds of group gratitude. Finally, we suggest some ways in which group liturgical gratitude can prove beneficial. More specifically, we argue that a kind of liturgical "loafing" might take place, whereby those who cannot express gratitude to God in a fully formed way (either through circumstance or capacity) can participate in and contribute to a grateful community. While the literature on loafing is typically negative (i.e., it seeks to explore the ways in which individuals avoid contributing to the actions of the group), we show that reflecting on a theological understanding of group liturgical gratitude provides a surprising role for loafing in a more positive light.

GRATITUDE AND ATTENTION

As Liz Gulliford and colleagues note,[9] there is no unified account of what gratitude is. Gratitude, they note, has been characterized as an action (e.g., engaging in a behavior that shows one is grateful) and as an emotion (for instance, "gratitude is an emotion, the core of which is pleasant feelings about the benefit received").[10] Alternatively, within a virtue ethics framework, Gulliford and colleagues suggest that gratitude might be conceived of in episodic terms (i.e., as a sequence of behaviors that combine to form an expression of gratitude), or it may be described as a trait (i.e., the property of an individual who consistently displays grateful behavior). Gulliford and colleagues thus conclude that the study of gratitude currently resembles a "complicated network of overlapping and criss-crossing concepts"[11] and suggest that "psychologists slow down their hurry to publish papers on the effects of gratitude to spend more time examining key conceptual issues."[12]

Our aim here is not to try to provide a singular definition of gratitude[13] but instead to focus on sub-concepts that might provide helpful points of contact with other relevant domains of investigation in psychology and philosophy, specifically those that have explored the various joint and collective facets of human experience and behavior related to the themes of jointness and joint attention we have been exploring so far in this book. By drawing upon preexisting conceptual resources, it is possible to chart a path forward for understanding the various complexities of group gratitude. In each case, we identify a sub-concept that has previously been discussed in the gratitude literature and link it with a corresponding area of research that has explored joint or collective instances of that sub-concept.

First, it is important to see the connections between gratitude and attention.[14] It has been argued in various places that gratitude is about directing one's own attention from the negative to the positive. For instance, Emmons and Stern maintain that

> gratitude practice is systematically paying *attention* to what is going right in one's life . . . Gratitude practice is intentionally shifting your *attention* from the negative to the positive.[15]

Similarly, writing on the positive subjective effects of gratitude for those who are depressed, Philip C. Watkins writes,

> I propose that gratitude may mitigate depression by directing one's *attention* away from oneself to others. Research has shown that depressed individuals engage in self-focus that exacerbates their dysphoria . . . I submit that a grateful disposition and practice should result in directing one's *attention* more to others and what they are providing for one, and away from maladaptive self-preoccupation.[16]

Naturally, we think that there are some helpful links between the role of "attention" (according to Emmons and Watkins) and the concept of joint attention we have been exploring throughout this book. As we have seen, joint attention has been described as enabling co-attenders to achieve a shared or mutual awareness of features of the world, whether concrete or abstract.[17] In the case of gratitude, it is thus plausible that just as individual gratitude involves attending to a source of gratitude (e.g., to the positives in one's life),[18] so joint attention can involve jointly attending to some shared source of gratitude. For example, while two partners can individually be grateful for the arrival of their new child, they can also jointly attend to this source of gratitude. To do so jointly is plausibly a distinct kind of experience to doing so individually, as we will go on to explore.

Moreover, this focus on the role of joint attention in gratitude goes beyond providing us with a conceptual account of how objects of gratitude can be jointly attended to. Joint attention also seems to play a role in achieving a shared experience of subjective inner states in expressing gratitude.[19] Through responsive engagements with others, participants are able to achieve a sense of commonality between their private subjective experiences.[20]

Moreover, as outlined in chapter 2, shared experiences lie on a scale of jointness.[21] While the strongest kinds of jointness involve active, communicative, physically present engagements, there are also minimal joint experiences that can occur in the total absence of others.[22] As we will argue, group gratitude experiences can be similarly diverse, from a couple celebrating together, to an individual who is aware that others are also grateful for the actions of healthcare workers during a time of national crisis. Thus, understanding gratitude through the lens of joint attention is a helpful place to begin if we are to understand how multiple subjects can be grateful to God.

A TAXONOMY OF GROUP GRATITUDE

To see the different ways in which gratitude might be expressed jointly in the context of liturgy, first consider more generally how we might conceive of gratitude in group contexts.[23] Instances of group gratitude (such as those described in the introduction) are not just occasions to jointly attend to an object. They also appear to involve communities *expressing* gratitude together. If we think of gratitude as involving an expression (of that gratitude), then we might think that the entity making such expressions is sometimes more than one person. Consider the following examples:

1. You receive a Christmas present addressed to your whole family and send a note to thank the gift giver, signed "The Smith family."
2. You receive a thank-you gift from a couple after letting them stay with you for a few days.
3. On your last day at work, your organization sends you a letter of thanks and a large check thanking you for all your hard work over many years.

Who is expressing gratitude in these examples? You individually, or the whole family? The couple, or each individual? The individual members of your workplace, your boss, or the organization? There are further questions that arise regarding the emotional experiences involved in such cases. If your brother is not grateful for the joint gift but you are, is your family still grateful for the gift? If one of your colleagues did not contribute towards your leaving gift, is gratitude still being expressed by the *whole* organization? These are complex questions. To begin to answer them, we need some clear ways of distinguishing between different kinds of gratitude phenomena in these contexts. Thus, to understand what is going on in acts of liturgical gratitude, we need to reflect on the group dynamics present.

Individual and Group-Context Gratitude

The first kinds of gratitude we consider are *individual* gratitude and *group-context* gratitude. These levels are similar in that there is a single grateful agent in each case. However, the difference that marks cases of group-context gratitude is that while gratitude is experienced or expressed in a group setting, the grateful agent is an individual rather than a group. Consider Tsang's example. She imagines a community stricken by natural disaster receiving money to fund the rebuilding of the whole town.[24] Such a case, Tsang thinks, is different from a case in which an individual's house is rebuilt after a natural disaster. For in the group case, the individual beneficiary, the recipient of a new house, is nested in a broader community, the town. While the beneficiary of the benefit in such cases is a group, gratitude is still described as something primarily attributable to individuals. All that the group provides is the context for such gratitude.[25]

In such cases, one is not experiencing gratitude jointly with others, nor is an organization or community said to express gratitude in any meaningful sense; it may occur in total absence of interaction with or presence of others. Furthermore, we can further divide contextual group gratitude between "offline" and "online" cases (note, these are technical psychological terms, rather than references to virtual and embodied contexts). Offline contextual group gratitude requires a minimal awareness that one shares a reason for gratitude with others, but with no sense that others are doing so at the same particular moment. A relevant example is "vaccine gratitude": one can be grateful that they have received a flu vaccination, knowing that others across the country are also grateful, despite these acts of gratitude not necessarily occurring simultaneously. The act is not entirely individual, as one knows one's gratitude is likely to be occurring in the same broad time frame as that of others.

However, it is offline because it is not clearly occurring simultaneously with others. In contrast, online contextual group gratitude requires awareness that one's individual gratitude is occurring simultaneously with others who are also being grateful for the same reason or reasons. For example, the "clap for carers" movement in the UK had people across the country expressing gratitude (by clapping, banging pans, or playing music) at a particular time each week during the national lockdown brought on by COVID-19. Even those who did not (or could not) actively participate, or lived away from others (i.e., could not express gratitude *jointly*), could take a moment to be grateful for the nation's carers, aware that many others were doing so at that specific moment. Here, we had something like Siposova and Carpenter's "attention monitoring,"[26] where another agent or agents' attention is part of one's individual-level experience. But in many cases, it did not rise to the level of joint gratitude, since there was no communication or joint attention present in the expressions of gratitude.[27]

In the context of liturgy, individual and group-context gratitude will often occur. In gathering to sing hymns, or engage with written liturgical scripts, there are many ways individuals may be prompted to be grateful to God for what they have received. This might involve group-context gratitude, such as when a community is invited to reflect on the ways in which each of them are grateful for the life of an individual who has recently passed away. This group-context gratitude may even (to preempt some of the reflections in the following chapter) be embedded within the wider community of God's people over time. The ways in which we have been describing the nesting effects of jointness provide a helpful way of seeing how the context of individual gratitude might be located. We think it is even possible that most instances of liturgical gratitude are of this individual kind, in which liturgy provides an occasion for members of the community to express their gratitude to God. But it is also important to see that there are many other instances of group gratitude present in liturgy than merely individual or group-context gratitude.

Joint Gratitude

Next, consider joint gratitude. Joint gratitude involves (1) jointly attending to the source of gratitude, (2) co-attenders actively signaling to each other that they have a grateful attitude to that source (even if this attitude is not always identical in all participants), and (3) jointly responding with some kind of grateful action.

Here, it will be helpful to consider in more detail how we might understand joint action (which we briefly considered in chapter 2). A helpful distinction is made in the work of Deborah Tollefsen between "joint action" (which we explain in this section) and "collective action" (which we explain in the next section).[28] Tollefsen describes joint action as "the ability of individuals to engage in joint actions such as moving a table together, painting a house together, or playing a game of chess."[29] In contrast, collective action refers to groups which "have a structure and a decision-making process."[30] The actions of the Labour Party, for example, cannot be easily explained by referring to the coordinated actions of its members; we also need to know something about who is authorized to perform which actions. In other words, collective action requires a kind of structure to enable group action.

Let us explore what is meant by joint action. As we started to examine in chapter 2, if we consider examples of groups acting together, whether sports teams, orchestras, or actors, for example, there is a sense in which some group activities go beyond the actions of each individual. As Woodworth articulates,

> two boys, between them, lift and carry a log which neither could move alone. You cannot speak of either boy as carrying half the log . . . Nor can you speak of either boy as half carrying the log . . . The two boys . . . achieve a result which is not divisible between the component members of this elementary group.[31]

What, then, marks a coordinated action as joint? Philosophical accounts have generally argued that the latter case involves some kind of "shared intention" or "we-intention."[32] There has been significant debate regarding how exactly to characterize shared intentions and how to identify the processes involved in joint rather than parallel actions,[33] an issue akin to the question of the jointness of joint attention.[34] These discussions have spawned a large and growing literature on joint action in the psychological sciences. Amongst the differing theoretical approaches in this literature, there is a general agreement that joint actions involve qualitatively different processes to those involved in acting alone or in parallel with others.[35]

Turning to the intersection of joint action and gratitude, it would seem reasonable to suggest that there are cases in which grateful actions are joint actions. If, for example, a couple received a gift from a friend, they could express gratitude individually; one might bake the generous friend a cake, and the other could write the friend a letter. But there can also conceivably be cases in which the grateful response is joint; both individuals bake a cake for the friend, or both write a letter together. In such cases, it would appear that the most appropriate way to understand these grateful actions is as jointly grateful actions, which cannot be credited half to one person and half to the other, but must be attributed wholly to both.

Joint action also provides a useful way of understanding liturgical expressions of gratitude. Different religious traditions engage in communal activities such as prayers, ceremonies, and fasts that are understood as active expressions of gratitude.[36] For example, Terence Cuneo argues that in the example of singing in liturgy, participants are required to sing *together* not merely to sing as individuals; "to engage in group singing . . . requires that I adjust my singing to yours and that you adjust your singing to mine in 'real time', often in ways that are not dictated by the score that they are following."[37] These ways might include the sharing of eye contact, the reading aloud of text, or simply the awareness that the person nearby is slowing their tempo unexpectedly. In liturgical singing there are joint intentions present, such that individuals intend to sing the liturgy *together* rather than to act as individuals. While in cases of group-context gratitude, individuals may happen to express the same intention at the same time, in acts of joint liturgical gratitude, individuals must attempt to mesh or merge their intentions, such that the subject expressing gratitude is "we," not "I." If I try to speak at the same time as my fellow congregants, or to coordinate my movements such that I raise my hand in worship when the worship leader sings the line "so we raise up holy hands to praise the holy One," then liturgical gratitude is a kind of joint gratitude.[38]

An interesting possibility of joint grateful actions (which we will explore in more detail in the final section) is that one can participate without the emotional experience of gratitude. Using our example, John might know that the generous friend had obtained their money through illegal activity, and thus is not grateful for their gift. However, rather than reveal this knowledge, he may choose to jointly act in a grateful manner with Betty. One might argue that both actors must experience grateful emotions for a genuine case of joint grateful action. But for Betty, it seems plausible to say that there would be no difference in her experience.

It is also important to see that joint gratitude involves shared awareness of both the source of gratitude and individuals' response to it. Similarly to individual cases, a group of jointly grateful individuals can be assigned the trait of gratitude if they persistently engage in grateful behaviors. However, it is important to note that joint gratitude need not involve *identical* levels of experience and involvement amongst all participants. Not only will participants have a distinct subjective experience,[39] but they do not necessarily all contribute equally to jointly grateful actions.[40]

Collective Gratitude

Finally, consider what we call collective gratitude. Collective gratitude occurs when organizations or social groups are organized such that they can act gratefully in response to benefits identified at the collective level. Note that unlike the other kind of group gratitude, collective gratitude is not dependent on joint attention, and there is no collective-level phenomenology. The individuals on whom the collective actions depend may attend to group-level benefits, but the collective as the subject of gratitude can only *identify* benefits, through decision-making procedure (such as voting, or group hierarchy).[41]

To see how we might understand this, return to Tollefsen's concept of "collective action." To explain collective action, it is helpful to first see the limits of joint action. As Stephanie Collins describes, joint action "rises and falls with the specific joint commitment that defines it—for example, a joint commitment to paint the house or go for a walk."[42] If one person fails to uphold their commitment while a motivated individual might still finish painting the house, only the part of the house that was painted by both can be understood as having been painted jointly. But not all instances of group action seem to rise and fall in quite this way. For example, large organizations appear to persist even when key members leave, and this does not mean that they are unable to continue to perform group actions or to act virtuously (or indeed, viciously). Consider how a newspaper might be said to display the virtue of courageous journalism. While a team of investigative journalists might display courage through joint actions (such as the *Boston Globe*'s exposure of abuse, as depicted in the movie *Spotlight*), we might also say of a newspaper that it is courageous over a long period of time (i.e., we might say that the *Boston Globe* has consistently acted courageously in pursuit of the truth for the past two decades, even though its editorial team has changed entirely over this period). Collective-action accounts allow us to talk about the actions of groups over longer periods of time, whereas joint-action accounts do not allow us to say much of the long-term actions or virtues of a group, given the ways in which action is tied to the specific instance of joint commitment.

In large, dispersed groups in which work is delegated, accounts focusing on joint action fail to capture a plausible account of the group's acting. It is plausible that one might contribute to the actions of a group without having any awareness of the aims of the larger group. For example, the *Boston Globe* might recruit a journalist to write an article that involves a long-term covert investigation (i.e., because of its sensitive nature), such that the rest of the staff is not aware of the journalist's actions and the journalist is unaware of the actions of the group. When the article is eventually published, it is still the case that *The Boston Globe* has produced a piece of courageous journalism. But it does not do this in virtue of joint action of any discernible kind. The same would clearly apply to cases of group gratitude. That is, there are, plausibly, instances of gratitude in which large, dispersed groups might be said to act gratefully. And so, we must look beyond joint gratitude if we wish to provide a comprehensive taxonomy of group gratitude.

Consider an example. Suppose a university receives a large financial gift from one of its donors. The university hierarchy meets together to decide what the best response to this donation might be, and after some deliberation, decides to send a letter to the donor on behalf of the university, as well as name one of their faculty buildings after the donor. In the letter, the university principal writes the following words: "On behalf of the university, I would like to express my deep gratitude for your donation; this gift will benefit many students for many years to come." Who is the beneficiary in this instance? Not the principal, or at least not primarily. Not a group of students who are jointly grateful for the gift, either. Rather, we suggest, the *university* is the beneficiary of the donation, and the principal's letter expresses gratitude on behalf of the university as a group.

How should we make sense of such claims? According to some philosophers,[43] collectives can be thought of as agents, capable of performing actions (such as a corporation spilling oil in the North Sea), and even as moral agents capable of displaying virtues and vices (such as a corporation having the vice of greed). While joint action clearly plays a role in what is happening in these cases, for the reasons suggested above, it cannot be said to give a complete account of group action. The reason for this is that members of groups do not all contribute to each action a group performs. Typically, in collectives there are authorizing members (i.e., those who permit others to act on their behalf, like fee-paying members of a trade union) and active members (i.e., those who are authorized to act on behalf of the group, say by lobbying an employer on behalf of a trade union). As List and Pettit argue, in a collective

> two types of members are typically present and often overlap. In a participatory group like a voluntary association, members have the same status within the group agent; they equally authorize the

> group agent and take roughly equal parts in acting on its behalf. In a hierarchical organization, such as a commercial corporation or a church, there may be differences in the members' roles, for example through holding different offices or through belonging to subgroups with different tasks.[44]

Return to our example of the university's letter. In an organization such as a university, some are authorized to speak on behalf of the collective.[45] The principal of a university is elected or appointed to have such authority, but there are likely many layers of authority beneath this too. Committees are appointed to make decisions on behalf of the university in issues of policy and governance. But then there are many members of the university who are unable to contribute to its agency directly; an undergraduate student does not have the authority to write a letter of thanks *on behalf* of the university. However, by becoming a member of the university, she authorizes (even if only implicitly) the principal to express gratitude on her behalf. Thus, in order to explain collective gratitude, we need to provide an analysis of what it is for that group to act, that is, to explain who is authorized to act on behalf of the group and who is authorized to participate as a member of the group.[46]

While we might seek to distinguish between cases of individual gratitude by referring to emotional states, clearly this option is not available in the context of collective gratitude, since organizations and institutions cannot feel grateful.[47] But this does not mean we cannot distinguish between such cases at all.[48] Take a parallel example: "greenwashing," where corporations appear to offer environmentally friendly products in order to attract environmentally conscious consumers, though the company shows a disregard for how sustainable their products really are. Many activists are deeply troubled by these practices, and rightly so. But this is not because they want companies to have *emotions* concerning the planet but rather because they want companies to act for the right *reasons*. They want companies who are committed to the end goal of sustainability rather than solely of profit. Similarly with grateful institutions, what might distinguish genuine gratitude is the reason (or reasons) for the grateful action. Is the board committed to expressing thanks to its benefactors, or does it merely wish to look good on social media? We can make these distinctions without invoking any emotional states.[49]

Finally, let us reflect on how liturgical gratitude might be thought of as a kind of collective gratitude. It seems plausible to think that the liturgical "we" (e.g., in a line of liturgy) refers sometimes to a broader group than is captured by the joint-action account. Consider the following prayer that a minister might pray in liturgy:

> Lord, we are so grateful for what you are doing in the life of our community. Thank you for your Word and its challenge to us this morning to thank you in all circumstances. We pray you would make us a thankful people. In Jesus' name. Amen.

The expression of gratitude in this prayer seems to refer not only to the individuals present in the liturgy, or those jointly enacting the liturgy, but also to the community more widely. For instance, Betty, a long-standing member of the congregation, might have been in bed with a fever on the morning of this prayer, but arguably the pastor's prayer still applies to her as she is a member of the community. Similarly, Jon may have been distracted when the prayer was being said and failed to attend to the pastor's words. But in some sense, the words still apply to the collective in which he is a member. In other words, group gratitude sometimes describes an action that is performed by a wider community, beyond instances of joint action.

Finally, this collective sense of "we" in the context of liturgical gratitude may extend to a much broader group, namely the whole of the Church. Return to Underhill's remarks that in worship, the participants of the liturgy form "part of a social and spiritual complex with a new relation to God; an organism which is quickened and united [by the Holy Spirit]."[50] In expressing gratitude to God in liturgy, individuals are brought into a group that extends beyond what an individual is currently aware of, either in congregational structure or through jointly intentional action.[51]

THE VALUE OF GROUP GRATITUDE

We have now considered how to make sense of the group nature of liturgical gratitude. We can now consider the potential benefits of engaging in gratitude in this context. First, it seems reasonable to think that many of the benefits of communal prayer discussed in chapter 3 also equally apply to liturgical gratitude. Given existing work on the influence of co-attention on emotions, it is plausible to argue that grateful feelings are amplified when shared.[52] That is, rather than a situation in which individuals in a group setting are encouraged to bring to mind reasons they are each individually grateful to God, all members of the group express gratitude to God together. This is not to claim that shared grateful experiences are *always* stronger than individual grateful experiences but that sharedness is just one of many factors that might influence an individual's emotional experience.

Similarly, just as communal prayer might lead to social bonding, it has been shown that gratitude serves to promote affiliation between benefactor and recipient.[53] But it is also plausible that there are effects that promote cohesion within larger groups.[54] For example, individuals that experience gratitude towards a fellow group member (in one study by Algoe et al., a fellow sorority member[55]) also feel more integrated within that social group (the sorority). Algoe and colleagues propose that this is because the dyadic-level sense of social value that comes with gratitude to a particular group member serves to enhance one's sense that one is a genuine member of the larger group. It is plausible that this is also the case at the joint level; sharing gratitude with others helps create a sense of being part of an integrated group that experiences common benefits.

Here, particular features of gratitude to God (rather than gratitude to other sources) are also relevant. Tsang suggests that group-based benefits (those that help an individual but are not specifically for that individual, such as healthcare, civil liberties, etc.) typically generate weaker grateful feelings than individual benefits (e.g., someone paying for another's operation).[56] She suggests that this is because in the individual case it is clearer how a specific relationship benefits, which has the further effect of there being a clearer sense of a benevolent motivation. However, as Tsang goes on to suggest, if the benefactor is God, it is possible that a specific sense of relationship, and thus sense of benevolence, can emerge. This means that group-based benefits that usually generate weak grateful feelings can generate stronger feelings if the benefactor is believed to be God, and with whom one has a personal relationship, rather than some more diffuse category ("the government," "British society," and so on). We might also expect different effects in the case of liturgy, where the sense of group is at both the collective and joint level. Here, the sense of the group in which one is benefiting may be collective (i.e., the Church) but also distinctly local (i.e., this church), in which case the sense of group benefit is likely to be much more specific and thus generate stronger grateful feelings.

The benefit we wish to explore in most detail is that of "liturgical loafing." It has been shown that by engaging in intentional gratitude practices (such as journaling[57]), individuals can facilitate an increase in grateful feelings, regardless of their emotional state at the point of deciding to engage in such practices or while actually engaging in the practice. But what if one does not feel grateful when participating in liturgy?

For many, participating in acts of liturgical gratitude may be difficult. In any congregation, there will be those who are experiencing personal difficulties such as grief, depression, or perhaps even a sense of apathy. Moreover, some scholars have even argued that, for some people, a feeling of gratitude to God might rarely or never be present. For example, in a recent paper, Kent Dunnington argues that if we

> focus on what is supposedly the essence of gratitude—grateful feelings—I suspect many Christians will agree that they fail to live up to the calling to be grateful to God. For many Christians, feelings of gratitude to God fall short of what one would expect given what Christians allege to be God's extraordinary beneficence.[58]

It seems possible, if not likely, that many cases of liturgical gratitude (whether group-context, joint, or collective) include those who participate without the concomitant grateful feelings. Are such people really expressing gratitude? Are they participating in the life of a grateful community?

To respond to these questions, it will be helpful to make a distinction that we borrow from the psychological discussion of forgiveness. Everett L. Worthington Jr. argues that "decisional forgiveness" (i.e., a willful act to forgive someone who has wronged you) and "emotional forgiveness" (i.e., the feeling of no longer holding wrongdoing against a transgressor) can be differentiated in complex ways. Worthington writes, "People could decide to forgive and not experience emotional forgiveness. They also could experience sudden compassion for a transgressor . . . and realize that unforgiveness had disappeared even though no decision had been made to forgive."[59] It is not always the case, Worthington thinks, that emotional forgiveness precedes decisional forgiveness or vice versa. While it is typically the case that decisional forgiveness leads to emotional forgiveness, this might not always be so; one's affective response to a perpetrator might change and lead to a decision to forgive. It seems plausible to think that a similar distinction might be made between decisional and emotional gratitude.[60]

Making this distinction allows us to say something more nuanced about the role of emotion in liturgical gratitude. Such gratitude typically involves a kind of decisional gratitude in which the participant chooses to engage in acts of thanksgiving to God. Moreover, in many cases of expressing liturgical gratitude, it may be the case that participants do not respond emotionally to God. But as the distinction above alludes to, participating in grateful liturgies by deciding to be grateful may still have the effect of increasing one's gratitude emotions in the long term. As Worthington argues, acts of decisional forgiveness may be a cause of emotional forgiveness; it seems reasonable to think something similar could occur in the case of gratitude. Indeed, as we have seen in our discussion of liturgical formation (chapter 1), there may be some value in participating in liturgy even if one is not "feeling it." Regularly engaging in confession teaches one how to forgive and be forgiven. Regularly petitioning God teaches one how to pray. Similarly, liturgical acts of gratitude provide a kind of training for how to act gratefully. And this may have the result of leading to an increase in emotional gratitude towards God, even if this outcome is not instantaneous. Indeed, one might argue that the function of a gratitude diary, a method used widely in the gratitude literature,[61] is precisely to develop gratitude in this way. By repeatedly *deciding* to record things that one is grateful for (regardless of one's feelings in that particular moment), one can become more grateful, in the sense of having grateful emotional experiences more often.

But regardless of whether one is *feeling* grateful, the benefit of thinking about liturgical gratitude in group terms is that we can find ways of carrying those who cannot express gratitude in a fully formed way, such as those whose life circumstances make it difficult to be thankful. The importance of the Church as a community to carry those who are struggling is stressed in many places in Scripture. Paul emphasizes that the community of the Church should bear "each other's burdens" (Gal 6:2). Elsewhere, he writes of the interconnectedness of the suffering of each member of Christ's body ("If one part suffers, every part suffers with it" [1 Cor 12:26]). It seems crucial to accommodate this need for community and gathered worship to those who cannot participate in gratitude.

We can see this by considering a phenomenon some social psychologists have called "social loafing," in which the group carries members who do not or cannot contribute to joint actions.[62] This might occur in a case where the individual is unwilling (such as in the case of an unwilling participant in a grateful group), but it might also occur in cases where the individual is unable. For example, a person may not fully participate in the gratitude of the group because they are having a difficult time in life or because of a difference in abilities that limits their participation.

Whether full participation is hindered by being unwilling or unable, those that are not feeling or expressing gratitude as an individual have a means to express gratitude by virtue of being nested within a grateful joint action or a grateful collective. In the case of joint action, even minimal participation (e.g., being present for a ritual expressing thanks but not being willing or able to join in the actions) constitutes a form of participation and is thus a means of expressing gratitude or having gratitude expressed on one's behalf. In cases where an individual does not or cannot contribute to joint grateful actions (e.g., choosing not to join or being physically unable to join a joint action), they can still be part of a grateful collective as a member as long as they align with the membership conditions for that collective. For example, an elderly congregant who watches a church's services online because they fear contracting an illness is still a member of that community.

To the extent that the unwilling cases are distinct from the unable cases, we would suggest that collective membership conditions are typically more lenient towards unable cases. There is also a question of the extent to which joint action participation relates to membership of the collective; it seems reasonable that an individual needs to be willing to participate in at least some of the joint actions of a group to be considered a member of the collective, but precise boundaries are difficult to draw and likely to vary between different collectives (e.g., a business would quickly jettison an employee who rarely participated in the joint actions of the company, but an amateur sports club might allow a member who rarely attends practices and matches).

Consider an example. Bob is leaving his workplace after many years of employment. The manager decides to email all of the staff to ask them to contribute to a financial leaving gift for Bob. John has especially deep pockets and contributes £500, making up almost a third of the total. Other employees are struggling and can offer only £10 or £20. Mike is having a really hard time and cannot afford to contribute anything to the gift, but he still signs the card. Who should Bob be grateful to for his leaving gift? Most of us would find it frustrating if John decided to reveal that he was the most generous giver and Mike did not contribute a penny. Why is this? Because such a revelation defeats the point of having a gift given on behalf of the whole community. If we think of this gift as only a summation of each of the givers' offerings, then we have missed the point. The community has given Bob a generous gift, even if Mike is a "loafer" to this action, at least with regard to the financial aspect.

This seems especially pertinent in the context of liturgy. Those that are struggling to feel or express gratitude as an individual have a means to participate in an expression of gratitude by virtue of being nested within a grateful community and a group grateful action. Even if illness or ability limit how much an individual can directly contribute to a group's grateful action, they are still a participant by virtue of their membership in that grateful community (the limits of jointness are something we consider in more detail in chapter 6). Understanding liturgical gratitude through this group gratitude lens helps us to see the importance of expressing gratitude together. Liturgical gratitude is not merely an opportunity to express gratitude to God for one's own blessings (although it may be this), but it also is an opportunity to offer an expression *together*, in which all are included no matter how grateful they feel that day.

In the business case, loafing is primarily a negative phenomenon that seeks to highlight how some members of the team do not contribute effectively to the actions of the whole. The wider aim is to eradicate ineffective freeloaders and organize workplaces in such a way that everyone contributes fairly. But the community of the Church is a community in which the priorities of the world are to be reversed and challenged. Consider Paul's use of familiar imagery in 1 Corinthians: "the body is not made up of one part but of many. Now if the foot should say, 'Because I am not a hand, I do not belong to the body,' it would not for that reason stop being part of the body. And if the ear should say, 'Because I am not an eye, I do not belong to the body,' it would not for that reason stop being part of the body" (12:14–16). Scholars widely agree that Paul's imagery is not original here; the body is used as an analogy for social harmony in many ancient texts, and Paul's choice of body parts even mirrors some of these texts.[63] But unlike these texts, which are typically used to show how weaker parts of society should know their place, Paul subverts the political imagery to show that weaker parts have a greater importance: "God has put the body together, giving greater honor to the parts that lacked it, so that there should be no division in the body, but that its parts should have equal concern for each other. If one part suffers, every part suffers with it; if one part is honored, every part rejoices with it" (1 Cor 12:24–26). We put Paul's point like this: In the community of the Church, social loafing is vital. In creating communities in which people can participate despite their abilities, social status, mental health, or simply how grateful they "feel," there is a kind of subversion of the expectations that everyone ought to *pull their weight*. In the liturgies of the Church, those who cannot express gratitude individually are nested within a collective and joint gratitude that can hold them through times of difficulty and darkness.

The hope, in emphasizing the ways in which liturgical loafing occurs, is that in being held in a community that expresses gratitude, individuals might also relearn this expression of gratitude in a context that values and honors them. Much like the way Worthington thinks that decisional forgiveness can precipitate emotional forgiveness (e.g., in the case of insisting a child apologizes to their sibling), liturgical loafing might have a similar effect on those who do not or cannot feel grateful. That is, in being incorporated into the actions of a community that is marked by gratitude to God, the liturgy of the Church, at its healthiest, might provide a classroom for thankfulness and praise in which gratitude becomes habitual and fully formed, whatever is going on in the lives of the members of the community. This is not to say that it is not possible to loaf in an unhealthy way in the community of the Church; there will still be some for whom loafing does not bring any benefit, and some who would abuse their position as loafer. We are not suggesting that loafing is *always* a good phenomenon in the Church but only that its possibility provides helpful ways of thinking about how the Church can support those who are unable to participate.

SUMMARY

Practices of gratitude are primarily practices of attention; they prompt individuals to focus on the good benefits they have received. Liturgy is one of the primary places in which gratitude is expressed in the life of the Christian. The ways in which gratitude is expressed in liturgy are complex and varied. The ways in which a sense of jointness is nested provide a fruitful way of seeing the relationship between these different kinds of gratitude. That is, individual gratitude to God expressed in liturgy is nested in the broader context of the group, and it might also be expressed jointly through some liturgical act such as singing. Broader still is the sense of jointness that is expressed at a group level through participation in the community and even the wider Church. Across all these levels, there is a sense of jointness that helps to make sense of what it is to express gratitude to God, even if the psychological mechanisms may differ in each case.

Reflecting on not only the content of liturgy but also the shape and forms of liturgy will raise important questions about how gratitude is cultivated in the life of the community. Who is authorized to express gratitude and how? Who is included in the act of collective gratitude? Under what conditions should we identify a collective as genuinely grateful? And how can participation in group expressions of gratitude be encouraged? These questions are not merely theoretical; they are questions that must be answered in context by reflecting on the liturgical life of the community.

5

ACTS OF REMEMBRANCE

Making the Past Present, Together

RITES OF REMEMBRANCE

Through the ritual of Communion (or the Eucharist, or the Lord's Supper), church congregations eat and drink together "in remembrance" of Christ (Luke 22:19; 1 Cor 11:23–26).[1] This is a liturgy that has its roots in the Hebrew tradition of remembrance through ritual. For instance, the Seder meal, the Jewish celebration of the Exodus story (and the occasion on which Jesus instituted the liturgy of Communion), is celebrated each year in families across the world.[2] The meal is a response to the biblical command—*Zakhor* (Remember)! Much like the practices of prayer and gratitude, these rituals of remembrance involve fostering a sense of jointness, in which a community gathers together and is shaped by participation with others.

Many of the issues regarding understanding jointness examined in previous chapters are relevant to rituals that focus on remembrance. For example, in chapter 3, we considered the limits of what it means for prayer to be joint, and the same question might be asked of remembrance rituals. For example, think of the practice of "reserve sacrament" (in Anglican or Roman Catholic traditions), in which the consecrated bread and wine from the eucharistic service are taken to the homes of those who are unable to gather with others in the church building because of sickness. Or, consider the more controversial question of whether the sacrament can be celebrated online.[3] Much of what we said in chapter 3 about prayer extends very straightforwardly here. That is, it is plausible that the Eucharist gets its sense of jointness from interactive joint attention (e.g., people sharing bread and wine in the building) or from a broader sense of jointness such as the knowledge that one is participating in the communal meal of the church from one's sickbed. Similarly, in chapter 4, we discussed the significance of contextualizing gratitude in a wider group and the possibilities of "liturgical loafing" for those who do not feel grateful on that particular day. Likewise, one might enter into the eucharistic meal with a sense of resentment or bitterness (noting that Eucharist means "thanksgiving") but allow the community to enact gratitude on your behalf despite your personal struggles to adopt a grateful attitude.

So, as liturgical rites that are geared towards creating a sense of jointness, rituals of remembrance share many of these features described above. But rituals of remembrance raise unique challenges. These challenges center not just on the spatial or affective limits of jointness, but on the temporal limits of jointness. For both the Eucharist and the Seder meal purport to join their participants not just with the community of the living but also with those who are now dead. In doing so, they seek to establish a sense of historical continuity, one that enables those still living to experience themselves as part of a diachronically extended community. In doing so, those living in the present are connected by an unbroken thread to the formative events of their community's history. Moreover, as Ryan P. O'Dowd argues, rituals of remembrance play a crucial epistemological role in the community: "Israel's access to knowledge is performative by virtue of the roles Deuteronomy creates for the community. Reading, hearing, writing, singing, remembering and obeying the Torah actualise the ontological realities of Israel's relationship with Yahweh."[4]

So, how can a sense of jointness extend to those who are no longer living? This is the question we seek to explore in this chapter. In responding to this question of temporal jointness, we explore two related issues. The first discussion pertains to the notion of *actualization* that has been highlighted in discussions of memory in the Seder and the Eucharist. It has been suggested that memory in these rituals goes beyond fact recollection, instead involving a sense of *participation* in the events of the past. Second, given the explicitly communal emphasis of memory in these rites, and the communal emphasis of actualization in particular, a further important challenge is to articulate how a community might actualize the past together. Drawing upon recent psychological and philosophical work on memory and joint reminiscing, we offer a novel articulation of the concept of actualization and its function in shaping communal practices and identity. In doing so, we emphasize the way in which rituals of remembrance highlight the interconnections between past, present, and future.

REMEMBERING TOGETHER

So how might observance of the commands to remember be understood? There are a variety of possibilities. One could say, "Our ancestors were enslaved in Egypt and suffered at the hands of Pharaoh." Assuming a person accepts this as true, they have now achieved the appropriate form of remembrance that their ancestors were enslaved and suffered at the hands of Pharaoh. Or, one could say, "I want you to imagine what happened to our ancestors. Close your eyes and imagine the pain of slavery; the bitter tears you would weep as you slave away making bricks." Perhaps this provides a more evocative form of remembrance than simple, impersonal presentation of a story. Or, one could eat and drink the symbolic foods of Jewish ritual. In eating *karpas* (parsley or celery) dipped in salt water, one might more vividly be drawn into reflecting on the bitterness of slavery, both for those in the past and for those who remain in slavery today.

These different ways of remembering have connections with some of the ways psychologists and philosophers think about memory today. In contemporary psychological and philosophical work, it is common to distinguish between different aspects of memory. A typical taxonomy includes "episodic," "semantic," and "procedural" memory.[5] Episodic memory refers to a memory of an event at which the individual was present, and includes a phenomenal experience in which one relives the sense of what that past event was like. For example, we might say, "I can still see his face" or "I spent all night reliving the traumatic interview experience." Semantic memory refers to cases of fact recollection in which one remembers some fact or that some event has occurred. This need include neither the phenomenological component or episodic memory, nor the requirement that the event actually be experienced. For instance, one might recall that Sheffield Wednesday won the FA Cup in 1935, even if this occurred before one's birth. Semantic and episodic memory are both "declarative," that is, "their contents can in principle be articulated."[6] These kinds of memory loosely correlate to the distinctions often made by philosophers between phenomenal knowledge (i.e., knowledge of what something is like) and propositional knowledge (i.e., knowledge-that). Procedural memory, in contrast, is not declarative and aligns closely to what philosophers have called "practical knowledge" (i.e., knowledge-how). For example, one may remember how to drive a manual car, even if the summation of what this amounts to cannot be articulated.[7]

This taxonomy can help us to make some connections between the ways in which memory is described in some Biblical texts, and the discussions of remembering in contemporary psychology and philosophy. We do not intend to give a complete overview of the ways in which memory is described in Jewish and Christian Scripture, but it is helpful to identify how discussions of memory in the Jewish and Christian traditions involve parallels with episodic, semantic, and procedural memory.[8] It is important to note that this taxonomy of memory does not fit neatly onto, for example, biblical texts or rabbinic discourse, but this does not mean that we cannot draw helpful comparisons between conceptions of memory in Judeo-Christian thought and the ways in which contemporary psychology and philosophy define memory.[9]

Take an example from Deuteronomy 5:15. Moses tells the Israelites to "remember *that* they were slaves in Israel!" While, at face value, a straightforward English reading of the sentence might be to see Moses urging for a kind of semantic recollection of the past events, this reading oversimplifies the complexity of remembrance in this context. The sense of memory found in the Hebrew scriptures appears to interweave aspects of episodic, semantic, and procedural memory. Semantic memory clearly must have some role in the passing down of the Israelites' corporate identity; the retelling and writing of history, at a very basic level, must involve a recording of the bare facts, which surely includes the memory that "once we were slaves."

Yet, semantic memory is not sufficient for preserving the memory of Israel, and it is not clear that it is always necessary either. We can see this clearly in the repeated admonishment to remember the commandments (Num 15:40, for instance). Remembering the commandments must involve something semantic (i.e., knowing that the commandments forbid murder), and indeed such a case might appear to be a prime example of where the kind of remembrance at stake is predominantly semantic. However, as Brevard S. Childs argues in his overview of memory in the Hebrew Bible,

> the commandments are not expressions of abstract law, but are events, a part of God's redemptive history toward Israel. . . . Memory serves to link the present commandments as events with

> the covenant history of the past. . . . The commandments given to a former generation continue to lay claim anew on each generation. Yet one cannot separate instruction in the law from covenant history. . . . Historical memory establishes the continuity of the new generation with the decisive events of the past. God's plan for Israel unfolds in her history.[10]

There is something much richer communicated in the command to remember than the mere recollection of fact, even in cases in which what is remembered is some law or commandment.[11] Remembrance serves to create a connection between past events and present events by locating one's present story within the stories of the past.

Thus, remembrance clearly involves something like an episodic memory. What is preserved by the past generations is not simply the knowledge that some event happened but also the phenomenal experience of this event as *participating in the past* in some way.[12] What exactly this amounts to we will explore in more detail later, but in the Jewish sense of memory, there clearly seems to be an emphasis on *participating* or *joining*. The term used for this sense of participating, in many of the discussions of memory in Hebrew Bible scholarship, is "actualization." As Childs puts it, "The act of remembering serves to actualise the past for a generation removed in time from those former events in order that they themselves can have an intimate encounter with the great acts of redemption. Remembrance equals participation."[13] Returning to the discussion of Deuteronomy 5, Childs writes, "Memory does not serve to arouse a psychological reaction of sympathy for slaves. Rather, quite the reverse is true. Israel observes the Sabbath *in order to* remember her slavery and deliverance. . . . Memory functions as an actualization of the decisive event in her tradition."[14]

Implicit in Childs' discussion of actualization is the role of ritual practices of remembrance—here, the practice of the Seder meal and the observation of the Sabbath.[15] In tasting the bitter herbs in the Seder, the aim is not merely to recall the bitterness of Israel's oppression but to experience some of this bitterness for oneself; to participate in the bitterness as a member of the same community who experienced these past events firsthand.[16] Notable Jewish historian Yosef Hayim Yerushalmi argues that on Passover, an important purpose is to "take each person at the Seder back to Egypt."[17] In both discussions, there is some sense of participating or joining with some event in the past, and the term *actualization* can be used to cover this sense of participation. In both discussions, there is some sense of participating or joining with some event in the past. At this point, our working definition of actualization is "a form of remembrance involving a sense of participation in the events of the past." But can this concept be fruitfully unpacked by drawing upon the resources of current research on memory in psychology and philosophy?

Of the senses of memory described above, actualization appears to involve something akin to episodic memory, given the way it implies an event experienced in the past rather than recollection of some abstract fact. However, the role of episodic memory here is not straightforward; typically, psychologists think of episodic memory as something that must be connected to past events that one has experienced oneself. Thus, the application of psychological approaches to memory must be careful on both counts, seeking to accurately contribute to articulating notions of "intimate encounter" and "taking back" without incorrectly claiming a memory process is occurring (i.e., episodic memory) when it is not.

Much of this discussion of remembrance and actualization carries over to thinking about remembering together in the Eucharistic meal. Clearly, there is an important sense of continuation between these rituals, given the last supper takes place in the context of the Jewish Passover. But there are also some similarities in the acts involved in each ritual. As N. T. Wright reflects,

> Eating the Passover said: it happened, once for all, and we are part of the people to whom it happened. Jesus' words over the bread transformed this, so that it now said: the new Passover *is about to happen*, and those who share this meal thereafter will be constituted as *the people for whom it had happened* and through whom it will happen in the wider world.[18]

While there is not space here for a detailed analysis of the overlap between Passover and the Eucharist, it seems plausible that remembrance in the Eucharist involves a similar process of actualization. It is important to note, however, that actualization of the past is not all that takes place in the Eucharist. In some traditions, it is important that these rituals are focused on the present as well as the past; the *Book of Common Prayer*, for instance, includes the lines "grant that we receiving these thy creatures of bread and wine, according to thy Son our Saviour Jesus Christ's holy institution, in remembrance of his death and passion, may be partakers of his most blessed Body and Blood."[19] Our discussion does not assume nothing occurs in the present during Communion, but rather, we specifically focus on the acts of remembrance in this ritual.[20]

JOINTNESS AND ACTUALIZATION

Actualization in rites of remembrance is presented as allowing individuals to somehow participate in the events of the past in a way that goes beyond mere fact recollection. We have suggested that there are parallels with the psychological concept of episodic memory, insofar as each involves some sort of revisiting the past. However, the application is not direct. Our view is that one significant reason for this indirectness is that actualization is typically a communal activity.

Rituals of remembrance are *joint* acts of remembrance. In the Hebrew scriptures, it is the *community* that is urged to remember the events of its past. Deuteronomy (the book in which much of the discussion of memory in the Hebrew Bible is focused) uses the term *zakar* (to remember) most commonly in the context of addressing the people of Israel. When Moses uses the words "Remember that you were a slave in the land of Egypt" in Deuteronomy 5:15, he is addressing all of God's people rather than just posing this point to individuals. The Hebrew Bible less frequently uses the noun *zikkaron* to describe memorial signs, as in Exodus 13:9, which describes the unleavened bread as providing a "sign . . . so that the teaching of the Lord may be on your lips." Again, the context is corporate—the memorial sign of unleavened bread serves to allow Israel to remember the work of God and to continue to train the people of Israel in worship of God.

It is this second sense of remembrance that is closest to the use we find in 1 Corinthians (the Greek term used here is *anamnesis*, which the Septuagint uses to translate *zikkaron*), which is used in the context of the Church's practice of the Eucharist in Corinth, and so, again, the context is communal. As we will see, this joint dimension of memory is crucial for the sense in which memory is used in the religious rites of Communion and Passover. In remembering together using these rituals, the community of faith is connected to the events of the past. The rituals help in maintaining a coherent autobiographical narrative—a shared story regarding the past experiences of the community. The creation of this shared narrative strengthens the community's shared identity.

Not only is the *context* of the remembrance meal communal, but the purpose of the meal is unitive. Consider Paul's remarks in 1 Corinthians 10:17: "Because there is one loaf, we, who are many, are one body, for we all share the one loaf." Writing on this passage, the New Testament scholar Gordon Fee argues that

> there can be little doubt that Paul intends to emphasize the kind of bonding relationship of the worshipers with one another that this meal expresses. . . . Paul has chosen to interpret the bread in light of the present argument, an interpretation that emphasizes the solidarity of the fellowship of believers created by their all sharing "the one loaf."[21]

For Paul, rituals of remembrance create joint experiences to bring about a deeper sense of community. It is for this reason that he goes on to stress the importance of order in the celebration of the meal, encouraging the Corinthians to ensure they are well fed before participating and to avoid getting drunk from the Eucharistic cup (1 Cor 11:17–22). Reflecting on the social context can help us to see why this is important. As Richard B. Hays explains,

> We must bear in mind that the Christian gatherings were held in private homes, not in large public spaces . . . the dining room . . . of a typical villa could accommodate only nine persons, who would recline at the table for the meal. Other guests would have to sit or stand in the atrium, which might have provided space for another thirty to forty people . . . The host of such a gathering would, of course, be one of the wealthier members of the community. It is reasonable to assume, therefore, that the host's higher-status friends would be invited to dine in the [dining room] . . . while lower-status members of the church . . . would be placed in the larger space outside.[22]

In other words, the meal of remembrance was supposed to be a symbol of community, fostering a sense of jointness amongst its participants by joining in this act of remembering together. But in Corinth, the actions of some had made it difficult for other members of the community to join in this act, thereby undermining the very purpose of the ritual.

We might even describe the events occurring in 1 Corinthians through the lens of joint attention or shared situations: in not waiting for all members of the community before starting the meal, and in segregating the spaces in the house, those who celebrate the meal place hard social and material boundaries on this act of remembrance (issues we address in more detail in chapter 6). The person arriving late to the meal has no means of joining in the shared situation, because it has been established without them.

More generally speaking, it seems plausible to think that the sense of jointness fostered in both the Seder and the Eucharist can be thought of in terms very similar to how we have conceived of prayer and gratitude. That is, in gathering together to enter the narratives of the past, the people are able to jointly attend to these past events in God's presence. Moreover, both rituals are nested in a broader sense of jointness; at the time of Passover, one is conscious of the fact that one is joining not only with those who are gathered around the table but with God's people all over the world. Similarly, in sharing bread and wine, Christians create a sense of jointness that extends beyond one's own tradition and community; Christians throughout the world regularly share in this meal of remembrance. Thus, through both active joint attention and through broader experiences of shared situations, rites of remembrance create a sense of jointness for those who participate.

But, as we have seen, one of the distinctive features of this sense of jointness is that the limits of who is included do not extend only to the gathered congregation or the worldwide body of believers; somehow the meal joins its participants to those who have gone before. It is this notion of bringing the past to the present and the present to the past that requires some further reflection, we think. We now turn to consider how psychological and philosophical work on group forms of remembering might further illuminate this notion of joining with the past.

UNPACKING ACTUALIZATION

We have seen the importance of the concept of actualization—understood as "a form of remembrance involving a sense of participation in the events of the past"—and its role in the rituals of remembrance in both Jewish and Christian communities. Thus far, we have suggested that there are points of contact between the concept of actualization and the concept of episodic memory. To unpack these connections in more depth, it is important to provide a more detailed exposition of how episodic memory is investigated and understood in psychological and philosophical research, focusing on the concept of "Mental Time Travel." Then, emphasizing the communal nature of actualization, we explore the role of *joint reminiscing*, understood as *joint attention to the past*.[23]

Joint reminiscing connects the personal dimension of episodic memory with the group level of experience. Moreover, evidence suggests that the development of *autobiographical memory* ("a term describing knowledge and schemata that form the memorial basis of the self"[24]) depends on first participating in joint acts of reminiscing. Thus, our account draws together these threads by arguing that actualization involves creating a sense of participation through joint attention to the past events of one's community, where these past events are understood as involving oneself by virtue of one's own membership of "the people to whom it happened."[25]

Episodic memory has proven a difficult concept to pin down in psychology. When first proposed by Endel Tulving,[26] it was suggested it could be defined informationally, in terms of memory with information about What took place, Where, and When.[27] Recently, it has been more popular to define episodic memory in terms of its *autonoetic* character.[28] This refers to the phenomenological properties of episodic memory recall: the distinctive subjective character of such memories as previously experienced. This phenomenological dimension of episodic memory has been widely linked to the ability to engage in "mental time travel" (MTT).[29] The capacity to recall specific personal experiences enables individuals to engage in MTT.[30] Such a view emphasizes recall of episodic memories as involving a process of *reliving* the events of the past as they are remembered.[31] To say that episodic memory involves MTT, and MTT involves reliving past events, is not to say that such memories are perfect snapshots of the past. In fact, memory has been demonstrated to be a highly flexible and constructive process. That is, memories are not pure reflections of past events but rather are encoded, stored, and retrieved according to the attention and motivations of the agent.[32]

Why might human memory have such "flaws"?[33] An influential approach has been to connect MTT to the past with MTT to the future.[34] The flexibility of memory of the past enables imaginative construction of future or fictional events. Similarities between past and future MTT have been identified at the neural and cognitive levels.[35] There are two properties of particular relevance.[36] First, the sensory and contextual features of past, future, and imagined events are highly similar.[37] Each involves the mental construction of particular spatiotemporal settings.[38] Episodic memories by definition involve a particular event in a particular time and place as experienced from a particular perspective. To mentally conceive of an event therefore requires simulated construction of a time and place. This is true whether it involves MTT to the past or to the future. Indeed, it has been argued that past memories provide the building blocks for constructing possible events in the future.[39] In order to simulate how a future event might appear and play out, an agent needs the mental resources with which to build that simulated environment. For example, Szpunar and McDermott found that participants constructed more elaborate future scenarios taking place in recently experienced settings (e.g., at a university campus) compared to unfamiliar settings (e.g., the North Pole) or temporally distant settings (e.g., at their former secondary school).[40]

Second, it is also important that such processes, which are necessarily experienced from a particular perspective, have intrinsic relevance to the self.[41] Past events are experienced as having happened to *me*, and thus my reactions in that context form an integral part of being able to identify the kind of person that I am and have been. MTT therefore enables agents to revisit and reimagine the past in order to consider questions such as "What might I have done differently?" or "What would have happened if . . . ?"[42] By reflecting on such events, individuals can learn more effectively from past events. Similarly, individuals can imagine how the future might play out, allowing them to weigh which path to take prior to having to commit to any one option.[43] This flexibility means memory can be both a help (in reflection and planning) and a hindrance (in its susceptibility to manipulation and failure). This flexibility also allows individuals to create meaning from past events, an ability critical to the formation of a coherent sense of self.[44]

Let us take stock of the account so far and consider the relevance of this literature for our discussion of actualization. A distinctive part of human memory is episodic memory. Episodic memory has been characterized as involving MTT, allowing individuals to mentally reconstruct scenes from their past. This reconstruction is flexible, involving similar processes to those used in imagination and future thought. Recall of episodic memories involves a process of imaginative reliving, meaning these memories serve an important role in the construction of a narrative about the self, which enables a sense of the self as something continuous in time.

Given the theological emphasis on actualization as joining in the events of the past, in some sense participating in the past rather than merely recalling it, episodic memory would appear to play some role in a psychologically informed account of actualization. However, there are issues that emerge. Most pressingly, episodic memory is emphasized as involving autonoetic consciousness. We are not aware of any who claim that participants in the Seder or the Eucharist literally take on the memories of those in the past. How, then, might the human capacity for MTT still be said to be of relevance?

First, we think that the connections between MTT and imagination are key. The experience of the Seder provides the tools for an imaginative reliving of the events of the Exodus. The bitterness of the maror (bitter herbs) fuels the imagination of the pain of slavery, just as the act of reclining evokes the feeling of freedom from slavery; they serve as the impetus to imagine life under slavery and the feeling of freedom and deliverance. The simple act of eating, in the context of the ritual, functions to "take each person at the Seder back to Egypt" as they imagine the past.[45] Following the findings of Szpunar and McDermott,[46] wider cultural and historical knowledge of the context of remembered events may also help participants to imaginatively enter into these scenes in more rich and vivid ways.[47] However, one might imagine themselves experiencing a past event without any notion of personal participation. Imagination alone is not sufficient to capture the concept of actualization. This is where the identity-shaping function of episodic memory comes to the fore, particularly when integrated with the communal emphasis of rituals of remembrance.

The imaginative participation that is promoted through practices like the Seder is necessarily conducted as part of *our* memory; one imagines in order to identify. This way, the events of the Exodus take on a particular immanence and relevance to the identity of the participant and the remembering community. They are what the nation of Israel experienced in the past, therefore having consequences for the present-day identity of Jewish people as their descendants.

Something similar might be said of the Eucharist—the drinking and eating of bread and wine, and the words of the liturgy (however this might be formalized), serve to actualize the events of the Last Supper and allow participants to participate in this pivotal moment in the Gospel story. Borrowing from Wright's description, this *new Passover* meal provides a connection to the present reality, and the participants are "constituted as *the people for whom it had happened* and through whom it will happen in the wider world."[48] Moreover, identity draws on not only what one has done in the past but how one may act or plans to act in the future.[49] I might conceive of myself as "somebody who will one day play football for England" and take that on as part of my identity.

So, to understand this challenging sense of participation, our view is that we must move from individual accounts of memory to group accounts. While no one individual was there at the events of the Passover, the theological claim, as we interpret it, is that each individual participates as part of the community who experienced these events firsthand. Thus, to the extent that the Passover Seder involves a participation in the past, it is because it is the community and not the individual that is remembering.

JOINT REMINISCING AND GROUP ACTUALIZATION

How then ought we to understand such group forms of remembering? The literature on MTT focuses not only on individuals but also on communities. Group MTT is a recent but growing subfield in memory research.[50] As part of a wider increased interest in group memory in psychology and philosophy,[51] group MTT has emerged as an area of study that might provide fresh insight into how groups remember together. With MTT so closely connected to episodic memory and its characteristic subjective phenomenology, care is needed with understanding such a concept.[52] Even in the light of ongoing debates about mentality in groups,[53] few would want to claim that there is such a thing as collective phenomenology. More tractable is the idea that groups can construct joint representations of events in the past and the future, in a manner that bears some resemblance to individual MTT.[54] When, for example, a couple imagines life with their new baby, they might imaginatively transport themselves to future situations and discuss how they would react as a couple.[55] However, each would have their own unique phenomenological experience of how that scene might look.[56]

We want to focus on a particular kind of group MTT. Rather than considering the way in which large groups such as nations construct such shared representations, we want to focus on how this is achieved in small-scale groups through the process of *joint reminiscing*. Intuitively, reminiscing refers to the revisiting of past experiences. In this vein, recent philosophical treatments of joint reminiscing have defined it as *joint attention to the past*.[57] As a reminder, we define joint attention as a situation in which two or more agents share some feature of the world together with mutual awareness of this joint focus.[58] While in development, joint attention is typically towards objects or events, it can also be towards abstract objects.[59] Past memories are one such example of an abstract target of attention.

Why is joint attention to the past a fruitful way of conceiving of joint reminiscing? Joint attention involves a dynamic process of coordinating attention.[60] Similarly, joint reminiscing involves the contribution of different perspectives and details, enriching the memories through integration of others' experiences. Joint attention involves establishing what is truly shared rather than simply common knowledge between participants (i.e., not "out in the open"). For example, individuals can avoid sharing some detail in the past by failing to recognize it or publicly acknowledge it.[61] An individual can refuse to reminisce with another about a memory that is embarrassing for them by denying they recall that experience. Regardless of the sense of the "elephant in the room" that may be experienced by the interacting persons, this memory is not *truly* joint until it is made open between the individuals through some kind of communicative acknowledgment.

There remains an open question about how groups of more than two might come to jointly attend together.[62] Putting aside the details of this issue, the main claim we want to support is that joint attention to the past provides a special kind of group memory, one that has much more in common with episodic memory than collective representations of the past on a large scale. Reminiscing, understood as jointly attending to the past, can provide a way of linking the personal nature of episodic memory with a sense of group remembrance. To further buttress this line of argument, it is also beneficial to examine the development of autobiographical memory. There is evidence that, in line with our broader view that social experiences are typically the developmental foundation for individual experiences,[63] children first engage in reminiscing before they are capable of episodic memory. Reminiscing thus not only is the important developmental context for the emergence of individual, autonoetic episodic memories but continues to play a role in shaping individual and communal autobiographies.

AUTOBIOGRAPHICAL MEMORY

Having considered in detail the psychological and theological nature of actualization and mental time travel, we can now explore questions related to the value of remembering together and, particularly, its role in shaping a community's sense of identity in a manner akin to "autobiographical memory." Autobiographical memory refers to the formation of coherent narrative regarding oneself out of past memories.[64] The key ingredients of autobiographical memory are episodic memories, given their particular significance for the self.[65] However, these are supplemented by semantic and procedural memories.[66] Autobiographical memories, while characterizing an individual self, are in some sense public as well as private.[67] This is true of not just semantic and procedural memories but episodic memories too. While episodic memories are inherently private, multiple individuals can have episodic memories about a common event, as is the case in joint reminiscing. By communicating their different perspectives on the same event, a form of communal autobiographical memory can emerge, in which individuals can each play a role in shaping the group's shared experience of the past and mutually shaping how each other recalls the episode.[68]

For example, a group of friends might gather together many years after attending a wedding together. Because each friend sat at a different table during the dinner reception, their perspective and memory of the event is slightly different. As they each reminisce about aspects of the day ("remember when Grandma fell asleep in the speech!" or "wasn't it funny that Frank got red wine on his tie!"), they add details that other members of the group might not have realized. In piecing together this group perspective on the event, each member of the group has their own individual memory of the wedding enhanced and enriched.

This kind of joint reminiscing is key to the development of autobiographical memory. In keeping with the broadly sociocultural approach we have drawn upon in previous chapters,[69] a large body of research has highlighted the significance of maternal reminiscing style[70] on the development of children's autobiographical memory.[71] For example, Reese and Farrant presented longitudinal data on the development of children's autobiographical memory from nineteen to forty months of age.[72] They found that children are able to report memories with higher quality and quantity of detail when their mothers adopt a "highly elaborative" reminiscing style. This style involves asking children questions that encourage elaboration, rather than forcing children to head towards a predetermined topic.[73] The topic is not rapidly changed, and instead, children are guided to progress the narrative in a coherent manner. Children are encouraged to elaborate themselves, rather than mothers filling in all the details. When this style was adopted, a bidirectional relationship between mother and child reminiscing styles emerged. For example, children's reminiscing style at twenty-five months was both predicted by maternal reminiscing style at nineteen months and successfully predicted later maternal reminiscing style at thirty-two and forty months.[74] More recently, evidence has suggested that maternal sensitivity has an influence from even earlier in childhood, prior to production of verbal narratives.[75] Maternal sensitivity is defined as the ability of a mother to understand the wants and needs of their child and to respond in a way that respects the child's autonomy. Maternal sensitivity at eight months predicted how elaborative mothers and children were when describing a scary event at three-and-a-half years of age. The general picture is that children's ability to reminisce and construct autobiographical memory is initially dependent on parental scaffolding, before more autonomous reminiscing emerges at around four years of age.[76]

As well as in the parent-child dyad, reminiscing can be a family activity.[77] Formation of a clear "autobiographical" family narrative has been shown to be connected to children and adolescents' psychosocial well-being.[78] Both childhood and adolescence are key stages in the formation of self-narratives: childhood as the time of emergence, and adolescence as a time of forming overarching life narratives.[79] The role of the family is of relevance throughout, and the way families remember is significant. For example, families can remember either as an assembly of individuals contributing their own separate perspectives or, in a truly shared manner, with each member contributing.[80] There is evidence that the former style leads to adolescents that are more self-efficacious, whereas the latter relates to higher adolescent self-esteem.[81] However, if reminiscing involves one individual dominating or involves repeated disagreement, no such benefits are observed.[82] Families that tell stories of the past that provide more emotional detail, and have a clearer understanding of how emotional conflicts were resolved, typically have adolescents that are more socially and academically competent.[83] The data suggest that family reminiscing has important though varied effects, depending on the manner in which the family shares memories together.

AUTOBIOGRAPHICAL MEMORY AND LITURGY

These reflections on the importance of community "autobiography" provide a fruitful way of understanding remembrance in the context of liturgy. What these studies and others suggest is that humans' ability to effectively form narratives about the self emerges out of dynamic, reciprocal social engagements throughout ontogeny.[84] This view complements theological discussions of actualization, which emphasize both the communal dimension of such acts of remembrance as well as the necessary role in community identity formation. The Seder and the Eucharist are conducted in a manner that bears strong similarity to a family reminiscing together, and each is to be told not just as *a* story but as *our* story.

As a group chooses what to share about the past, it can form a communal identity around these shared memories. As the same stories are repeatedly revisited in a process of "shaping and reshaping,"[85] groups go beyond mere factual recall and begin to ascribe meaning to past experiences.[86] A group might leave out their own failings in order to fashion a story that emphasizes past successes, or they might find a way to process a traumatic experience that emphasizes the opportunities for growth rather than the sufferings experienced.[87] Consider how one might remember the Exodus: as a story of suffering and pain, or as one of redemption and freedom. By what and how a group chooses to remember, they make a choice about the identity they will forge.

The Seder bears a particular resemblance to family reminiscing, given the central role given to the dialogue between the children of the family and the adults. The children ask questions and the parents provide answers, making the ceremony necessarily a didactic, dialogic activity. While this teaching involves the transfer of semantic truths about the past, it is given narrative form, rather than being a dry transfer of facts. It is as if an act of family reminiscing is being captured in a ritual format, but this structured format is then given new life as each family comes to it, not merely repeating the words to fulfill the roles given but truly embracing the narrative, reminiscing character. The Eucharist also bears some resemblance to family reminiscing, yet the role of children is perhaps more contentious. In most traditions, there is at least some participation for children, even if this is a simple prayer of blessing.

Just as the notion of memory required to understand actualization is complex, so is the notion of identity needed. In our view, identity should be understood as incorporating information from a number of different timescales and on a variety of levels. Consider the following quote by historian Jan Assmann:

> Memory is knowledge with an identity-index, it is knowledge about oneself, that is, one's own diachronic identity, be it as an individual or as a member of a family, a generation, a community, a nation, or a cultural and religious tradition.[88]

The key detail of this quote is the description of the multiply embedded nature of persons in a number of communities. To participate in the Seder involves participating as a family, which itself is a subset of the Jewish people in both a synchronic and diachronic sense. Similarly, to participate in the Eucharist is to do so as part of a family, a church, and a people. The simultaneous occurrence of these levels of participation does not mean they blur together; rather, each provides a different but interconnected mode of experience. As participants enact the Seder, they reminisce about their shared history as a family and as a people. They reminisce about the way their family has uniquely told the story, while also remembering how their people have continually told the story. These modes of remembering cannot be neatly separated; it is the nature of the interplay between interwoven identities that provides a richer sense of a holistic identity.

To summarize, our account of actualization is that it requires a process of *joint reminiscing*, understood as *joint attention to the past*. The focus on reminiscing draws upon the personal, imaginative, and identity-shaping facets of episodic memory without requiring its autonoetic character. Furthermore, reminiscing in this sense is an inherently joint activity. Indeed, we suggest that reminiscing is developmentally primary in that episodic memory is built on a foundation of social interactions involving joint attention to the past. Because reminiscing is conducted as part of a community, it can draw upon memories that belong to that community—rather than those belonging to any particular individual. In this way, those involved in actualizing the past are participating—because they are part of the people to whom these formative events happened and who continue to be shaped by these definitive events.

SUMMARY

The notion of actualization and the more contemporary discussion of group MTT and reminiscing help us to expand the account of jointness we have been exploring in this book so far. As we stated in the introduction, rituals of remembrance share many features with other liturgical acts, such as liturgies expressing gratitude and petitionary prayer. These rituals are enacted by communities and create a sense of jointness that extends beyond the spatial limits of a gathered congregation. The discussion of group MTT and actualization has shown the ways in which this sense of jointness is extended not just *spatially* but also *temporally*.[89] As James Torrance puts it,

> at the Lord's Table we do not merely remember the passion of our Lord as an isolated date from nineteen hundred years ago. Rather, we remember it in such a way that we know by the grace of God we are the people for whom our Saviour died and rose again, we

> are the people whose sins Jesus confessed on the cross, we are the people with whom God has made a new covenant in the blood of Christ, we are the Israel of God to whom God has said "I will be your God and you shall be my people." We today are the people whose sorrows and cries Jesus bears in his kingly heart as he intercedes for us and constitutes himself the eternal Memorial for all his creatures before God. We are what we are today by the grace of God, because of what God did for us then.[90]

By entering into the events of the past together, those gathered extend the sense of jointness to include themselves in the narrative of God's people throughout history.

The psychological discussion of group MTT and reminiscing helps us understand one way in which communities might participate in the memories of the past, rather than simply recall them as abstract facts or even solely imagine the events. Through reminiscing, living members of the community can preserve a sense of connection and jointness with those who came before. They belong to one community that extends back in time from the present day to those alive at the time of the formative events of the tradition. By preserving this connection, the living community strengthens its identity and cohesion. Israel must remember God's deliverance from Egypt lest she cease to be Israel; the Church must enact the Eucharist to continue to be the body of Christ on earth.

6

BAPTISM AND THE BOUNDARIES OF JOINTNESS

WHO IS INCLUDED IN LITURGY?

Throughout the book so far, we have been outlining an account of liturgical jointness and its limits.[1] We have argued that all liturgy creates a sense of jointness that unites its participants to one another and to God. We have seen that this sense of jointness can extend beyond the confines of physical space, allowing individuals to be united to those geographically distant from them (chapter 3), and we have also seen that this sense of jointness can include even those who are unable to muster the appropriate affect (chapter 4). And in the previous chapter (chapter 5), we considered how liturgy can even enable a sense of jointness with those in the past.

But an important question lingers behind many of these conversations: Who is included in the community? And who is excluded? If I happen to watch the live stream of a church service on YouTube,[2] am I included in the community in some way? If I bring my one-day-old baby to a Eucharist service, does she play any meaningful role in the sense of jointness of those gathered? These questions raise important issues about just who is acting together and who is not. As we saw in the powerful example of celebrating the Eucharist in the days of the early church in Corinth (chapter 5), the ways in which one chooses to enact liturgies can provide powerful markers of who is included—and excluded—from an experience of jointness.

It is important to stress that the question of social belonging and its psychological implications has received substantial interest in the fields of social psychology[3] and developmental psychology[4] as well as in theological work.[5] It is well beyond the scope of this chapter to offer a full treatment of this topic. While there are many ways one might address these issues from a psychologically and theologically informed perspective, our approach, consistent with the rest of the book, is on joint attention and liturgical practices. Our focus is on the expression of social boundaries and structures through the actions and attention of the gathered community. How do the joint liturgical practices of a community delineate who is included?

We explore two dimensions of this issue. First, we examine the case of baptism, a liturgy that explicitly serves to mark new members of a community in a manner that establishes their membership as common knowledge. In doing so, the liturgy itself offers an explicit and potent means of defining the boundaries of that community. In the second section, we look more generally at how liturgies express a community's view of its social boundaries and roles. Not all liturgies have the specific function of marking social boundaries in the manner that baptism does. However, we argue that the practices of a community reveal its implicit views regarding the inclusion, role, and contributions of community members. We articulate a broader view of participation, in which all, including newborn infants, are genuine and valuable participants in the gathered activities of the community.

BAPTISM AS INITIATION

Theological views regarding who can and should be baptized vary widely. Some traditions see baptism as welcoming to the community all those who willingly make a public profession of faith, as baptism itself is understood as symbolizing a personal move from unbelief to belief. Others view baptism as a community marker that is inclusive of young children and those with psychological differences, regardless of their intellectual capacities or ability to make public statements of belief. Despite these disagreements, on both sides of this theological debate is a shared commitment to the idea that baptism expresses something fundamental about community identity and its boundaries. As the theologian N. T. Wright describes,

> baptism is a community-marking symbol, which the individual then receives, not first and foremost as a statement about him- or herself, but as a statement which says, "This is who we are." . . . Baptism marks out this community, the messianic-monotheist,

> new-exodus, crucified-and-risen community, which like Israel of old then requires a commensurate way of life of its members.[6]

Moreover, while the practice of baptism in the context of liturgy has significant variations across traditions, there are again some common features to observe. Most traditions of the church include some combination of the following liturgical features: profession of faith (by the candidate or a representative of the candidate, such as a parent or godparent), promises of the candidate (or representative) and the community, immersion or sprinkling with water, anointing with oil, and a welcome into the community of the church. All these features of baptism liturgy involve a *public* and *communal* declaration made by the community as a whole or a representative subset or individual. In other words: one cannot get baptized alone. Rather, in Scot McKnight's words, *it takes a church to baptize.*[7] Reflecting on these public features of baptism in his own Anglican context, McKnight writes,

> A baptism is a big event . . . as it witnesses to God's grace of new life in Christ, the purification of the water, the welcoming of a new child into our church, and the participation of the family and the whole church in a public commitment to support this child in the faith. In baptism we welcome a child into the family of faith. If an adult is being baptized, we welcome the adult.[8]

Publicly welcoming someone serves to make explicit the identity of this individual as a member of the community. In turn, this can play an important role in fencing the boundaries of who is in the community of faith and who is outside. Some of these boundaries are formal and explicit. For example, in many churches, baptism is the means of deciding who is invited to the eucharistic meal and who is excluded. Baptism may also be the grounds on which one decides who can formally vote in church matters of church polity. Some of these boundaries may be implicit. For example, baptism may determine how one relates socially to others who gather for worship and who one listens to. For as Luis Weil describes, "All the baptized are equal and integral participants in its [the Church's] common life, bearing witness week after week to the God whom they acclaim as the Creator, the Incarnate Lord, and the Holy Spirit."[9]

If baptism is the primary marker of the boundaries of this common life, then there are significant implications to the theological decision of who can be baptized. For example, Benjamin Connor writes about his friend Trey, who has learning difficulties. He states, "Only the community that denies Trey baptism can claim that the learning impairment is his alone, not the community's responsibility."[10] Because of the very public nature of baptism, it can serve as a powerful means of including and excluding individuals from the church. It is this sense of inclusion into the community that some theologians have been keen to stress is an important reason for extending the practice of baptism to children. As John Calvin puts it,

> children receive some benefit from their baptism: being engrafted into the body of the church, they are somewhat more commended to the other members. Then, when they have grown up, they are greatly spurred to an earnest zeal for worshipping God, by whom they were received as children through a solemn symbol of adoption before they were old enough to recognize him as Father.[11]

Regardless of whether one agrees with Calvin's view regarding who should be baptized, his point stresses the value of inclusion for those who are regarded as members of the church. In being recognized as equal members of the church,[12] we might expect that children are more likely to grow up with a sense of belonging and sharing in the common life of the community, even before they lack the comprehension to articulate this for themselves.

BAPTISM AND COMMON KNOWLEDGE OF MEMBERSHIP

As we have seen, one of the reasons baptism is such a powerful initiation rite is that it creates an explicit public mark of group membership and belonging. In keeping with the line of argument we have presented throughout the book, we argue that a key reason that the practices involved in baptismal liturgies are significant is that they create a shared situation in which the whole community jointly attends to the candidates' initiation into their common life. The acts themselves ritually enact an important set of transitions—the theologically significant visual of death to life and the socially significant shift from being without the community to being within it. But it is their publicly conducted character that is key.

Part of the importance of this public ritual involving the joint attention of the community is that it creates common knowledge. As discussed in chapter 3, one reason common knowledge is an important part of social life is because it involves more than a particular fact being known by each individual member of a group. Rather, in addition to having this knowledge, the members of that group are aware that this knowledge is shared by other group members. Recall the example of the Super Bowl advert for the Apple Macintosh; more than just ensuring numerous individuals had knowledge of the product, the advert relied on the recipients being aware that everyone else would be watching the same advert.

This notion of common knowledge has been used to help understand the notion of communal responsibility. For example, Margaret Gilbert argues that the foundation of all social groups is a kind of "joint commitment" in which all parties of the group openly express their "personal readiness" to belong to this group.[13] Moreover, Gilbert thinks, it is important "that these expressions have been made openly must be common knowledge in the relevant population."[14] On the basis of such public declarations, people can be held accountable and regarded as members of the same social group.

The very public nature of baptism liturgies lends itself well to this notion of common knowledge; in publicly professing faith and being publicly welcome into the community of the church, both the initiated candidate and the community make common knowledge that this person belongs to this group. As Cockayne puts it elsewhere,

> Not only does one make a joint commitment with God in the baptism liturgy, but one also makes a joint commitment with the other members of the Church . . . the commitments involved in baptism stand one in a new relation to the community of the Church.[15]

Thus, in the case of baptism, the ritual not only marks that the candidate has joined the group but ensures this knowledge is instantly spread throughout the community, without effort, controversy, or caveat. Moreover (as we have argued in chapters 2 and 3), this act is conducted in the attention of God; the community thus not only knows together with each other but is reminded of God's participation in the joining of the candidate to the community. To subsequently seek to exclude this individual is contesting an authority that is not merely social, but divine.

This line of argument focuses specifically on the local expression of a church community. However, as we have argued in chapters 2 and 3, an advantage of thinking in terms of shared situations is that it affords an appreciation of the nested structure of joint experiences. When a particular gathered community participates in a liturgy, they are also doing so within the larger activity of the global Church (and many other potential levels besides, e.g., the denomination of which they are a part). In the case of baptism, there are specific effects on the local gathering, as only by jointly attending within that shared situation can common knowledge of community membership be established. However, baptismal liturgies serve to promote an awareness of the ways in which the local activity is embedded within a larger community. As the Apostle Paul puts it, "There is one body and one Spirit, just as you were called to one hope when you were called; one Lord, one faith, one baptism; one God and Father of all, who is over all and through all and in all" (Eph 4:4). The welcome into the family of the church in baptism is not merely a welcome into a particular community but is also a sharing in the life of the one Church. Thus, baptismal liturgies, while primarily serving as public events that join a new member to the local community, also typically seek to also instill the sense that this act is also conducted within the larger community of the Church.

FROM INCLUDING LITURGIES TO INCLUSIVE LITURGIES

While the discussion around initiation is a helpful starting point for answering the question of who is included and who is excluded, it surely cannot be the end of the matter. For the explicit function of the majority of liturgies is not to mark entry of a new member into the community. However, this does not mean that other liturgies do not play an important role in defining the social boundaries of a community.

For example, consider the following descriptions of how children might be incorporated into the liturgies of gathered worship:

1. The children never enter the main space in which the community is gathered. They remain in a different adjacent space.
2. The children first enter the main space in which the community gathers. They then leave the space to an adjacent space at some point during the service. They may return to the main space at some later point in the service.
3. The children remain in the main space in which the community gathers, but are positioned at a location to the back or the side of the space.
4. The children remain within the same space as the gathered community through the service, positioned amongst the community.

Each of these arrangements conveys how each community understands the role of children in that environment.[16] In case 1, it is apparent that there is an especially marked point of difference between the role of children and the role of adults within the community, whereas in case 4, this is less stark. In cases like example 2, the moments at which children are present with the larger community are significant. But these examples do not tell us everything about the inclusion of children either; are they welcome to participate only in sung worship or also in communion? In other words, there might be variation in the extent to which children take an active role in the liturgical practices of the community.

Our point here is not to insinuate that the above examples represent a scale from minimally inclusive to maximally inclusive. A church using the arrangement of example 4 is not inherently inclusive; if it makes no effort to involve its younger members (and assumes its female members will corral the bored and restless children), it can become exclusionary. Rather, we seek to highlight how aspects of practice such as the physical location of community members can reveal how that community understands the role and contribution of its members. But the question of *where* children are located does not tell us everything. Even if present in the midst of the gathered community, children are surprisingly perceptive of when they are being included and excluded from worship. Consider the following example:

> One Sunday, my three-year-old attended worship in an Anglican church in which he usually received Holy Communion. It was difficult to know how much he understood about what was going on, and whether he could differentiate his after-church snack from the consecrated wafer received at the altar rail. One Sunday, when the rector was on holiday, a visiting priest presided at Holy Communion. After receiving only a prayer of blessing, my son screamed all the way back to his seat "but I wanted communion!"[17]

There is evidence that a capacity for social evaluation emerges early in ontogeny, followed by a sensitivity to group membership.[18] There is a range of evidence that infants in their first few years of life display a preference for prosocial rather than antisocial agents.[19] For example, there is evidence that infants as young as six months prefer an agent who they observe helping another agent rather than hindering them (e.g., by helping push them up a hill rather than blocking their progress).[20] There is also evidence that toddlers (aged nineteen to twenty-three months) also prefer prosocial agents, being more likely to give a treat to a prosocial rather than antisocial agent (e.g., indexed by either helping another agent to open a box they were struggling to open or deliberating hindering their efforts by jumping on the box).[21]

As they get older, children will use minimal cues to group membership as a basis for forming social preferences and allocating resources. For example, children randomly assigned a particular color of T-shirt to wear will view other children wearing that color as more likable and prefer to give them resources (e.g., toy coins) over children wearing a different color.[22] The moral implications of children's social evaluations and biases are not our focus here. Rather, our aim is to highlight that children, including infants, should not be viewed as either unaware or neutral regarding the social boundaries and organization of a community.

It seems a reasonable assumption that considerations of children's social awareness and sensitivity to exclusion are rarely considerations that are high on the agenda of churches—especially for children that are less than five years of age. However, in many cases, it is also not clear how church practices would change even if communities became convinced that young children are influenced by these different approaches. Even church communities that do care about children's inclusion may feel it is impossible to avoid children feeling excluded for at least some aspects of a service—which is precisely why children are placed outside the main location of liturgical practice. In other cases, children's inclusion is not all that important; the assumption is that children do not really understand what is going on and they are not old enough to properly engage with liturgical forms such as preaching or confession. Indeed, the organization of many church liturgies implies that worship is *really* for adults and that children should be accommodated or included in the liturgy only insofar as they can avoid distracting the adult participants. The barriers are thus intellectual: not many children under the age of twelve will have the capacity to properly engage with a dense thirty-minute sermon aimed at adults (with constant appeals to what it says "in the Greek").

This worry returns us to the question we began the book (chapter 1) by asking: How does liturgy form its participants, given the kind of creatures they are? Liturgical traditions that exclude children on the basis of intellectual capacity have arguably bought into the implicit anthropology that human beings are primarily thinking things, that the kind of thinking that matters is explicit and propositional, and that liturgy is primarily about changing explicit, propositional beliefs. It is difficult to see how, in such traditions, the sense of jointness experienced in liturgy could extend beyond those who have the cognitive capacity to keep up with the intellectual demands of liturgy.

It is important to see that the risk of such a view of liturgy is not just that children feel excluded and thereby miss the benefits of being included in the community of faith (as important as this is). The problem is bigger than this. As we have already highlighted in the case of baptism, it excludes those who are differently abled. It is likely also to be exclusionary towards many neurodiverse people and is a mode of engagement that may be unfamiliar or uncomfortable in a range of cultural contexts. In fact, an adult-centric or intellectual-centric view of liturgy seeks to rob *everyone* of the potential for liturgical formation. Jerome Berryman, the founder of the Godly Play movement, writes,

> Ignoring children in the church is an unrealized defensive act. Children present a powerful challenge to what adults conceive of as spiritual maturity. Jesus was very forthright when speaking about this error, made by his disciples, as well as us. He said that if you want to become spiritually mature, you have to become like a child.[23]

Thinkers such as Sofia Cavalletti, the founder of the Catechesis of the Good Shepherd,[24] maintain that good liturgy is playful and that engaging with liturgy playfully has an important role in the development of faith in children. Building on the work of Berryman and Cavalletti, philosopher Faith Pawl has recently argued that children are the exemplars of liturgical participation.[25] This claim raises a puzzle, for, as Pawl discusses, each of the following propositions appears initially plausible:

1. In order to participate meaningfully in liturgy, one must understand the propositional content of what is expressed in liturgy.
2. Children lack the requisite understanding of the propositional content of liturgies.
3. Children are exemplary participants in liturgy.[26]

Pawl goes on to give good reasons for rejecting premise 1, citing recent work by Nicholas Wolterstorff on the relationship between liturgical action and liturgical understanding. But it is Pawl's rejection of premise 2 that is of most interest here. In rejecting this claim, she writes,

> Children might not fully grasp the meaning of the statements in the Nicene Creed or the prayers in the Liturgy of the Hours or

> the Book of Common Prayer. By this I simply mean they might not have many of the words of those texts in their vocabularies, or they may not know what propositional content is ruled out as contrary to the positive affirmations expressed through creeds and prayers. However, children can understand the essential elements of the Gospel message . . . understanding isn't something that one simply comes to possess like water poured into a bucket, but is rather an intellectual virtue that is cultivated and nurtured—both in children and adults.[27]

Pawl is clear that the kind of understanding children gain will not often look like understanding in an adult. But, drawing on Cavaletti, she observes that children have rich spiritual lives that are sometimes underappreciated. As Cavaletti puts it, the depth of children's faith often comes "with ephemeral moments, like a flash of light that shines vibrantly then fades away . . . The fact that we are dealing with flashes does not invalidate their importance, because it is proper to the child to live at first in a discontinuous way the riches he possesses, which only gradually and through the aid of the environment later becomes a constant habitus in him."[28] If by "understanding," we mean something akin to the capacity to grasp creeds and listen to long sermons, then clearly children cannot participate. Indeed, it is not clear how many adults can truly and consistently participate. But if we think of understanding in holistic terms including both explicit and implicit beliefs as well as the engagement of the body and affect (see chapter 1), then children can understand in ways that sometimes adults fail to.[29]

Finally, Pawl highlights well the myth that all participants lie on a scale from "no understanding" to "full understanding." This assumes that the kind of understanding that a child provides is simply an underdeveloped version of adult understanding. However, an alternative view is that children's understanding represents a *qualitatively different kind* of understanding. Children are not simply preadults but experience a different form of life.[30]

Pawl's strategy is helpful for a number of reasons. For sometimes when talking of liturgical inclusion, the emphasis is on fitting children into an adult mode of engagement. The risk of this approach is a failure to see how children can benefit the wider community. It might lead to making them passengers (or, perhaps loafers, see chapter 4) in the context of liturgical actions, without appreciating what they can genuinely *contribute*. Instead, Pawl thinks, it is important to begin to see that children are genuine liturgical exemplars; they display the openness and wonder that everyone should strive to bring to liturgy. She writes that, "while children may exhibit over-confidence in some of their beliefs, it does seem that they are able to sit in contemplation of the mysteries of the faith, to ask questions over and over again, to hear the same stories, and to be open to the possibility that what they know of reality is not the whole story."[31] On this account, learning from children is important for the liturgical life of the Church. As C. B. Matthews explains,

> the adult has a better command of the language than the child, and, latently anyway, a surer command of the concepts expressed in the language. But it is the child who has fresh eyes and ears for perplexity and incongruity. And children typically have a degree of candor and spontaneity that is hard for the adult to match. Since each party has something important to contribute, the inquiry can easily become a genuinely joint venture, something otherwise rather rare in adult encounters with children.[32]

Matthews' usage of the phrase "genuine joint venture" is notable here. In keeping with our line of argument, it places an emphasis on joint activity in the life of the Church community. But it also draws out a further important point. A joint venture does not require equal allocation of understanding or role. In fact, it is precisely such asymmetries—for example, between adults' conceptual familiarity and children's eye for the novel—that can enrich liturgical practices and community life.

EMBRACING ROLE ASYMMETRY IN LITURGICAL PRACTICES

Pawl's argument concerning the place of children in the liturgical life of the Church is compelling. But we worry that it does not go far enough. Pawl's account may widen the goalposts to include those who have a childlike but profound understanding of the gospel, but it is difficult to see how the same might be said of a newborn infant or those with profound differences in intellectual ability. In other words, while endorsing Pawl's inclusion of children in the liturgical life of the Church, we need to go further if we wish to give an account of inclusion that involves human participants in all their cultural, psychological, and bodily diversity.

In trying to emphasize the inclusion of children in worship, it is possible to make the assumption that liturgical participation is a monolithic category. That is, the temptation is to think that inclusion means everyone has to be doing the same thing or else there is a risk of excluding someone. Ironically, this emphasis on a generic kind of equality can sometimes lead to a more exclusionary view of liturgy. For example, consider an all-age worship service that is not dynamic enough to keep young children entertained, but too simplified to engage their parents. The aim is noble—that all participants are included—but the outcome is a widespread experience of distraction and disengagement. Trying to appeal to everyone can mean appealing to no one.

Moreover, it is not difficult to see how an emphasis on children as liturgical exemplars might lead us to think that the ideal of liturgy is some form of play, inviting adults into a childlike engagement with liturgical forms—replacing sermons with stories, hymns with crafts, and prayers with sensory activities. To be clear, we are not claiming that this is Pawl's claim, nor are we saying that this form of liturgy does not have its place. The highly successful Messy Church movement has engaged many people for many years; they describe their liturgy as: "a way of being church for families and others. It is Christ-centered, for all ages, based on creativity, hospitality and celebration."[33] But note that Messy Church essentially takes the reverse line on inclusion to traditional church—rather than accommodating children in a service "for adults," Messy Church aims primarily at engaging children and families. If Messy Church is to be understood as a model for how a church organizes its liturgy, there are parallels with the adult-centric approach: it takes a monolithic view of liturgy, in which the goal is for all to engage in the same way.

There are reasons to doubt this monolithic approach. For instance, writing in the context of Hebrew rituals, Dru Johnson asks,

> If rituals dispose Israelites to know, then must they dispose them disparately? A child in the crowd at Yom Kippur is disposed to know something differently than the High Priest. The ritual shapes the husband whose wife offers impurity sacrifices, but surely the rite impresses him differently than it does his wife who offers. Moreover, the one laying the hand on the head of sacrificial animals must be disposed distinctly from those who watch. What I am attempting to draw out in these examples is the presumption of disparity in the text itself. Like our cultural biases against ritual, these disparities might grate against egalitarian sensibilities. Although most all countries in the West grasp the necessity of representation, hence the proliferation of representational democracies, our sense of fairness might impose itself at this juncture.[34]

Johnson's point here is instructive in the contemporary discussion of liturgy, we think. A properly inclusive view of liturgy will make space for individuals to participate in a variety of modes. This need not mean giving up on the challenging and profound task of learning from one another, for which Pawl advocates, but it may mean recognizing that there can be space for different groups to engage in different ways. For example, taking children out of the primary worship space to engage in age-appropriate liturgies and activities may end up being more inclusive than trying to engage everyone at the same time. Moreover, in cases where participants are unable to engage outwardly with liturgies (e.g., very young infants and differently abled individuals), we can still make sense of their participation in the same liturgy. If we have space to allow for there to be liturgical leaders of some form, whose role is distinct from most of the congregation (whether these are priests, worship leaders, or ministers), then we can surely think of newborn babies, for instance, as full liturgical participants, whose contribution differs from the majority. But this raises an important question: What do such participants contribute to liturgy, and do they gain from participation in any meaningful way? Let us take each of these questions in turn.

First, what might a newborn baby contribute to the liturgical life of the community? Consider a more trivial example: After dinner each night, a family with two young (two- and four-year-old) children engage in the important business of the kitchen dance party. They put on a piece of music, dim the lights, and freestyle in the kitchen before doing the washing up. When, later that year, the latest arrival to the family is born, they continue to do the same after-dinner ritual, placing the baby in a seat while the rest of the family dance haphazardly around the kitchen. Is the baby part of this family activity? At a week old, the baby is unable to make out shapes more than a few centimeters in front of his face, let alone distinguish the movements of his siblings. The baby is not obviously contributing to the dance in the *same way*, that is, he does not contribute by dancing. But he does contribute to the sense of jointness of the experience.

It is worth stressing our focus here on *jointness* rather than *joint attention*. The perspective that we have articulated throughout the book is that joint attention is the foundational context for the experience of jointness, but that jointness plays a role in a much broader range of cases and experiences (e.g., the sense of jointness achieved by believing that others are attending to the same focus). In stressing this sense of jointness, it is important to acknowledge the infant as a person, rather than an object. Even if the infant is not proactively shaping the joint experience, their role is different to that of a spatula or microwave.

But even if we make this step, this does not get us all the way to treating the infant as a participant. There are still many scenarios in which persons are present but not part of a joint experience. In chapter 2 we gave the example of the train station, in which many individuals attended to a common locus (the screen displaying timetables) but were not jointly attending. Presence plus attention to the same target equates only to jointness in its most minimal sense.[35] The infant's role in the family dance party seems to be more than this. Personhood only identifies the infant as having the *potential* to join a joint experience, just as the others attending to the screen with me are those with whom I *could* share the experience—for example, by noting how many of the trains are running late. Their attention, to borrow a term from John Campbell, is a constituent of the experience of the others who are present. As he puts it:

> The individual experiential state you are in, when you and another are jointly attending to something, is an experiential state that you could not be in were it not for the other person attending to the object. The other person enters into your experience as a constituent of it.[36]

Note that Campbell's definition of joint attention differs from our own, as does his sense of what it means to be a co-attender. But the overarching point is a helpful one; the presence of other persons shapes our own sense of engagement. For example, the joint experience and activity is influenced by the infant's experience—the music is perhaps not played quite so loudly, and the parents might frequently glance across to ensure the infant is still content. The nature of the joint experience is different when the infant is present. One might accept the infant as a participant to the extent that others are influenced by their presence. But it is another step to suggest that the infant themselves, with their limited ability to grasp the situation (or even limited perceptual capabilities to see what is occurring), can benefit in some way from being a participant. So how might such participants benefit from being included?

There is no clear line that an infant crosses in order to move from nonunderstanding to understanding. Indeed, most communities implicitly grasp this, hence the use of initiation rituals (such as baptism) that provide objective points of social transition. An understanding of liturgy that sees babies and those with profound differences in ability as waiting until they are able to join in "properly" is one that fails to take seriously the scope of liturgical jointness. It may be true that such participants understand little, if anything, of what goes on, and that they cannot actively participate in liturgical actions, but this does not mean that they do not contribute to the experience of jointness. Continuing with our dance party example, consider two different approaches to inclusion:

1. The parents decide that the baby is too young to participate in the dance party (he cannot even walk, let alone pirouette), and so they decide to hold their dance parties exclusively at nap time, at least until the baby is old enough to properly participate.
2. The parents include the baby in the dance party and try to engage him at some level. They make regular eye contact while they are dancing and encourage his siblings to move his arms and legs in time to the music. Over time, as he develops, the baby begins to move in time to the music. Eventually, as he learns to walk independently, he is able to dance in the same manner as his siblings.

Which approach will more effectively facilitate the infant in becoming an active participant? And which case is most likely to lead to the child learning to dance? And which is most likely to lead to a stronger sense of family identity? These are testable claims, but the intuitive answer to all the above seems obviously to be the second. Full inclusion in this ritual influences not just the family but also the baby. In recent years, there have been numerous campaigns across the world that encourage parents to socially engage with their infant from birth (and in some cases before), informed by a robust foundation of evidence regarding the influence of caregivers on infant social, emotional, and cognitive development.[37] For example, the large literature on the development of communication and language development demonstrates the ways in which social engagement and exposure to speech influences infant development during pregnancy and across their first year.[38] The clear consensus is that the shaping of the very early learning environment of infants is vital for their subsequent development and flourishing, even while some of the precise mechanisms through which these influences occur are not fully understood.

While this does not amount to a set of concrete predictions regarding the influence of a dance party on an infant's development, it does reinforce the notion that these experiences are contributing to the infant's formation in nontrivial ways. The same point is surely true of liturgical inclusion; finding ways to include infants in the liturgies of the Church is beneficial to their formation in the life of the community. This provides a helpful way of unpacking Calvin's point, which we considered previously:

> being engrafted into the body of the church, they are somewhat more commended to the other members. Then, when they have grown up, they are greatly spurred to an earnest zeal for worshipping God, by whom they were received as children through a solemn symbol of adoption before they were old enough to recognize him as Father.[39]

The practical consequences of this engrafting will differ from community to community. But the key point to stress is that *all* members of the community have a role to play in shaping the sense of jointness, even if they cannot contribute in the same way. Even the simple act of being physically present and influencing the liturgical actions of others shapes how everyone participates. By embracing the influence of these members of the community, churches might find new ways of understanding the Apostle Paul's view that "the members of the body that seem to be weaker are indispensable" (1 Cor 12:22).

SUMMARY

Throughout the book we have been exploring the sense of jointness that is at the heart of all liturgies. In liturgy, participants are joined with others across spatial and temporal barriers. Here, we have asked where the boundaries of community might lie. First, the explicit inclusion of those who are regarded as part of the community through rites of initiation, like baptism, provide boundaries that are made common knowledge in the life of the community. In baptism, individuals are welcomed into the local community of the church, which is nested in the broader community of the mystical body of the Church.

Second, we have seen that baptism is not the only relevant factor in determining the boundaries of jointness. The structure and shape of liturgy play a significant and ongoing role in this matter. Where and how children are included is significant both for an infant's experience of jointness in the community and also for the adult's sense of jointness, and whether this includes infants or not. *How* infants are included is more complex; reflecting on Pawl's recent discussion of liturgical play, we have seen the importance of seeing children as liturgical exemplars, not just accommodating children but seeking to learn from them. But children vary massively from early infancy to late childhood, and thus including children requires carefully considering their age and stage of development.

We have also seen the need to provide a pluralistic mode of participation in liturgy, one which can make sense of the idea that even very young infants are included in the liturgical life of the Church. Including infants in this way promises to shape the sense of jointness of all who participate and to provide an environment where holistic liturgical formation can take place. We have focused specifically on the issue of the inclusion of children, but a similar discussion may be had regarding those with physical differences, the elderly, or those across different cultural contexts and, indeed, any group that may find itself excluded in some form from church practice. Thus, reflecting on how the youngest participants might be included in a community will help as we consider how all people, in all of their diversity, can be included in the shared worship of the Church.

CONCLUSION

Gathered and Sent

Gathering with other people matters. Throughout this book, we have explored the nature and significance of gathering with others for acts of prayer, confession, praise, and remembrance. Most gathered worship—in which these liturgical acts can be found—ends with another liturgical act, namely dismissal. The presiding minister may use some words (e.g., some formal liturgy such as "go in peace to love and serve the Lord!") or may end the gathering with an informal prayer of God's blessing. The liturgical act of dismissal signifies that the community that was gathered at the beginning of worship is now dismissed, sent into different parts of the world.

We might instinctively think, therefore, that gathering ceases when the congregation is dismissed. In a certain sense, this is right—the acts of interactive joint attention can no longer occur when the congregation is not physically present in the same building. But as we have explored throughout this book, the jointness that is expressed in its most ideal form in embodied, gathered liturgy cannot be contained to the liturgical acts between gathering and dismissal.

In fact, to limit our thinking only to such acts risks reducing the community of the Church to our own actions and attempts to worship. To do so is to risk missing a central pillar of Christian theology. As Torrance argues, a view of worship in which human agents are primary is widespread but mistaken. In such a view,

> We go to church, we sing our psalms and hymns to God . . . No doubt we need God's grace to help us do it. We do it because Jesus taught us to do it and left us an example as how to do it. But worship is what *we* do . . . In theological language, this means that the

> only priesthood is our priesthood, the only offering our offering, the only intercessions our intercessions.[1]

The reason Torrance thinks that this view of worship is misplaced is that it fails to see that Christian worship is primarily aimed at participation in the life of the Triune God, rather than existing only as a set of acts which human participants are to perform. A properly Trinitarian view of worship states that even one's best efforts of gathering to worship God must be understood as acts of *joining* in the communion that already exists between Father, Son, and Holy Spirit. The offering and intercession Torrance speaks of are thus understood as a participation in the offering and intercession of the Triune God. Following Torrance, the liturgical act of gathering is itself not an act of *constituting* worship but of participating in something that is ongoing, even when the congregation is dismissed by the minister's blessing.

Through this theological lens, gathering for worship is always nested within the jointness of the Church as a work of the Triune God. Gathering matters not just because it creates an act of worship in and of itself but because it participates in a deeper reality. The psychological work we have drawn on throughout this book helps to provide a framework for understanding this nesting of worship within a broader communal life, avoiding the temptation to make cheap and simplistic binaries between in-person worship (good!) and other worship (bad!). For the Christian, all worship, however alone and isolated, has potential to derive a sense of jointness from its location within the worshiping life of God, the community of saints, and the gathered men and women in one's particular location.

We started our exploration of this account of liturgical jointness with an anthropology that sought to avoid two pitfalls. On the one extreme, a brains-on-sticks approach makes thinking primary; liturgy shapes participants by changing their beliefs from false or inaccurate beliefs to true and accurate beliefs. But a hearts-on-legs model, though rightly emphasizing the role of the body and affect in liturgical formation, is a flawed solution insofar as it reinforces the unhelpful binary between thinking and feeling. Liturgy surely does shape one's body and one's affect, but not as a first step before the shaping of cognition can begin. In contrast with these approaches, we proposed a psychologically holistic approach where none of cognition, affect, or behavior is treated as more fundamental than the other. In doing so, we highlighted the need for a *developmental* perspective, one that emphasizes that cognition and affect are both present from the very earliest stages of development and insists that we will only understand these processes if we understand their developmental origins. This perspective requires a nuanced view of thinking that recognizes that cognitive processes range from implicit to explicit. While thinking is often associated with slow, conscious, explicit modes of cognition, psychologists have highlighted that there are other fast, nonconscious, implicit cognitive processes that are present in early development and continue to play a role throughout the life span. Building on this view of cognition, we discussed evidence for the deeply *social* origins of explicit cognitive thought, considering both evolutionary and developmental perspectives. Indeed, we think that humans' profoundly social nature is such that the role of social engagement must be recognized in any discussion of human thought, feeling, or action. Taken together, this anthropological framework leads to a view of liturgical formation where the totality of the human person is shaped through engagement with others.

This anthropological foundation led us to explore the importance of joint attention for human development more generally and for liturgical development more specifically. Our approach has been twofold: first, to explore the *nature* of joint liturgical acts, and second, to understand the distinctive *value* of joint liturgical acts.

First, we made a number of claims about the nature of joint liturgical acts. We explored the psychological concepts of joint attention and shared situations, and the ways these both contribute to a wider sense of jointness. Drawing upon these concepts, we provided a framework for thinking about how liturgy can be shared with others across a wide range of contexts—from physically copresent gatherings, to Zoom prayer and even certain forms of personal liturgy. A nested approach to jointness provided us with a helpful way of understanding a variety of different forms of liturgy. In communal prayer, we claimed, jointness can be expressed in many different ways and on many different levels. Some prayer relies on joint attention involving direct interaction with others, whereas other forms of prayer derive their sense of jointness from their context and background beliefs (e.g., the belief that the Church is praying at the same time as me). We also examined the way in which these senses of jointness could be extended to differing conceptions of group gratitude to God—from the small-scale acts of individual gratitude embedded within communal life, to acts of joint intentionality with others such as expressing worship to God through song, and also to acts of collective gratitude, in which whole communities unite to show gratitude at an organizational or institutional level. This account of jointness was also applied to acts of remembrance. The sense of jointness which is established throughout communities in the present can, in a sense, extend to the past. Exploring the notion of actualization in the Hebrew scriptures, we offered a way of conceiving of the nature of jointness extending over time through acts of ritualized remembrance. Concluding our reflections on liturgical jointness, we proposed ways of thinking about the limits of jointness, asking how the concepts we have unpacked help us look more specifically at who is included and who is excluded from communal liturgical acts.

Second, in reflecting on the nature of joint liturgical acts we also explored something of their distinctive value. For example, communal prayer said with others provides opportunities for social cohesion and bonding, and an alignment of knowledge and purpose in response to God. We also discussed the way in which prayers of confession might allow a deepening of relationship within communities and highlighted the importance of vulnerability in joining acts of worship with others. On the theme of gratitude, we showed how accounts of liturgical jointness allow for a beneficial form of loafing in which group acts can include those who are unable or unwilling to join in the actions of the church, in ways that allow the church to be a community of safety and learning. In reflecting on joint acts of remembrance, we showed how a sense of jointness with those who have come before can fuel a community's imagination about its future. It is worth acknowledging that, while these distinctive values were highlighted in relation to specific liturgical acts (i.e., cohesion with prayer, loafing with gratitude), these links were not meant to be exclusive. Many of the distinctive values of liturgical jointness are both connected to each other and translate to different liturgical acts. For example, the concept of liturgical loafing surely applies as much to acts of petition (e.g., when those undergoing personal tragedy lack the right words to petition God) as it does to acts of gratitude. Similarly, social bonding and bodily synchrony are surely present in the consuming of the eucharistic meal. The point was not to tie these values to the particular acts but to show concrete cases of how a concept of liturgical jointness might enrich our understanding of the distinctive value of gathered worship of its many forms.

The significance of a project like this, we hope, is not confined only to *what* we have argued, but also to *how* we have argued it. At the beginning of the book, we stated that our goal throughout this book was a kind of mutual enrichment between psychology and theology. Rather than offer reductive or competitive accounts of liturgy, we have sought to show the ways in which disciplines might complement and inform one another. It is not the case that the psychological discussions were written only by a psychologist and the theological discussions only written by a theologian. As the project has unfolded, what has emerged has come through dialogue, not delegation. It is interesting to reflect on the ways in which some of the concepts we have explored have provided enrichment in both directions.

For psychologists, we hope that this book illustrates the broad relevance and applications of the concept of joint attention beyond its role in human social development. For example, work on joint attention has largely existed separately from psychological research on ritual, gratitude, and memory. We think that concepts taken from the joint attention literature can supplement and enrich these other domains, in which interaction and shared experience play a key role. The emphasis of the book has been as much on *jointness* as it has been on joint attention, and we have sought to contribute new ways of thinking about how jointness can extend beyond the two-agent context. There are few conceptual accounts of joint attention beyond two agents or outside of physically copresent engagements,[2] and empirical work is somewhat limited in this regard.[3] We (like others[4]) think that there is still much more to be understood about the role of joint attention in human social life, and that jointness and joint attention are more complex phenomena than is sometimes assumed.

We also hope that this book has illustrated the value of taking seriously the theological rationales and frameworks of meaning that underpin religious practices. For example, we can certainly understand communal prayer solely as an exercise in knowledge sharing and social bonding. However, by engaging with the belief that prayer involves jointness with God, we can talk more specifically about what differentiates prayer from other communal activities, and are thus better placed to understand how it may have differing consequences to other forms of socially unifying activity.

For theologians, we hope this dialogue has illustrated the value of engaging with other disciplines in thinking through important theological questions. Let us consider two examples. While many theologians and practitioners may instinctively agree that worship should be inclusive of those who cannot participate in specific liturgical acts, the exploration of the psychological concept of loafing in relation to our account of liturgical jointness (in chapter 4) provides a concrete application of this important theological truth. In exploring the ways in which this concept has been described in psychology, we are forced to think practically about what it means to carry one another's burdens (Gal 6:2) in the context of gathered worship. Similarly, the notion of actualization plays a crucial role in understanding rites of remembrance, both the Eucharist and the Seder meal (see chapter 5). In offering a psychological account of actualization, we have seen the richness of this abstract concept and the ways in which it can shape human experiences and their practices of worship. Exploring theological concepts through the lens of the psychological sciences allows us to glimpse with greater depth and richness the acts of gathering for worship in its many forms.

Finally, and relatedly, while our aim has been primarily theoretical and academic, our hope is that the conceptual resources of this book can enable church leaders and communities to engage in deeper reflection on their existing liturgical practices, prompting fresh practical ideas or providing new ways of articulating the value of existing practices. Our goal has not primarily been to develop a practical theology, but we hope that the novel conceptual contributions of the book might enable new ways of approaching familiar challenges. Indeed, a value of avoiding prescriptive guidelines and focusing on conceptual clarity is that it allows for an embracing of diversity in practices. For example, the discussion of "liturgical loafing" in chapter 4 offers a way of thinking about participation in church life that comes with a range of pastoral consequences such as thinking about how to include those who cannot participate in a normative way: Where are the spaces within gathered worship for people to participate differently or to remain inactive throughout liturgical acts? How do we recognize and uphold those who cannot participate in typical ways? Similarly, chapter 6 approaches inclusion as something expressed in the choices that communities make when gathering together and engaging in liturgical practices. We hope that our account can help leaders and communities make intentional decisions about their practices—such as what children are doing, and when—rather than resorting to familiar norms or introducing new approaches without consideration of the consequences.

We hope we have shown that gathering together really does matter. These mundane liturgical acts of eating, listening, singing, and speaking (whether mediated through laptop screens or church buildings) are means of participating in the communal life of the Church, and promise to shape the experience not just of these liturgical acts but, more widely, of one's human experience. Seeing the simple acts of prayer and gratitude as nested within multiple and complex layers of jointness means that even when the congregation is sent from the gathered act of worship, their working, their sleeping, their relationships, and their families are located within a community of worship. This promises to color even those acts that might seem far removed from the gathered worship of the church.

Moreover, while we have spoken to something of the value of these acts, the fundamentality of jointness for living whole lives of worship presses us to move beyond instrumentalization. While communal prayer might lead to social cohesion, and group gratitude to social inclusion, pursuing the life of worship solely for its social benefits is missing a crucial part of the theological impetus for worship, and even attempts to naturalize liturgy must engage with its theological rationale: liturgy provides a means of joining attention with one who is worthy of worship, praise, and adoration. "For from him and through him and to him are all things. To him be the glory forever. Amen" (Rom 11:36).

NOTES

INTRODUCTION

1 See Priya Parker, *The Art of Gathering: How We Meet and Why It Matters* (London: Penguin, 2020) for a fuller exploration of the importance of gathering. Parker writes, "The way we gather matters. Gatherings consume our days and help determine the kind of world we live in, in both our intimate and public realms. Gathering—the conscious bringing together of people for a reason—shapes the way we think, feel, and make sense of the world." Parker, *Art of Gathering*, 1.

2 See World Health Organization, "COVID-19 Pandemic Triggers 25% Increase in Prevalence of Anxiety and Depression Worldwide," March 2, 2022, https://www.who.int/news/item/02-03-2022-covid-19-pandemic-triggers-25-increase-in-prevalence-of-anxiety-and-depression-worldwide.

3 This emphasis stems from the Jewish roots of the Christian tradition, which likewise emphasize the shared nature of worship. Consider, for example, the Jewish practice of minyan prayer, a ritual that is performed by at least ten adults. Minyan prayer is said to provide a context where the imperfect prayers of individuals can be drawn together into the prayer of the congregation, to whom God will be attentive. See Aryeh Citron, "Minyan: The Prayer Quorum," *Chabad*, accessed November 7, 2024, https://www.chabad.org/library/article_cdo/aid/1176648/jewish/Minyan-The-Prayer-Quorum.htm. While this book will primarily focus on the Christian tradition, we recognize that this cannot be understood entirely separately from the Jewish traditions that precede it, and elsewhere we consider Jewish practices in greater depth (e.g., chapter 5).

4 All biblical references are to the New Revised Standard Version unless otherwise stated.

5 We explore some of this literature in more detail in chapter 1. See, for example, Warren S. Brown and Brad D. Strawn, *The Physical Nature of Christian Life: Neuroscience, Psychology, and the Church* (Cambridge: Cambridge University Press, 2022); Brad D. Strawn and Warren S. Brown, *Enhancing Christian Life: How Extended Cognition Augments Religious Community* (Lisle, Ill.: InterVarsity, 2020); C. Andrew Doyle, *Embodied Liturgy: Virtual Reality and Liturgical Theology in Conversation* (New York: Church Publishing, 2021); Deanna A. Thompson, *The Virtual Body of Christ in a Suffering World* (Nashville: Abingdon, 2016); W. David O. Taylor, *A Body of Praise: Understanding the Role of Our Physical Bodies in Worship* (Grand Rapids: Baker Books, 2023).

6 Taylor, *Body of Praise*, 26.

7 Strawn and Brown, *Enhancing Christian Life*, 3.

8 See Ian G. Barbour, *When Science Meets Religion: Enemies, Strangers, or Partners?* (London: SPCK, 2000).

9 See Peter Harrison, ed., *The Cambridge Companion to Science and Religion* (Cambridge: Cambridge University Press, 2010).

10 See Alister E. McGrath, "Response: Science and Religion—The State of the Art," *Zygon* 57, no. 1 (2022): 267–86.

11 When we use the term *psychology*, our focus will be on psychological science. The term *psychology* can be inclusive of practical applications of psychological science, such as in counseling and psychotherapy.

12 See Justin L. Barrett, *TheoPsych: A Psychological Science Primer for Theologians* (Knoxville: Blueprint 1543, 2022).

13 At least not in the sense used by Varela and colleagues. See Francisco J. Varela, Evan Thompson, and Eleanor Rosch, *The Embodied Mind: Cognitive Science and Human Experience*, rev. ed. (Cambridge, Mass.: MIT Press, 2017).

14 See Barrett, *TheoPsych*.

15 Andrew Davison, "Science and Specificity: Interdisciplinary Teaching Between Theology, Religion, and the Natural Sciences," *Zygon* 57, no. 1 (2022): 235.

16 John Perry and Joanna Leidenhag, "What Is Science-Engaged Theology?" *Modern Theology* 37, no. 2 (2021): 247.

17 Perry and Leidenhag, "What Is Science-Engaged Theology?" 248.

18 McGrath, "Response: Science and Religion," 276, quoting Alister E. McGrath, *The Territories of Human Reason: Science and Theology in an Age of Multiple Rationalities* (Oxford: Oxford University Press, 2018).

19 Malcom A. Jeeves and Thomas E. Ludwig, *Psychological Science and Christian Faith: Insights and Enrichments from Constructive*

Dialogue (West Conshohocken, Pa.: Templeton Foundation Press, 2018), 95–96.

20 Barrett, *TheoPsych*, 146.

21 See Jeeves and Ludwig, *Psychological Science and Christian Faith*.

22 James K. A. Smith, review of *Ritualized Faith: Essays on the Philosophy of Liturgy* by Terence Cuneo, *Scottish Journal of Theology* 71, no. 1 (2018): 118–19, https://doi.org/10.1017/S0036930617000126.

23 See James K. A. Smith, *Desiring the Kingdom: Worship, Worldview, and Cultural Formation*, vol. 1 of *Cultural Liturgies* (Grand Rapids: Baker Academic, 2009); Bruce Ellis Benson, *Liturgy as a Way of Life: Embodying the Arts in Christian Worship*, The Church and Postmodern Culture (Grand Rapids: Baker Books, 2013); Terence Cuneo, *Ritualized Faith: Essays on the Philosophy of Liturgy* (Oxford: Oxford University Press, 2016); Nicholas Wolterstorff, *Acting Liturgically: Philosophical Reflections on Religious Practice* (Oxford: Oxford University Press, 2018).

24 Michael Tomasello, *The Cultural Origins of Human Cognition* (Cambridge, Mass.: Harvard University Press, 1999).

25 M. Scaife and J. S. Bruner, "The Capacity for Joint Visual Attention in the Infant," *Nature* 253, no. 5489 (1975): 265–66.

26 Roger Bakeman and Lauren B. Adamson, "Coordinating Attention to People and Objects in Mother-Infant and Peer-Infant Interaction," *Child Development* 55, no. 4 (1984), 1278–89; Elizabeth Bates et al., *The Emergence of Symbols: Cognition and Communication in Infancy* (New York: Academic Press, 1979); Malinda Carpenter et al., "Social Cognition, Joint Attention, and Communicative Competence from 9 to 15 Months of Age," *Monographs of the Society for Research in Child Development* 63, no. 4 (1998): 1–143.

27 Naomi Eilan, ed., *Joint Attention: Communication and Other Minds; Issues in Philosophy and Psychology* (Oxford: Oxford University Press, 2005); Axel Seemann, ed., *Joint Attention: New Developments in Psychology, Philosophy of Mind, and Social Neuroscience* (Cambridge, Mass.: MIT Press, 2011).

28 Jeremy I. M. Carpendale and Charlie Lewis, "Constructing an Understanding of Mind: The Development of Children's Social Understanding Within Social Interaction," *Behavioral and Brain Sciences* 27, no. 1 (2004): 79–96; Tomasello, *Cultural Origins of Human Cognition*; Michael Tomasello, *Becoming Human: A Theory of Ontogeny* (Cambridge, Mass.: Harvard University Press, 2019); Samuel P. L. Veissière et al., "Thinking Through Other Minds: A Variational Approach to Cognition and Culture," *Behavioral and Brain Sciences* 43 (2020), https://doi.org/10.1017/S0140525X19001213.

29 Garriy Shteynberg, "A Collective Perspective: Shared Attention and the Mind," *Current Opinion in Psychology* 23 (October 2018): 93–97; Garriy Shteynberg, "Shared Attention," *Perspectives on Psychological Science* 10, no. 5 (2015): 579–90; Barbara Siposova and Malinda Carpenter, "A New Look at Joint Attention and Common Knowledge," *Cognition* 189 (2019): 260–74.

30 Malinda Carpenter and Kristin Liebal, "Joint Attention, Communication, and Knowing Together in Infancy," in *Joint Attention: New Developments*, ed. Axel Seemann, 159–81; R. Peter Hobson, "What Puts the Jointness into Joint Attention?" in *Joint Attention: Communication and Other Minds; Issues in Philosophy and Psychology*, ed. Naomi Eilan, 185–204; Michael Tomasello, "Joint Attention as Social Cognition," in *Joint Attention: Its Origins and Role in Development*, ed. Chris Moore, Philip J. Dunham, and Phil Dunham (Sussex: Psychology Press, 1995), 103–30.

31 Siposova and Carpenter, "A New Look at Joint Attention."

32 Harrison, in the introduction to his *Cambridge Companion to Science and Religion*, 10.

33 Barrett, *TheoPsych*, 14.

34 McGrath, "Response: Science and Religion."

35 McGrath, "Response: Science and Religion," 282–83.

36 For an example of this usage, see Timothy P. Racine and Jeremy I. M. Carpendale, "The Role of Shared Practice in Joint Attention," *British Journal of Developmental Psychology* 25, no. 1 (2007): 3–25.

37 Psychologists and cognitive anthropologists use the term "goal demotion" to describe cases where participants are unaware of why they or others are required to act in a certain manner, and use "causal opacity" to describe cases in which participants cannot articulate the mechanism by which a ritual achieves its purported effects (see Rohan Kapitány and Mark Nielsen, "The Ritual Stance and the Precaution System: The Role of Goal-Demotion and Opacity in Ritual and Everyday Actions," *Religion, Brain & Behavior* 7, no. 1 [2017]: 27–42). Our definition of ritual here draws primarily from Harvey Whitehouse and Jonathan A. Lanman, "The Ties That Bind Us: Ritual, Fusion, and Identification," *Current Anthropology* 55, no. 6 (2014): 674–95. But also, for a similar approach, see Cristine H. Legare and Mark Nielsen, "Ritual Explained: Interdisciplinary Answers to Tinbergen's Four Questions," *Philosophical Transactions of the Royal Society B* 375, no. 1805 (2020), https://doi.org/10.1098/rstb.2019.0419.

38 See Whitehouse and Lanman, "Ties That Bind Us"; Christopher M. Kavanagh et al., "Exploring the Pathways Between Transformative

Group Experiences and Identity Fusion," *Frontiers in Psychology* 11 (2020), https://doi.org/10.3389/fpsyg.2020.01172.

39 Moreover, while practices can involve the activity of individuals or dyads, liturgies typically involve larger communities. While we go on to discuss the role of sociality in practices, rituals, and liturgy, we put to one side the issue of precisely how these processes of transformation might occur.

1 THE FORMATIONAL POWER OF LITURGY

1 This chapter develops material originally published in Joshua Cockayne and Gideon Salter, "Liturgical Anthropology: A Developmental Perspective," *TheoLogica* 6, no. 1 (2022): 72–106. It is reprinted here with permission.

2 Harriet Over et al., "Ritual and the Origins of First Impressions," *Philosophical Transactions of the Royal Society B* 375, no. 1805 (2020), https://doi.org/10.1098/rstb.2019.0435; Nicole J. Wen et al., "Watch Me, Watch You: Ritual Participation Increases In-Group Displays and Out-Group Monitoring in Children," *Philosophical Transactions of the Royal Society B* 375, no.1805 (2020), https://doi.org/10.1098/rstb.2019.0437.

3 See, for instance, Smith, *Desiring the Kingdom*, whom we engage at length in this chapter; Dru Johnson, *Knowledge by Ritual: A Biblical Prolegomenon to Sacramental Theology* (Winona Lake, Ind.: Eisenbrauns, 2016), whose focus differs significantly from Smith's in tracing the theme of ritual through Scripture; Taylor, *Body of Praise*; Strawn and Brown, *Enhancing Christian Life*. See Legare and Nielsen, "Ritual Explained," for papers that represent the state of the art of ritual research across the domains of cognitive science, anthropology, and evolutionary biology.

4 Matthew Kaemingk and Cory B. Willson, *Work and Worship: Reconnecting Our Labor and Liturgy* (Grand Rapids: Baker Academic, 2020), 27.

5 Brown and Strawn, *Physical Nature of Christian Life*, 4.

6 Brown and Strawn, *Physical Nature of Christian Life*, 148–49.

7 Taylor, *Body of Praise*, 26.

8 Smith, *Desiring the Kingdom*, 47.

9 Smith, *Desiring the Kingdom*, 46.

10 Smith, *Desiring the Kingdom*, 50.

11 Smith, *Desiring the Kingdom*, 51.

12 Smith, *Desiring the Kingdom*, 58.

13 Smith, *Desiring the Kingdom*, 64.

14 Smith, *Desiring the Kingdom*, 63.

15 Smith, *Desiring the Kingdom*, 136.

16 A similar critique of Smith's epistemology can be found in Yoo Shin's recent work, *Pentecostalism, Postmodernism, and Reformed Epistemology: James K. A. Smith and the Contours of a Postmodern Christian Epistemology* (Lanham, Md.: Lexington / Fortress Academic, 2021).

17 To be clear: we are not arguing that a theological anthropology that sees love at the center of human existence can be scientifically falsified. In fact, the psychological perspective we develop in this chapter could easily affirm such an anthropology; it would seem strange to think that love is primarily affective rather than cognitive given how complexly these states interact. Intuitively, although we will not argue for it here, such an anthropology makes more sense on our holistic account than on an affect-first account.

18 Jerome S. Bruner, *Acts of Meaning* (Cambridge, Mass.: Harvard University Press, 1990).

19 Juan-Carlos Gómez et al., "Knowing Without Knowing: Implicit Cognition and the Minds of Infants and Animals [Saber sin saber: La cognición implícita y las mentes de niños pequeños y animales]," *Studies in Psychology* 38, no. 1 (2017): 37–62.

20 Cecilia M. Heyes and Chris D. Frith, "The Cultural Evolution of Mind Reading," *Science* 344, no. 6190 (2014): 1–6; Daniel D. Hutto, *Folk Psychological Narratives: The Sociocultural Basis of Understanding Reasons* (Cambridge, Mass.: MIT Press, 2008); Hugo Mercier and Dan Sperber, "Why Do Humans Reason? Arguments for an Argumentative Theory," *Behavioral and Brain Sciences* 34, no. 2 (2011): 57–74; Cathal O'Madagain and Michael Tomasello, "Joint Attention to Mental Content and the Social Origin of Reasoning," *Synthese* 198, no. 5 (2021): 4057–78.

21 See discussions in Fred Adams and Rebecca Garrison, "The Mark of the Cognitive," *Minds and Machines* 23, no. 3 (2013): 339–52; James A. Russell and Lisa Feldman Barrett, "Core Affect, Prototypical Emotional Episodes, and Other Things Called Emotion: Dissecting the Elephant," *Journal of Personality and Social Psychology* 76, no. 5 (1999): 805.

22 See Colin Allen, "On (Not) Defining Cognition," *Synthese* 194, no. 11 (2017): 4233–49, for an argument in favor of this approach.

23 Ken Aizawa, "What Is This Cognition That Is Supposed to Be Embodied?" *Philosophical Psychology* 28, no. 6 (2015): 755–75.

24 Brandon J. Schmeichel and David Tang, "Individual Differences in Executive Functioning and Their Relationship to Emotional Processes and Responses," *Current Directions in Psychological Science* 24, no. 2 (2015): 93–98.

25 There is a large and long-standing debate over how to define cognition. See Frederick Adams and Kenneth Aizawa, *The Bounds of Cognition* (Oxford: Blackwell, 2008); Adams and Garrison, "Mark of the Cognitive." On whether cognition is embodied, see Aizawa, "What Is This Cognition?" 755–75; Varela et al., *Embodied Mind.* While our perspective bears similarity to some arguments from embodied cognition theorists regarding the interdependence of cognition and action, we avoid entering specific conceptual disputes in this domain, as they are not relevant to our overarching argument.

26 Russell and Barrett, "Core Affect."

27 Katie Hoemann and Lisa Feldman Barrett, "Concepts Dissolve Artificial Boundaries in the Study of Emotion and Cognition, Uniting Body, Brain, and Mind," *Cognition and Emotion* 33, no. 1 (2019): 67–76.

28 Like cognition, there is no uncontroversial way to talk about affect or emotion; for example, see Jessica L. Tracy and Daniel Randles, "Four Models of Basic Emotions: A Review of Ekman and Cordaro, Izard, Levenson, and Panksepp and Watt," *Emotion Review* 3, no. 4 (2011): 397–405, versus Lisa Feldman Barrett, "Are Emotions Natural Kinds?" *Perspectives on Psychological Science* 1, no. 1 (2006): 28–58. The approach we have taken is one that fits well with our wider argument about the interconnection of cognition, affect, and behavior. It is beyond the scope of this book to provide a deeper exploration of competing theoretical positions and how they align with our account.

29 Bruner, *Acts of Meaning.*

30 Bruner uses the term "action" rather than "sensorimotor" or "bodily activity," but his intended meaning is similar.

31 Bruner, *Acts of Meaning*, 61.

32 Bruner, *Acts of Meaning*, 118.

33 It is important to note the three-part division here is not of central importance; one could opt to split affect into "emotion" and "motivation," or, as we go on to do, subdivide cognition into "implicit" and "explicit" cognition. The nature of the split is not as important as the ultimate unity and interdependence of any abstractly divided components.

34 In recent years, a number of theorists have made similar claims regarding the unity of psychological processes (see Jeremy R. Gray, "Integration of Emotion and Cognitive Control," *Current Directions in Psychological Science* 13, no. 2 [2004]: 46–48; Schmeichel and Tang, "Individual Differences"), with some arguing that cognition and affect are ultimately indistinguishable (see Seth Duncan

and Lisa Feldman Barrett, "Affect Is a Form of Cognition: A Neurobiological Analysis," *Cognition and Emotion* 21, no. 6 [2007]: 1184–211; Hoemann and Barrett, "Concepts Dissolve"; Luiz Pessoa, "On the Relationship Between Emotion and Cognition," *Nature Reviews Neuroscience* 9, no. 2 [2008]: 148–58).

35 Mary Catherine Bateson, "Mother-Infant Exchanges: The Epigenesis of Conversational Interaction," *Annals of the New York Academy of Sciences* 263, no. 1 (1975): 101–13.

36 It is possible that infants' social capacities can be traced back even earlier. There is substantial controversy over whether newborn infants can imitate others' facial expressions (see, for example, Jacqueline Davis et al., "Does Neonatal Imitation Exist? Insights from a Meta-Analysis of 336 Effect Sizes," *Perspectives on Psychological Science* 16, no. 6 [2021]: 1373–97; Andrew N. Meltzoff et al., "Re-Examination of Oostenbroek et al. [2016]: Evidence for Neonatal Imitation of Tongue Protrusion," *Developmental Science* 21, no. 4 [2018], http://doi.org/10.1111/desc.12609; Emese Nagy et al., "Positive Evidence for Neonatal Imitation: A General Response, Adaptive Engagement," *Developmental Science* 23, no. 2 [2020], https://doi.org/10.1111/desc.12894). Some recent research has even explored evidence of social capacities prenatally. Vincent M. Reid et al., "The Human Fetus Preferentially Engages with Face-Like Visual Stimuli," *Current Biology* 27, no. 12 (2017): 1825–28, https://doi.org/10.1016/j.cub.2017.05.044, presents evidence that third-trimester fetuses were more likely to turn their heads towards "face-like" configurations of laser dots (two over one) than the inverse configuration (one over two). However, our focus is on the capacity of infants to interact reciprocally with other agents, rather than just the ability to detect social stimuli. It is only from around two months that there is a general consensus that this is within the capacity of infants, so we begin our discussion from this age.

37 Gergely Csibra, "Recognizing Communicative Intentions in Infancy," *Mind & Language* 25, no. 2 (2010): 141–68.

38 Edward Tronick et al., "The Infant's Response to Entrapment Between Contradictory Messages in Face-to-Face Interaction," *Journal of the American Academy of Child Psychiatry* 17, no. 1 (1978): 1–13.

39 Lauren B. Adamson and Janet E. Frick, "The Still Face: A History of a Shared Experimental Paradigm," *Infancy* 4, no. 4 (2003): 451–73.

40 Mary D. Salter Ainsworth et al., *Patterns of Attachment: A Psychological Study of the Strange Situation* (Hillsdale, N.J.: Lawrence Erlbaum, 1978); Carl J. Dunst and Danielle Z. Kassow, "Caregiver

Sensitivity, Contingent Social Responsiveness, and Secure Infant Attachment," *Journal of Early and Intensive Behavior Intervention* 5, no. 1 (2008): 40–45; Elizabeth Meins, *Security of Attachment and the Social Development of Cognition* (Sussex: Psychology Press, 1997).

41 Tomasello, "Joint Attention as Social Cognition."

42 Scaife and Bruner, "Capacity for Joint Visual Attention."

43 Carpenter and Liebal, "Joint Attention," 159–81; Hobson, "What Puts the Jointness into Joint Attention?"; David A. Leavens et al., "Putting the 'Joy' in Joint Attention: Affective-Gestural Synchrony by Parents Who Point for Their Babies," *Frontiers in Psychology* 5 (2014), https://doi.org/10.3389/fpsyg.2014.00879.

44 Susan S. Jones and Hye-Won Hong, "Onset of Voluntary Communication: Smiling Looks to Mother," *Infancy* 2, no. 3 (2001): 353–70; Meaghan Venezia et al., "The Development of Anticipatory Smiling," *Infancy* 6, no. 3 (2004): 397–406.

45 Karen E. Adolph and Justine E. Hoch, "Motor Development: Embodied, Embedded, Enculturated, and Enabling," *Annual Review of Psychology* 70 (2019): 141.

46 We take this claim from Anderson and colleagues' (David I. Anderson et al., "The Role of Locomotion in Psychological Development," *Frontiers in Psychology* 4 [2013], https://doi.org/10.3389/fpsyg.2013.00440) reading of Mahler and colleagues (Margaret S. Mahler et al., *The Psychological Birth of the Human Infant: Symbiosis and Individuation* [New York: Basic Books, 1975]).

47 Anderson et al., "Role of Locomotion"; Amanda C. Brandone, "Infants' Social and Motor Experience and the Emerging Understanding of Intentional Actions," *Developmental Psychology* 51, no. 4 (2015): 512–24; though see Amanda C. Brandone et al., "Intentional Action Processing Across the Transition to Crawling: Does the Experience of Self-Locomotion Impact Infants' Understanding of Intentional Actions?" *Infant Behavior and Development* 60 (2020), https://doi.org/10.1016/j.infbeh.2020.101470.

48 Joseph J. Campos et al., "Travel Broadens the Mind," *Infancy* 1, no. 2 (2000): 149–219.

49 James F. Sorce et al., "Maternal Emotional Signaling: Its Effect on the Visual Cliff Behavior of 1-Year-Olds," *Developmental Psychology* 21, no. 1 (1985): 195–200.

50 Karen E. Adolph, "Psychophysical Assessment of Toddlers' Ability to Cope with Slopes," *Journal of Experimental Psychology: Human Perception and Performance* 21, no. 4 (1995): 734–50.

51 Samantha Ehli et al., "Determining the Function of Social Referencing: The Role of Familiarity and Situational Threat," *Frontiers in*

Psychology 11 (2020), https://doi.org/10.3389/fpsyg.2020.538228. A further argument for this view draws upon evidence of dissociations between infants' predictions and actions. For example, there can be a mismatch between visual attention and reaching behavior when infants track an object following an irregular, nonlinear trajectory that moves within their reach (Claes von Hofsten et al., "Predictive Action in Infancy: Tracking and Reaching for Moving Objects," *Cognition* 67, no. 3 [1998]: 255–85). This implies that multiple separate systems are involved in processing incoming perceptual information and subsequently acting on this information. If multiple systems are implicated in prediction and action, it becomes more difficult to claim that any one system is primary or basic. With thanks to an anonymous reviewer for prompting us to explore this issue.

52 Adams and Garrison, "Mark of the Cognitive"; Gómez et al., "Knowing Without Knowing."

53 Jean Piaget, *The Origins of Intelligence in Children*, trans. Margaret Cook (London: W. W. Norton, 1952).

54 Jonathan T. Delafield-Butt and Colwyn Trevarthen, "The Ontogenesis of Narrative: From Moving to Meaning," *Frontiers in Psychology* 6 (2015), https://doi.org/10.3389/fpsyg.2015.01157.

55 Renée Baillargeon et al., "Object Permanence in Five-Month-Old Infants," *Cognition* 20, no. 3 (1985): 191–208; Mark H. Johnson et al., "Components of Visual Orienting in Early Infancy: Contingency Learning, Anticipatory Looking, and Disengaging," *Journal of Cognitive Neuroscience* 3, no. 4 (1991): 335–44.

56 Baillargeon et al., "Object Permanence."

57 In Kyeong Kim and Elizabeth S. Spelke, "Infants' Sensitivity to Effects of Gravity on Visible Object Motion," *Journal of Experimental Psychology: Human Perception and Performance* 18, no. 2 (1992): 385–93.

58 Gergely Csibra, "Teleological and Referential Understanding of Action in Infancy," *Philosophical Transactions of the Royal Society of London. Series B: Biological Sciences* 358, no. 1431 (2003): 447–58.

59 J. Kiley Hamlin et al., "Social Evaluation by Preverbal Infants," *Nature* 450, no. 7169 (2007): 557–59.

60 Josep Call et al., "'Unwilling' Versus 'Unable': Chimpanzees' Understanding of Human Intentional Action," *Developmental Science* 7, no. 4 (2004): 488–98; Brian Hare et al., "Do Chimpanzees Know What Conspecifics Know?" *Animal Behaviour* 61, no. 1 (2001): 139–51; Christopher Krupenye et al., "Great Apes Anticipate that Other Individuals Will Act According to False Beliefs," *Science* 354, no. 6308 (2016): 110–14.

61 Christophe Boesch and Hedwige Boesch, "Tool Use and Tool Making in Wild Chimpanzees," *Folia Primatologica* 54, no. 1–2 (1990):

86–99; Andrew Whiten et al., "Conformity to Cultural Norms of Tool Use in Chimpanzees," *Nature* 437, no. 7059 (2005): 737–40.

62 Nathan J. Emery and Nicola S. Clayton, "The Mentality of Crows: Convergent Evolution of Intelligence in Corvids and Apes," *Science* 306, no. 5703 (2004): 1903–7.

63 Lori Marino et al., "Cetaceans Have Complex Brains for Complex Cognition," *PLoS Biology* 5, no. 5 (2007), https://doi.org/10.1371/journal.pbio.0050139.

64 Richard W. Byrne et al., "Elephant Cognition in Primate Perspective," *Comparative Cognition & Behavior Reviews* 4 (2009): 65–79.

65 Lars Chittka, "Bee Cognition," *Current Biology* 27, no. 19 (2017): 1049–53.

66 Daniel Kahneman, *Thinking, Fast and Slow* (London: Macmillan, 2011); Gómez et al., "Knowing Without Knowing." In a similar vein, discussions in philosophy of mind have highlighted the role of "tacit knowledge" (Martin Davies, "Knowledge [Explicit, Implicit and Tacit]: Philosophical Aspects," in *International Encyclopedia of the Social and Behavioral Sciences*, 2nd ed., ed. James D. Wright, vol. 13 [Elsevier, 2015], 74–90) and the distinction between "knowledge that" and "knowledge how" (Jason Stanley, *Know How* [Oxford: Oxford University Press, 2011]).

67 There is no clear consensus regarding how to define what constitutes implicit versus explicit processes, though some have suggested differences, such as implicit versus explicit being related to associative versus rule-based learning, sensorimotor versus abstract representations, simplicity versus complexity, or nonconscious versus conscious processes (Gómez et al, "Knowing Without Knowing"). It has also been highlighted that the acquisition of language plays a key role in explicit cognitive processes (see Lev S. Vygotsky, *Mind in Society: The Development of Higher Psychological Processes*, ed. Michael Cole et al. [Cambridge, Mass.: Harvard University Press, 1978]), but it is beyond the scope of this discussion to unpack these issues further.

68 Kahnemann, *Thinking, Fast and Slow.*

69 Peter Carruthers, "Mindreading in Infancy," *Mind & Language* 28, no. 2 (2013): 141–72; Hugo Mercier and Dan Sperber, *The Enigma of Reason* (Cambridge, Mass.: Harvard University Press, 2017).

70 Annette Karmiloff-Smith, *Beyond Modularity: A Developmental Perspective on Cognitive Science* (Cambridge, Mass.: MIT Press, 1992).

71 Though German mathematician and physicist Theodor Kaluza is said to have tried just this and lived to tell the tale.

72 Smith, *Desiring the Kingdom*, 50.

73 Vygotsky, *Mind in Society*, 57.

74 Heyes and Frith, "Cultural Evolution of Mind Reading"; Hutto, *Folk Psychological Narratives*; Mercier and Sperber, "Why Do Humans Reason?"; O'Madagain and Tomasello, "Joint Attention to Mental Content."

75 O'Madagain and Tomasello, "Joint Attention to Mental Content"; Bahar Köymen and Michael Tomasello, "The Early Ontogeny of Reason Giving," *Child Development Perspectives* 14, no. 4 (2020): 215–20; Henrike Moll and Andy Meltzoff, "Perspective Taking and Its Foundation in Joint Attention," in *Perception, Causation, and Objectivity: Issues in Philosophy and Psychology*, ed. Johannes Roessler et al. (Oxford: Oxford University Press, 2011), 286–304.

76 Daniel C. Dennett, "Beliefs About Beliefs (Commentary on Premack, et al.)," *Behavioral and Brain Sciences* 1 (1978): 568–70; Heinz Wimmer and Josef Perner, "Beliefs About Beliefs: Representation and Constraining Function of Wrong Beliefs in Young Children's Understanding of Deception," *Cognition* 13, no. 1 (1983): 103–28.

77 Henrike Moll et al., "Taking Versus Confronting Visual Perspectives in Preschool Children," *Developmental Psychology* 49, no. 4 (2013): 646–54; Gideon Salter and Richard Breheny, "Removing Shared Information Improves 3- and 4-Year-Olds' Performance on a Change-of-Location Explicit False Belief Task," *Journal of Experimental Child Psychology* 187 (2019), https://doi.org/10.1016/j.jecp.2019.104665.

78 Janet Wilde Astington and Jennifer M. Jenkins, "A Longitudinal Study of the Relation Between Language and Theory-of-Mind Development," *Developmental Psychology* 35, no. 5 (1999): 1311–20.

79 O'Madagain and Tomasello, "Joint Attention to Mental Content."

80 Denise Dellarosa Cummins, "Dominance Hierarchies and the Evolution of Human Reasoning," *Minds and Machines* 6, no. 4 (1996): 463–80; Mercier and Sperber, "Why Do Humans Reason?"

81 Jonathan Evans and David E. Over, *Rationality and Reasoning* (Hove: Psychology Press, 1996).

82 Mercier and Sperber, "Why Do Humans Reason?"; Mercier and Sperber, *Enigma of Reason*.

83 Andrea Kern and Henrike Moll, "On the Transformative Character of Collective Intentionality and the Uniqueness of the Human," *Philosophical Psychology* 30, no. 3 (2017): 319–37; Tomasello, *Becoming Human*.

84 Larry W. Hurtado, *One God, One Lord: Early Christian Devotion and Ancient Jewish Monotheism*, 3rd ed. (London: Bloomsbury, 2015), 108.

85 Hurtado, *One God, One Lord*, 104.
86 Hurtado, *One God, One Lord*, 129.
87 With thanks to Dru Johnson for bringing this to our attention.
88 Chris Seglenieks, *Johannine Belief and Graeco-Roman Devotion: Reshaping Devotion for John's Graeco-Roman Audience*, WUNT 2/528 (Tübingen: Mohr Siebeck, 2020), 204.
89 David Hay and Rebecca Nye, *The Spirit of the Child*, rev. ed. (London: Jessica Kingsley, 2006), 109.
90 Hay and Nye, *Spirit of the Child*, 110.
91 Hay and Nye, *Spirit of the Child*, 114.
92 Hay and Nye, *Spirit of the Child*, 113.
93 Hay and Nye, *Spirit of the Child*, 157.
94 Hay and Nye, *Spirit of the Child*, 157.
95 This idea is explored in Kahneman, *Thinking, Fast and Slow*.
96 Kevin Laland and Amanda Seed, "Understanding Human Cognitive Uniqueness," *Annual Review of Psychology* 72 (2021): 689–716.
97 Nicholas Wolterstorff, *The God We Worship: An Exploration of Liturgical Theology* (Grand Rapids: Eerdmans, 2015), 56.
98 Nicholas Wolterstorff, "Knowing God Liturgically," *Journal of Analytic Theology* 4 (2016): 13.
99 Sarah Coakley ("Beyond Belief," in *The Vocation of Theology Today: A Festschrift for David Ford*, ed. Tom Greggs et al. [Eugene, Ore.: Wipf and Stock, 2013], 131–45) makes a very similar claim concerning how liturgy might provide perceptual, nonpropositional knowledge of God over a long period of time.
100 Mercier and Sperber, "Why Do Humans Reason?"; O'Madagain and Tomasello, "Joint Attention to Mental Content."
101 Hay and Nye, *Spirit of the Child*, 109.
102 Susan Grove Eastman, *Paul and the Person: Reframing Paul's Anthropology* (Grand Rapids: Eerdmans, 2017), 105.
103 Simeon Zahl, "Beyond the Critique of Soteriological Individualism: Relationality and Social Cognition," *Modern Theology* 37, no. 2 (2021): 352.
104 Philippe Rochat et al., "Emerging Sensitivity to the Timing and Structure of Protoconversation in Early Infancy," *Developmental Psychology* 35, no. 4 (1999): 950.
105 Valentina Fantasia et al., "Changing the Game: Exploring Infants' Participation in Early Play Routines," *Frontiers in Psychology* 5 (2014), https://doi.org/10.3389/fpsyg.2014.00522; Nicole Rossmanith and Vasudevi Reddy, "Structure and Openness in the Development of Self in Infancy," *Journal of Consciousness Studies* 23, no. 1–2 (2016): 237–57; Barbara Rogoff et al., "Development Through Participation in Sociocultural Activity," *New Directions for*

Child and Adolescent Development 67 (Spring 1995): 45–65; Mary Spagnola and Barbara H. Fiese, "Family Routines and Rituals: A Context for Development in the Lives of Young Children," *Infants & Young Children* 20, no. 4 (2007): 284–99.

106 Vasudevi Reddy et al., "Anticipatory Adjustments to Being Picked Up in Infancy," *PLOS ONE* 8, no. 6 (2013), https://doi.org/10.1371/journal.pone.0065289.

107 Rochat et al., "Emerging Sensitivity."

108 Fantasia et al., "Changing the Game."

109 Rossmanith and Reddy, "Structure and Openness."

110 Legare and Nielsen, "Ritual Explained." In spite of their immaturity, young infants are still active participants in shared practices. Looking at the routine of picking up, Reddy and colleagues ("Anticipatory Adjustments") found infants as young as two months are capable of adjusting their body to make it easier for their mother to pick them up, and mother and infants are able to cofacilitate increasingly smooth pickups from two to four months. They suggest that these adjustments indicate a grasp of being the target of another's intentional action, a basic form of sociocognitive awareness. By around five months, infants are capable of raising their arms as a request to be picked up (see Jeremy Carpendale and Ailidh B. Carpendale, "The Development of Pointing: From Personal Directedness to Interpersonal Direction," *Human Development* 53, no. 3 [2010]: 110–26). This simple routine facilitates the infant's sociocognitive grasp of being the target of another's intentional action, charged with the positive affect involved in being reunited with one's caregiver, as well as involving increasingly complex sensorimotor control, which facilitates increasingly smoothly coordinated action. Furthermore, the infant's role changes as their ability to communicate develops, going from solely coregulator to potential initiator of the activity.

111 Jon Barwise, "The Situation in Logic," *CSLI Lecture Notes* 17 (1989); Joshua Cockayne and Gideon Salter, "Praying Together: Corporate Prayer and Shared Situations," *Zygon* 54, no. 3 (2019): 702–30.

112 Maxwell J. D. Ramstead et al., "Cultural Affordances: Scaffolding Local Worlds Through Shared Intentionality and Regimes of Attention," *Frontiers in Psychology* 7 (2016), https://doi.org/10.3389/fpsyg.2016.01090.

113 As well as facilitating communication and coordinated action, joint attention has also been highlighted for its crucial role in the transmission of cultural knowledge, the instrumental skills and social conventions of a community (see Legare and Nielsen, "Ritual

Explained"). When humans jointly attend with others, their attention is guided to particular features of the world, shaping how they subsequently act on and learn from the world (see Michael Tomasello et al., "Understanding and Sharing Intentions: The Origins of Cultural Cognition," *Behavioral and Brain Sciences* 28, no.5 [2005]: 675–735; Peter Mundy and Lisa Newell, "Attention, Joint Attention, and Social Cognition," *Current Directions in Psychological Science* 16, no. 5 [2007]: 269–74). Shared practices, understood as attention-shaping practices, thus facilitate the acquisition of cultural knowledge by making certain features of the world more salient and introducing practitioners to certain forms of activity. Over time, the shaping of attention and activity through joint engagements and shared practices enculturates infants into the community in which they are embedded, enabling them to become competent cultural participants.

2 THE SHARED NATURE OF LITURGY

1 This chapter and the next are a development of the article: Joshua Cockayne and Gideon Salter, "Praying Together: Corporate Prayer and Shared Situations," *Zygon* 54, no. 3 (2019): 702–30. Material is reproduced here under the Creative Commons license.

2 Quoted in Chris Gunby, "Advantages of Meta Quest 3, Quest 2, and Quest Pro for Corporate Training," *Virtual Speech*, September 27, 2023, https://virtualspeech.com/blog/advantages-oculus-training.

3 Perhaps, it might be argued, this intuition is only sound because virtual reality is not yet sophisticated enough to create realistic joint experiences. This point may well be true, but it does not undermine the basic point we are making here: that jointness comes in degrees. Our current virtual reality clearly lacks something crucial regardless of what possibilities there may be in the future. With thanks to Ryan Winterbottom for this clarification.

4 Tomasello et al., "Understanding and Sharing Intentions," 675–91.

5 John R. Searle, "Collective Intentions and Actions," in *Consciousness and Language*, ed. John R. Searle (Cambridge: Cambridge University Press, 2002), 92.

6 John R. Searle, *Making the Social World: The Structure of Human Civilization* (Oxford: Oxford University Press, 2010), 45.

7 See Searle, *Making the Social World*; Michael E. Bratman, *Shared Agency: A Planning Theory of Acting Together* (Oxford: Oxford University Press, 2013); Raimo Tuomela, *Social Ontology: Collective Intentionality and Group Agents* (Oxford: Oxford University Press, 2013), for the key positions in the debate.

8 We here follow others in claiming that shared intentionality takes different forms (Michael Tomasello, *A Natural History of Human Thinking* [Cambridge, Mass.: Harvard University Press, 2014]; Dan Zahavi and Glenda Satne, "Varieties of Shared Intentionality: Tomasello and Classical Phenomenology," in *Beyond the Analytic-Continental Divide: Pluralist Philosophy in the Twenty-First Century*, ed. Jeffrey A. Bell et al. [London: Routledge, 2016]), from engagements with a particular other, to "forms that go beyond the here and now and involve the construction of a common cultural ground (involving conventions, norms and institutions)." See Zahavi and Satne, "Varieties of Shared Intentionality," 2.

9 See Nameera Akhtar and Morton A. Gernsbacher, "On Privileging the Role of Gaze in Infant Social Cognition," *Child Development Perspectives* 2, no. 2 (2008): 59–65; and Maria Botero, "Tactless Scientists: Ignoring Touch in the Study of Joint Attention," *Philosophical Psychology* 29, no. 8 (2016): 1200–1214.

10 See Tomasello, "Joint Attention as Social Cognition," 103–30.

11 For more detailed accounts that take a second-person perspective, see Juan-Carlos Gómez, "Second Person Intentional Relations and the Evolution of Social Understanding," *Behavioral and Brain Sciences* 19, no. 1 (1996): 129–30; Chris Moore and John Barresi, "The Role of Second-Person Information in the Development of Social Understanding," *Frontiers in Psychology* 8 (2017), https://doi.org/10.3389/fpsyg.2017.01667; Vasudevi Reddy, *How Infants Know Minds* (Cambridge, Mass.: Harvard University Press, 2008); and Leonhard Schilbach et al., "Toward a Second-Person Neuroscience," *Behavioral and Brain Sciences* 36, no. 4 (2013): 393–414.

12 This line of argument is not to deny the importance of third-person modes of social cognition in how we understand others' minds. Rather, it emphasizes that shared experiences have their basis in interactive, reciprocal engagements.

13 Moll and Meltzoff, "Perspective Taking," 286–304; Siposova and Carpenter, "New Look at Joint Attention," 260–74.

14 This notion of jointness appears under different terms, such as a sense of something being "between us" (Charles Taylor, *Human Agency and Language*, vol. 1 [Cambridge: Cambridge University Press, 1985]) or "mutually manifest" (Dan Sperber and Dierdre Wilson, *Relevance: Communication and Cognition*, 2nd ed. [Malden, Mass.: Blackwell, 1995]).

15 Margaret Gilbert, "Mutual Recognition, Common Knowledge, and Joint Attention," in *Hommage à Wlodek: Philosophical Papers Dedicated to Wlodek Rabinowicz*, ed. T. Rønnow-Rasmussen et al. (Department of Philosophy, Lund University, 2007), https://

www.fil.lu.se/hommageawlodek/site/papper/GilbertMargaret.pdf; Siposova and Carpenter, "New Look at Joint Attention."

16 See Leon de Bruin et al., "Reconceptualizing Second-Person Interaction," *Frontiers in Human Neuroscience* 6 (2012), https://doi.org/10.3389/fnhum.2012.00151.

17 Dan Zahavi, "You, Me, and We: The Sharing of Emotional Experiences," *Journal of Consciousness Studies* 22, no. 1–2 (2015): 84–101.

18 Moore and Barresi, "Role of Second-Person Information."

19 John Campbell, "Joint Attention and Common Knowledge," in *Joint Attention: Communication and Other Minds; Issues in Philosophy and Psychology*, ed. Naomi Elian et al. (Oxford: Clarendon Press, 2005), 289.

20 Axel Seemann, "Joint Attention: Toward a Relational Account," in *Joint Attention: New Developments in Psychology, Philosophy of Mind, and Social Neuroscience*, ed. Axel Seemann (Cambridge, Mass.: MIT Press, 2011), 199.

21 Ulf Liszkowski et al., "Pointing Out New News, Old News, and Absent Referents at 12 Months of Age," *Developmental Science* 10, no. 2 (2007): F1–F7; Ulf Liszkowski et al., "Prelinguistic Infants, but Not Chimpanzees, Communicate About Absent Entities," *Psychological Science* 20, no. 5 (2009): 654–60.

22 O'Madagain and Tomasello, "Joint Attention to Mental Content."

23 Lucas Battich et al., "Coordinating Attention Requires Coordinated Senses," *Psychonomic Bulletin & Review* 27, no. 6 (2020): 1126–38.

24 For arguments in favor of using "joint attention" to describe such cases, see O'Madagain and Tomasello, "Joint Attention to Mental Content."

25 Evelyn Underhill, *Worship* (London: Mayflower, 1936), 14, quoting R. R. Marett, *Faith, Hope and Charity in Primitive Religion* (New York: Macmillan, 1932), 56.

26 Underhill, *Worship*, 86.

27 Underhill, *Worship*, 86.

28 Eleonore Stump, "Omnipresence, Indwelling, and the Second-Personal," *European Journal for Philosophy of Religion* 5, no. 4 (2013): 30.

29 Stump, "Omnipresence," 30.

30 Søren Kierkegaard, *Upbuilding Discourses in Various Spirits*, ed. and trans. Howard V. Hong and Edna H. Hong, Kierkegaard's Writings 15 (Princeton, N.J.: Princeton University Press, 2009), 124.

31 Kierkegaard, *Upbuilding Discourses*, 124.

32 Kierkegaard, *Upbuilding Discourses*, 125; emphasis original.

33 Adam Green, "Reading the Mind of God (Without Hebrew Lessons): Alston, Shared Attention, and Mystical Experience," *Religious Studies* 45, no. 4 (2009): 462. Note Green's use of "shared attention," rather than "joint attention." There are differences in terminology in the literature; where possible, we have attempted to provide consistency here.

34 Green, "Reading the Mind of God," 463.

35 Adam Green and Keith A. Quan, "More than Inspired Propositions: Shared Attention and the Religious Text," *Faith and Philosophy: Journal of the Society of Christian Philosophers* 29, no. 4 (2012): 426.

36 Joshua Cockayne et al., "Experiencing the Real Presence of Christ in the Eucharist," *Journal of Analytic Theology* 5 (2017): 187–88.

37 But there are discussions which seek to broaden the focus to think about the role of community. Cockayne and Efird think that jointly attending to God in liturgy can broaden one's own knowledge and experience of God in important ways. See Joshua Cockayne and David Efird, "Common Worship," *Faith and Philosophy: Journal of the Society of Christian Philosophers* 35, no. 3 (2018): 299–325. In Derek S. King's work, it is argued that the revelation of Christ's presence is tied in important ways to the community of the Church, meaning that we cannot think of individuals as the recipients of relationship with God, thereby providing a novel response to the problem of divine hiddenness. See Derek S. King, *The Church and the Problem of Divine Hiddenness: Mirrors of God* (Abingdon-on-Thames: Routledge, 2022).

38 George Orwell, *1984* (New York: Signet Classics, 1981), 3–4.

39 Cockayne and Efird, "Common Worship," 320.

40 See Searle, *Making the Social World*; Tomasello, *Cultural Origins of Human Cognition*.

41 One type of examples that we do not consider are scenarios that have a sense of jointness but that clearly do not involve engaging with a perceived or real other. Green and Quan (see their article "More than Inspired Propositions") call these "as if" experiences, such as in their case of cooking along with a TV chef who asks viewers to look down at their mixing bowl. These examples have some phenomenological overlap with the examples we consider in this chapter, but we focus only on cases in which the sense of jointness is caused by a real or perceived other.

42 Barwise ("Situation in Logic," 285–88) uses the term *situation* as a way of referring to some corner of the world that an individual can access; a shared situation is some corner of the world that two or more individuals share together. Barwise has a technical notion of a situation that is part of his formal semantic theory. We do not

intend to commit to the whole of Barwise's project but rather to follow the spirit of his approach; in his words:

> Cognitive activity takes crucial advantage both of the agents' place in the environment and of regularities in their local environment. Moreover, the cognitive abilities of the agent have a certain "reach" which determines, at any given time, a situation, the largest portion of reality that the agent has access to . . . this situation may extend quite far in time and space ("The Situation in Logic," 223).

43 See Bryce Huebner, "Socially Embedded Cognition," *Cognitive Systems Research* 25–26 (2012–2013): 13–18; Evelyn B. Tribble and Nicholas Keene, *Cognitive Ecologies and the History of Remembering: Religion, Education and Memory in Early Modern England* (New York: Palgrave Macmillan, 2011).
44 Siposova and Carpenter, "New Look at Joint Attention," 260–74.
45 Tomasello et al., "Understanding and Sharing Intentions," 675–91.
46 Mardi Kidwell and Don H. Zimmerman, "Joint Attention as Action," *Journal of Pragmatics* 39, no. 3 (2007): 592–611.
47 Shteynberg, "Shared Attention," 579–90.
48 Evan F. Risko and Alan Kingstone, "Eyes Wide Shut: Implied Social Presence, Eye Tracking and Attention," *Attention, Perception, & Psychophysics* 73 (2011): 291–96.
49 Shteynberg, "Collective Perspective," 93–97. Shteynberg and colleagues have sometimes referred to this notion as "group attention" (Garriy Shteynberg et al., "Feeling More Together: Group Attention Intensifies Emotion," *Emotion* 14, no. 6 [2014]: 1102) and "collective attention" (Garriy Shteynberg et al., "Shared Worlds and Shared Minds: A Theory of Collective Learning and a Psychology of Common Knowledge," *Psychological Review* 127, no. 5 [2020]: 918). See also Bryan Chambliss, "Attending Together in Digital Environments," *Topoi* 43, no. 2 (2024): 311–22, in line with our argument.
50 Shteynberg et al., "Feeling More Together."
51 Garriy Shteynberg and Adam D. Galinsky, "Implicit Coordination: Sharing Goals with Similar Others Intensifies Goal Pursuit," *Journal of Experimental Social Psychology* 47, no. 6 (2011): 1291–94.
52 Gordon W. Allport, "The Historical Background of Social Psychology," in *The Handbook of Social Psychology*, 3rd ed., ed. Gardner Lindzey and E. Aronson (New York: Random House/Erlbaum, 1985), 1–46; Shteynberg et al., "Shared Worlds."
53 Eamon Flanagan, "Prayer and Sacred Spaces," website of St. Peter's Church, Phibsborough, accessed November 7, 2024, https://www.stpetersphibsboro.ie/prayer-and-sacred-places/.

54 Pierre Nora, "Between Memory and History: Les Lieux de Mémoire," *Representations* 26 (1989): 7–24.
55 Michael Suk-Young Chwe, *Rational Ritual: Culture, Coordination, and Common Knowledge* (Princeton, N.J.: Princeton University Press, 2001), 5.
56 Underhill, *Worship*, 81.
57 Underhill, *Worship*, 81.
58 The theological notion of oneness in the Church is explored in more detail in Joshua Cockayne, *Explorations in Analytic Ecclesiology: That They May Be One* (Oxford: Oxford University Press, 2023).
59 There is potentially a temporal-spatial distance, along with a dimensional distance; where and when the angels and saints in glory are praying is certainly beyond the scope of this discussion.
60 Stanley Hauerwas, *In Good Company: The Church as Polis* (South Bend, Ind.: University of Notre Dame Press, 1995), 157.

3 PETITION AND CONFESSION

1 For literature in theology and philosophy of religion on prayer, see, for instance, Vincent Brümmer, *What Are We Doing When We Pray? On Prayer and the Nature of Faith* (London: Routledge, 2017); Eleonore Stump, "Petitionary Prayer," *American Philosophical Quarterly* 16, no. 2 (1979): 81–91; Daniel Howard-Snyder and Frances Howard-Snyder, "The Puzzle of Petitionary Prayer," *European Journal for Philosophy of Religion* 2, no. 2 (2010): 43–68. There have also been a number of psychological works on prayer. See, for instance, Bernard Spilka and Kevin L. Ladd, *The Psychology of Prayer: A Scientific Approach* (New York: Guilford, 2012); Ann Belford Ulanov and Barry Ulanov, *Primary Speech: A Psychology of Prayer* (Louisville, Ky.: Westminster John Knox, 1982); Fraser Watts, *Psychology, Religion, and Spirituality: Concepts and Applications* (Cambridge: Cambridge University Press, 2017).
2 See, for instance, Giuseppe Giordan and Linda Woodhead, eds., *A Sociology of Prayer* (London: Routledge, 2015); Giuseppe Giordan, "Toward a Sociology of Prayer," in *Religion, Spirituality, and Everyday Practice*, ed. Giuseppe Giordan and William H. Swatos Jr., 77–88 (New York: Springer, 2011).
3 See, for instance, Caroline Humphrey and James Laidlaw, *The Archetypal Actions of Ritual: A Theory of Ritual Illustrated by the Jain Rite of Worship* (New York: Oxford University Press, 1994); Whitehouse and Lanman, "Ties That Bind Us."
4 See, for instance, Johannes Fabian, *Talk About Prayer: An Ethnographic Commentary* (London: Palgrave Macmillan, 2015).

5 This is not to say that Scripture *only* talks of communal prayer. The Christian tradition clearly affirms both private and communal acts of prayer. In the Gospel according to Matthew, for instance, Jesus instructs his hearers, "Whenever you pray, go into your room and shut the door and pray to your Father who is in secret" (Matt 6:6). We can also clearly see, in many places, Jesus' own practice of praying alone, such as in the garden of Gethsemane (Matt 26), for example.

6 Tanya M. Luhrmann, *When God Talks Back: Understanding the American Evangelical Relationship with God* (New York: Vintage, 2012), 49.

7 Yohang Chun, "Tongsung Kido (A Unique Korean Prayer)," *Upper New York Conference News*, May 10, 2017, http://www.unyumc.org/news/article/tongsung-kido-a-unique-korean-prayer.

8 Luke Childs, "How the Daily Office Is Different from a 'Quiet Time,'" *Anglican Compass*, November 19, 2018, https://anglicancompass.com/how-the-daily-office-is-different-from-a-quiet-time/.

9 John Perkin, "How Quakers Worship," *Quakers in Britain*, accessed November 7, 2024, https://www.quaker.org.uk/about-quakers/our-faith/how-quakers-worship.

10 Note, this is not to say that communal prayer is more valuable than private prayer; indeed, there are surely values to private prayer which are entirely lacking from communal prayer (e.g., the opportunity for intimate I-thou communication with God might be less available in some communal contexts).

11 Herbert H. Farmer, *The World and God: A Study in Prayer, Providence, and Miracle in Christian Experience* (London: Nisbet & Co Ltd., 1942), 261.

12 Farmer, *World and God*, 262.

13 Farmer, *World and God*, 263.

14 Farmer, *World and God*, 264–65.

15 Brümmer, *What Are We Doing When We Pray?* 66.

16 Brümmer, *What Are We Doing When We Pray?* 65; emphasis original.

17 Brümmer, *What Are We Doing When We Pray?* 66–67.

18 E. James Baesler and Kevin L. Ladd, "Exploring Prayer Contexts and Health Outcomes: From the Chair to the Pew," *Journal of Communication and Religion* 32, no. 2 (2009): 347–74.

19 Spilka and Ladd, *Psychology of Prayer*, 44.

20 Spilka and Ladd, *Psychology of Prayer*, 44.

21 David K. Lewis, *Convention: A Philosophical Study* (Cambridge, Mass.: Harvard University Press, 1969).

22 Chwe, *Rational Ritual*, 8.
23 Chwe, *Rational Ritual*, 11.
24 Shteynberg and Galinsky, "Implicit Coordination"; Gregory M. Walton et al., "Mere Belonging: The Power of Social Connections," *Journal of Personality and Social Psychology* 102, no. 3 (2012): 513–32.
25 Gharad Bryan et al., "Commitment Devices," *Annual Review of Economics* 2, no. 1 (2010): 671–98; Todd Rogers et al., "Commitment Devices: Using Initiatives to Change Behavior," *JAMA* 311, no. 20 (2014): 2065–66.
26 Nia Coupe et al., "The Effect of Commitment-Making on Weight Loss and Behavior Change in Adults with Obesity/Overweight: A Systematic Review," *BMC Public Health* 19, no. 1 (2019): 1–16.
27 Anne Marike Lokhorst et al., "Commitment and Behavior Change: A Meta-Analysis and Critical Review of Commitment-Making Strategies in Environmental Research," *Environment and Behavior* 45, no. 1 (2013): 3–34.
28 Margaret Gilbert, "Obligation and Joint Commitment," *Utilitas* 11, no. 2 (1999): 143–63; John Michael et al., "Observing Joint Action: Coordination Creates Commitment," *Cognition* 157 (2016): 106–13.
29 Michael et al., "Observing Joint Action."
30 Barbara Siposova et al., "Communicative Eye Contact Signals a Commitment to Cooperate for Young Children," *Cognition* 179 (2018): 192–201.
31 Jared Vasil and Michael Tomasello, "Effects of 'We'-Framing on Young Children's Commitment, Sharing, and Helping," *Journal of Experimental Child Psychology* 214 (2022), https://doi.org/10.1016/j.jecp.2021.105278.
32 Gilbert, "Obligation and Joint Commitment"; Michael Tomasello, "The Moral Psychology of Obligation," *Behavioral and Brain Sciences* 43 (2020), http://doi.org/10.1017/S0140525X19001742.
33 William H. McNeill, *Keeping Together in Time: Dance and Drill in Human History* (Cambridge, Mass.: Harvard University Press, 1997), 7.
34 McNeill, *Keeping Together in Time*, 8.
35 McNeill, *Keeping Together in Time*, 10.
36 McNeill, *Keeping Together in Time*, 66.
37 See M. Gallotti et al., "Alignment in Social Interactions," *Consciousness and Cognition* 48 (2017): 253–61; Deborah Tollefsen et al., "Alignment, Transactive Memory, and Collective Cognitive Systems," *Review of Philosophy and Psychology* 4, no. 1 (2013): 49–64.

38 Tanya L. Chartrand and John A. Bargh, "The Chameleon Effect: The Perception-Behavior Link and Social Interaction," *Journal of Personality and Social Psychology* 76, no. 6 (1999): 893–910.

39 Andrew N. Meltzoff, "Imitation and Other Minds: The 'Like Me' Hypothesis," in *Perspectives on Imitation: From Neuroscience to Social Science*, ed. Susan Hurley and Nick Chater, vol. 2 (Cambridge, Mass.: MIT Press, 2005), 55–77.

40 Ina C. Užgiris, "Two Functions of Imitation During Infancy," *International Journal of Behavioral Development* 4, no. 1 (1981): 1–12. A recent psychological discussion of communal worship and psychology can be found in Strawn and Brown, *Enhancing Christian Life*.

41 Tanya L. Chartrand and Rick van Baaren, "Human Mimicry," in *Advances in Experimental Social Psychology*, vol. 41, ed. Mark P. Zanna (London: Academic Press, 2009), 219–74.

42 Erica J. Boothby et al., "Shared Experiences Are Amplified," *Psychological Science* 25, no. 12 (2014): 2209–16.

43 Erica J. Boothby et al., "Psychological Distance Moderates the Amplification of Shared Experience," *Personality and Social Psychology Bulletin* 42, no. 10 (2016): 1431–44.

44 Brock Bastian et al., "Pain as Social Glue: Shared Pain Increases Cooperation," *Psychological Science* 25, no. 11 (2014): 2079–85.

45 Ronald Fischer et al., "How Do Rituals Affect Cooperation?" *Human Nature* 24, no. 2 (2013): 115–25; Michael I. Norton and Francesca Gino, "Rituals Alleviate Grieving for Loved Ones, Lovers, and Lotteries," *Journal of Experimental Psychology: General* 143, no. 1 (2014): 266–72; Rachel E. Watson-Jones and Christine H. Legare, "The Social Functions of Group Rituals," *Current Directions in Psychological Science* 25, no. 1 (2016): 42–46; Wen et al., "Watch Me, Watch You"; Whitehouse and Lanman, "Ties That Bind Us"; Sarah Jane Charles et al., "Religious Rituals Increase Social Bonding and Pain Threshold," preprint, *PsyArXiv*, January 31, 2020, https://doi.org/10.31234/osf.io/my4hs.

46 James B. Torrance, *Worship, Community, and the Triune God of Grace* (Milton Keynes: Paternoster, 1996), 34.

47 John D. Witvliet, "The Mysterious Mingling of Divine and Human Agency in Liturgical Participation," in *What Is Jesus Doing? God's Activity in the Life and Work of the Church*, ed. Edwin Chr. van Driel (Downers Grove, Ill.: InterVarsity Press, 2020): 223.

48 Siposova and Carpenter, "New Look at Joint Attention," 268.

49 Church of England, *1662 Book of Common Prayer* (Cambridge: John Baskerville, 1762), https://www.churchofengland.org/sites/default/files/2019-10/the-book-of-common-prayer-1662.pdf. The

title of this prayer is "The Order for the Administration of the Lord's Supper."

50 Church of England, "The Order for Morning Prayer" and "The Order for Evening Prayer," in *1662 Book of Common Prayer*; emphasis added.

51 W. S. T. Wright, "Confession in the Church of England," *Theology* 37, no. 220 (1938): 218.

52 Annemarie S. Kidder, *Making Confession, Hearing Confession: A History of the Cure of Souls* (Collegeville, Minn.: Liturgical Press, 2010), 287.

53 Kidder, *Making Confession*, 300.

54 Dietrich Bonhoeffer, *Life Together and Prayerbook of the Bible*, vol. 5 of *Dietrich Bonhoeffer Works* (Minneapolis: 1517 Media, 2004), 108.

55 Though we recognize, of course, that receiving unsolicited advice is a core part of being a parent.

56 Bonhoeffer, *Life Together*, 110; emphasis added.

4 GIVING THANKS TOGETHER

1 This chapter develops material originally written in Joshua Cockayne and Gideon Salter, "Liturgical Gratitude to God," *Religions* 13, no. 9 (2022), https://doi.org/10.3390/rel13090795; Joshua Cockayne and Gideon Salter, "Group Gratitude: A Taxonomy," preprint, *Journal of Value Inquiry*, January 12, 2023, https://doi.org/10.1007/s10790-022-09924-3. Reprinted with permission.

2 See Robert A. Emmons, *Thanks! How the New Science of Gratitude Can Make You Happier* (Boston: Houghton Mifflin Harcourt, 2007); Robert A. Emmons and Cheryl A. Crumpler, "Gratitude as a Human Strength: Appraising the Evidence," *Journal of Social and Clinical Psychology* 19, no. 1 (2000): 56–69; Robert A. Emmons and Robert Stern, "Gratitude as a Psychotherapeutic Intervention," *Journal of Clinical Psychology* 69, no. 8 (2013): 846–55; Jeffrey J. Froh et al., "Counting Blessings in Early Adolescents: An Experimental Study of Gratitude and Subjective Well-Being," *Journal of School Psychology* 46, no. 2 (2008): 213–33.

3 Liz Gulliford et al., "Recent Work on the Concept of Gratitude in Philosophy and Psychology," *Journal of Value Inquiry* 47, no. 3 (2013): 285–317; Michael E. McCullough et al., "Is Gratitude a Moral Affect?" *Psychological Bulletin* 127, no. 2 (2001): 249–66.

4 Jo-Ann Tsang, "(Un)Special Favors: Gratitude for Group-Based Benefits," *Journal of Positive Psychology* 16, no. 1 (2021): 27.

5 Tsang, "(Un)Special Favors," 27.

6 Wolterstorff, *God We Worship*, 11.
7 Church of England, "Holy Communion Service," *Common Worship*, 2000, https://www.churchofengland.org/prayer-and-worship/worship-texts-and-resources/common-worship/holy-communion-service.
8 Jim Reeves, "We Thank Thee," track 1 on *We Thank Thee*, RCA Victor LSP-2552, released 1962.
9 Gulliford et al., "Recent Work on the Concept of Gratitude."
10 Robert A. Emmons, "Gratitude, Subjective Well-Being, and the Brain," in *The Science of Subjective Well-Being*, ed. Michael Eid and Randy J. Larsen (New York: Guilford, 2008), 469.
11 Gulliford et al., "Recent Work on the Concept of Gratitude," 313.
12 Gulliford et al., "Recent Work on the Concept of Gratitude," 317.
13 The approach taken here is one of *fractionation* (Pascal Boyer and Brian Bergstrom, "Evolutionary Perspectives on Religion," *Annual Review of Anthropology* 37 [2008]: 111–30; Whitehouse and Lanman, "Ties That Bind Us"), whereby sub-concepts of the umbrella concept are identified and examined, rather than focusing on gratitude as a singular concept. For example, the actions involved in expressing gratitude can be discussed separately from questions regarding whether gratitude is a distinct emotional category or a mixed emotion. Indeed, as Gulliford and colleagues note, in "the earliest psychological writings about gratitude, there was no mention of a necessary emotional response. Bertocci and Millard defined gratitude as 'the willingness to recognize that one has been the beneficiary of someone's kindness, whether the emotional response is present or not'" (Gulliford et al., "Recent Work on the Concept of Gratitude," 294, quoting Peter A. Bertocci and Richard M. Millard, *Personality and the Good: Psychological and Ethical Perspectives* [New York: David McKay, 1963]). One can highlight how gratitude interacts with mental health (Emmons and Stern, "Gratitude as a Psychotherapeutic Intervention"), or one can discuss how religious people experience a sense of gratitude to God (David H. Rosmarin et al., "Grateful to God or Just Plain Grateful? A Comparison of Religious and General Gratitude," *Journal of Positive Psychology* 6, no. 5 [2011]: 389–96). The fractionation strategy has proved useful in discussions of other such nebulous concepts as "religion" (Boyer and Bergstrom, "Evolutionary Perspectives on Religion") and "ritual" (Whitehouse and Lanman, "Ties That Bind Us"; Rohan Kapitány et al., "Ritual Morphospace Revisited: The Form, Function and Factor Structure of Ritual Practice," *Philosophical Transactions of the Royal Society B* 375, no. 1805 [2020], https://doi.org/10.1098/rstb.2019.0436); by focusing on specific

sub-concepts, conceptual disagreement can be substantive rather than semantic. Indeed, there are parallels here with the specificity strategy discussed in the introduction.

14 Note the more general use of *attention* by Emmons, which should be distinguished from the specific concept of joint attention we have been exploring.

15 Emmons and Stern, "Gratitude as a Psychotherapeutic Intervention," 853; emphasis added.

16 Philip C. Watkins, "Gratitude and Subjective Well-Being," in *The Psychology of Gratitude*, ed. Robert A. Emmons and Michael E. McCullough (Oxford: Oxford University Press, 2004), 183; emphasis added.

17 O'Madagain and Tomasello, "Joint Attention to Mental Content"; Siposova et al., "Communicative Eye Contact Signals," 192–201.

18 Emmons and Stern, "Gratitude as a Psychotherapeutic Intervention."

19 See Curtis D. Hardin and E. Tory Higgins, "Shared Reality: How Social Verification Makes the Subjective Objective," in *The Interpersonal Context*, vol. 3 of *Handbook of Motivation and Cognition*, ed. Richard M. Sorrentino and E. Tory Higgins (New York: Guilford, 1996), 28–84; Gerald Echterhoff et al., "Shared Reality: Experiencing Commonality with Others' Inner States About the World," *Perspectives on Psychological Science* 4, no. 5 (2009): 496–521; Felipe León et al., "Emotional Sharing and the Extended Mind," *Synthese* 196, no. 12 (2019): 4847–67; Dan Zahavi and Philippe Rochat, "Empathy ≠ Sharing: Perspectives from Phenomenology and Developmental Psychology," *Consciousness and Cognition* 36 (2015): 543–53. Various theoretical accounts have highlighted that joint attention plays a key role in rendering subjective emotional experiences as shared. Echterhoff and colleagues ("Shared Reality") argue that by communicating attitudes to a common referent, individuals can achieve a sense of "shared reality": commonality with others' inner states about the world. León and colleagues ("Emotional Sharing and the Extended Mind") argue that shared emotions are achieved when individuals engage in joint attention to a common focus and allow their emotional responses to mutually influence one another (Peter Hobson and Jessica Hobson, "Joint Attention or Joint Engagement? Insights from Autism," in *Joint Attention: New Developments*, ed. Axel Seemann, 115–36 [Cambridge, Mass.: MIT Press, 2011]).

20 It is important to note that these various accounts of shared subjective feelings do not deny that there are differences in individually experienced phenomenology. Rather, they emphasize that through

joint attention, humans have a capacity to create a sense of jointness about their subjective experiences.

21 Siposova and Carpenter, "New Look at Joint Attention."

22 Shteynberg, "Collective Perspective," 93–97.

23 For more details on these distinctions, see Cockayne and Salter, "Group Gratitude."

24 Tsang, "(Un)Special Favors," 27.

25 This is not to say that Tsang discounts the possibility of other forms of group gratitude, only that individual response to contextual group gratitude was the focus of Tsang's study. With thanks to Jo-Ann Tsang for this clarification.

26 Siposova and Carpenter, "New Look at Joint Attention."

27 We might ask whether the clap for carers movement involved *collective* gratitude, which we define later in the chapter (e.g., such that the UK was grateful for the NHS, the National Health Service). While the movement could be understood as an attempt to demonstrate the collective gratitude of the UK for the NHS, it has been suggested that the apparent expression of gratitude was undermined by the poor working conditions faced by NHS workers throughout the pandemic (Jill Manthorpe et al. "Clapping for Carers in the Covid-19 Crisis: Carers' Reflections in a UK Survey," *Health & Social Care in the Community* 30, no. 4 [2022]: 1442–49). Both these positions would appear to presuppose we can talk meaningfully about collectives being grateful or not, in line with the approach we take here. As we qualify below, we are not yet in a position to fully define the conditions under which collectives ought to be considered truly (collectively) grateful, just that this is possible in principle.

28 Deborah Perron Tollefsen, *Groups as Agents* (Hoboken, N.J.: John Wiley & Sons, 2015), 3. Note that Tollefsen uses the terms "shared agency" and "joint agency." To avoid confusion, we talk instead of "joint agency" and "collective agency."

29 Tollefsen, *Groups as Agents*, 3.

30 Tollefsen, *Groups as Agents*, 3.

31 Robert S. Woodworth, "Individual and Group Behaviour," *American Journal of Sociology* 44, no. 6 (1939): 823–28, quoted in Günther Knoblich et al., "Psychological Research on Joint Action: Theory and Data," in *The Psychology of Learning and Motivation*, vol. 54, ed. Brian H. Ross (San Diego: Elsevier Academic, 2011), 60.

32 Searle, "Collective Intentions and Actions."

33 Knoblich et al., "Psychological Research on Joint Action," 59–101; Natalie Sebanz et al., "Joint Action: Bodies and Minds Moving Together," *Trends in Cognitive Sciences* 10, no. 2 (2006): 70–76.

34 Sophie J. Milward and Malinda Carpenter, "Joint Action and Joint Attention: Drawing Parallels Between the Literatures," *Social and Personality Psychology Compass* 12, no. 4 (2018), https://doi.org/10.1111/spc3.12377.

35 Psychologists have also distinguished emergent and planned joint action (Knoblich et al., "Psychological Research on Joint Action"). Emergent joint action refers to those cases in which joint action occurs spontaneously and without explicit planning, while planned joint action involves agents agreeing on a goal and working to achieve it. Studies of emergent joint action have typically come from researchers interested in temporal coordination of bodily action and the human tendency to synchronize bodily movements, even unconsciously (Michael J. Richardson et al., "Rocking Together: Dynamics of Intentional and Unintentional Interpersonal Coordination," *Human Movement Science* 26, no. 6 [2007]: 867–91; Richard C. Schmidt and Michael J. Richardson, "Dynamics of Interpersonal Coordination," in *Coordination: Neural, Behavioral and Social Dynamics*, ed. Armin Fuchs and Victor K. Jirsa [Berlin: Springer, 2008], 281–308). Investigations of planned joint action focus on higher-level cognitive representations such as intentions, beliefs, and commitments (Maria Gräfenhain et al., "Young Children's Understanding of Joint Commitments," *Developmental Psychology* 45, no. 5 [2009]: 1430–43; Natalie Sebanz et al., "Representing Others' Actions: Just Like One's Own?" *Cognition* 88, no. 3 [2003]: B11–B21), with a greater focus on the role of language (Herbert H. Clark, *Using Language* [Cambridge: Cambridge University Press, 1996]). In practice, there is typically an interplay between these different kinds of joint action (Knoblich et al., "Psychological Research on Joint Action").

36 Emmons and Crumpler, "Gratitude as Human Strength"; McCullough et al., "Is Gratitude a Moral Affect?"

37 Cuneo, *Ritualized Faith*, 138.

38 Note that on an account of joint liturgical gratitude, identifying who is picked out by the pronoun "we" is more complex than simply identifying those inhabiting the same space. For it might be the case that the "we" in liturgical contexts extends to anyone included in my joint intention. For example, in singing a hymn of gratitude, I might intend to sing with the whole congregation; here the meaning of "we" seems to extend to all those contained in my intention. However, if I am a member of the choir, seated at a distance from the rest of the congregation whom I am not consciously attending to, then plausibly, the meaning of "we" might only extend to

the members of the choir. In other words, joint gratitude cannot account for all instances of group gratitude in liturgy.

39 León et al., "Emotional Sharing and the Extended Mind."

40 See Robert C. Liden et al., "Social Loafing: A Field Investigation," *Journal of Management* 30, no. 2 (2004): 285–304; Steven J. Karau and Aric J. Wilhau, "Social Loafing and Motivation Gains in Groups: An Integrative Review," in *Individual Motivation Within Groups*, ed. Steven J. Karau (London: Academic Press, 2020), 3–51; Steven J. Karau and Kipling D. Williams, "Social Loafing: A Meta-Analytic Review and Theoretical Integration," *Journal of Personality and Social Psychology* 65, no. 4 (1993): 681–706.

41 We also note that the term "collective gratitude" has previously been used in the literature (e.g., Ryan Fehr et al., "The Grateful Workplace: A Multilevel Model of Gratitude in Organizations," *Academy of Management Review* 42, no. 2 [2017]: 361–81), but in reference to organizations that contain many grateful individuals, an approach that differs to ours here.

42 Stephanie Collins, *Group Duties: Their Existence and Their Implications for Individuals* (Oxford: Oxford University Press, 2019), 56.

43 See Christian List and Philip Pettit, *Group Agency: The Possibility, Design, and Status of Corporate Agents* (Oxford: Oxford University Press, 2011); Tollefsen, *Groups as Agents*; Collins, *Group Duties*.

44 List and Pettit, *Group Agency*, 36.

45 In extreme cases, such as a dictatorship or autocracy, there may be one active member who acts on behalf of the group and many more authorizing members who do not have the authority to act on behalf of this group. However, in cases of organizations like universities, the authority is typically more dispersed.

46 This need not commit us to thinking that there are mysterious entities called "groups" that exist beyond individual agents, to which we can ascribe virtues. Rather, the thought goes, certain organizational structures and decision-making procedures allow groups of individuals to act in such a way that they can be said to be the agents of certain actions. Collins suggests that collectives are groups which are "constituted by agents that are united under a rationally operated group-level-decision-making procedure that can attend to moral considerations" (Collins, *Group Duties*, 12). For example, the British government is constituted by the ministers of the cabinet, who, through a series of group decision-making procedures, deliberate on the "best" course of action for the country. Collectives, unlike groups involved only in joint action, have "an identity that can survive changes of membership," such as "a nation, a university, or a purposive organization" (List and Pettit, *Group Agency*, 31).

47 We concede that many psychologists will struggle to make sense of collective gratitude as an instance of genuine gratitude if they insist that emotions are a core component of gratitude. It is difficult to make sense of the notion of collective emotion or feeling, even if grateful organizations may foster grateful feelings in their members. Nevertheless, the phenomenon of collectives expressing gratitude still seems worthy of exploration in a number of contexts.

48 It is important to consider how individuals—and individual emotional responses—contribute to and are influenced by being a part of collectives that are categorized as being more or less grateful. Some previous work has discussed how to promote a "culture" or "climate" of gratitude in an organization, suggesting that it emerges as a result of many individual grateful experiences (Annamaria Di Fabio et al., "Gratitude in Organizations: A Contribution for Healthy Organizational Contexts," *Frontiers in Psychology* 8 [2017], https://doi.org/10.3389/fpsyg.2017.02025; Fehr et al., "Grateful Workplace"). Here, we suggest that gratitude in collectives may be more complex, allowing for a mismatch between the experiences of individuals and the categorization of organizations. An organization may express gratitude despite a lack of gratitude from its individual members, such as when the organization expresses gratitude for the purchase of a new building, but many members are resentful that they subsequently need to relocate. The inverse may also be true; members can be grateful for a pay raise achieved through collective bargaining, while the management resents this change.

49 Note that the analysis of collective gratitude we have given does not specify what the threshold is for being a case of genuine collective gratitude. As a next step, it would be beneficial to clearly articulate the conditions under which a group or organization can be said to be more or less grateful. If this can be achieved, organizations can assess the extent to which they have achieved this goal or can pursue measures that facilitate this end. However, given that collectives have no group consciousness, and thereby no feelings of gratitude, it may be the case that there are limitations on the kinds of questions that can be asked at the collective level versus the group-context and joint levels. The focus would primarily be on the way in which collectives make decisions, and the reasons for these decisions.

50 Underhill, *Worship*, 83.

51 Cockayne develops a detailed account of how we might think of the Church as a collective in Cockayne, *Explorations in Analytic Ecclesiology*.

52 Shteynberg et al., "Feeling More Together," 1102.

53 Sara B. Algoe et al., "Beyond Reciprocity: Gratitude and Relationships in Everyday Life," *Emotion* 8, no. 3 (2008): 425.

54 Sara B. Algoe, "Find, Remind, and Bind: The Functions of Gratitude in Everyday Relationships," *Social and Personality Psychology Compass* 6, no. 6 (2012): 455–69; Tsang, "(Un)Special Favors."

55 Algoe et al., "Beyond Reciprocity."

56 Tsang, "(Un)Special Favors."

57 Robert A. Emmons, *Gratitude Works! A 21-Day Program for Creating Emotional Prosperity* (Hoboken, N.J.: John Wiley & Sons, 2013).

58 Kent Dunnington, "Being Grateful and Feeling Grateful: Reconsidering the Phenomenology of Gratitude to God," *Journal of Positive Psychology* 19, no. 1 (2024): 1.

59 Everett L. Worthington Jr., *Forgiveness and Reconciliation: Theory and Application* (London: Routledge, 2013), 25.

60 Adapting Worthington's more detailed definitions of *decisional* and *emotional*, we can specify the differences as such:

Decisional Gratitude

1. arrived at rationally or by will
2. may come before or after emotional gratitude
3. may occur without emotional gratitude
4. aimed at controlling future behavior (not motives or emotions)
5. may make person feel "settled," calming emotion and motivation (i.e., might lead to emotional gratitude or at least reduce emotional ingratitude)
6. may give new meaning to situation
7. changes behavior

Emotional Gratitude

1. arrived at by emotional replacement
2. necessarily reduces ungrateful emotions
3. may come before or after decisional gratitude (but usually after)
4. may occur without decisional gratitude on rare occasions
5. aimed at changing emotional climate but inevitably triggers neoassociationistic networks leading to changes in motives, thoughts, and other associations

6. may give new meaning to situation
7. may change behavior
8. will change motivation
9. makes person feel less negative emotionally and perhaps more positive

Adapted from Worthington, *Forgiveness and Reconciliation*, 59, table 2.1.

61 See Emmons, *Gratitude Works!* 159–72, for example.

62 Liden et al., "Social Loafing: A Field Investigation"; Karau and Williams, "Social Loafing: A Meta-Analytic Review"; Karau and Wilhau, "Social Loafing and Motivation Gains."

63 Margaret M. Mitchell, *Paul and the Rhetoric of Reconciliation: An Exegetical Investigation of the Language and Composition of 1 Corinthians* (Louisville: Westminster John Knox, 1993), 157–59.

5 ACTS OF REMEMBRANCE

1 This chapter develops material from Joshua Cockayne and Gideon Salter, "Feasts of Memory: Collective Remembering, Liturgical Time Travel and the Actualisation of the Past," *Modern Theology* 37, no. 2 (2021): 275–95. It is reprinted here with permission.

2 Note that, as Dru Johnson helpfully points out to us (personal communication), the Seder is not a unified ritual over time. In Exodus it is a home rite. In Deuteronomy Israel is told to practice it gathered at the Tabernacle. After the fall of the Temple (70 CE), the Seder again became a home ritual, with embellishments of the ritual from synagogal Judaism. Nonetheless, the common feature of shared ritualized remembrance is surely present in all understandings of the ritual. It is this sense of jointness with the past that is the primary focus of our discussion here, rather than an attempt to give an analysis of any particular tradition. When we do focus on specific components of the Seder meal (e.g., the bitter herbs), we are talking about more recent iterations of the ritual.

3 This is a question considered at length in Thompson, *Virtual Body of Christ*; Doyle, *Embodied Liturgy*.

4 Ryan P. O'Dowd, "Memory on the Boundary," in *The Bible and Epistemology: Biblical Soundings on the Knowledge of God*, ed. Mary Healy and Robin Parry (Milton Keynes: Paternoster, 2007), 20.

5 See Kourken Michaelian, *Mental Time Travel: Episodic Memory and Our Knowledge of the Personal Past* (Cambridge, Mass.: MIT Press, 2016); Kourken Michaelian and John Sutton, "Collective Mental Time Travel: Remembering the Past and Imagining the Future Together," *Synthese* 196, no. 12 (2019): 4933–60. There is some overlap between our discussion in this section and the discussion

of memory in Miroslav Volf's discussion in *The End of Memory: Remembering Rightly in a Violent World* (Grand Rapids: Eerdmans, 2006). Both the aim and the details differ substantially, however. Volf aims to provide an account of memory that can help us to think about the role of memory in reconciliation and to consider when it is appropriate to forget past wrongs. Volf's taxonomy of memory is borrowed from Tzvetan Todorov's distinction between "literal" and "exemplary" memory, the key difference being that *exemplary* memory concerns the future as well as the past and takes the past to be guiding action in the present (Tzvetan Todorov, "The Abuses of Memory," *Common Knowledge* 5 [1996]: 6–26). This is something we touch on in our discussion, but our taxonomy follows the distinction in contemporary analytic philosophy of memory and the psychology of memory. Volf also discusses the role of the Eucharist and the Seder in religious communities and makes related points concerning the role of remembrance in forming religious identity (*End of Memory*, 97–99), in discussing its communal nature (99–100), and in helping communities to relate rightly to the future as well as the past (100–101). Our discussion is more focused on these points, and we provide a more detailed psychological discussion of the points raised in this brief section of Volf's book, without considering the application to reconciliation. To give an oversimplified summary of the difference: we are primarily focused on the "how" questions (i.e., how can communities remember together?), whereas Volf is focused on the "why" and "what" questions (i.e., what role does remembrance play in reconciliation between persons and communities? And why do communities remember or forget the past?).

6 Michaelian, *Mental Time Travel*, 141.

7 Of course, this will depend on the ongoing discussion of intellectualism and anti-intellectualism about practical knowledge.

8 Much of the discussion of liturgical remembrance (at least in philosophical theology) has focused on the memorial aspect of this discussion (i.e., on the noun, not the verb). Wolterstorff gives the following example to try to tease apart the connection between remembering and memorial:

> The Lincoln Memorial on the Mall in Washington DC, dedicated in 1922, is an example. Every American at the time was familiar with Lincoln from books on American history, biographies of Lincoln, informal conversations, recitations of Lincoln's Gettysburg Address, and the like. There was no prospect whatsoever of Lincoln fading from the memory of the American people. Or if there were some at the time who did fear that the memory of Lincoln was in danger of fading, why would they not have poured their efforts into school

> educational programs, documentary and quasi-documentary films, Lincoln biographies, and the like? Those would reach many more members of the public than would ever see the memorial. Clearly it was felt that even though Lincoln was well remembered, something was lacking. It was important to have a memorial of Lincoln. (Wolterstorff, *Acting Liturgically*, 179–80)

These remarks seem right to us. This need not rule out the possibility that memorial can thereby allow a community to remember. We circumvent this discussion by focusing our analysis on the act of communal remembrance (in the *zakar* sense) in religious rites, leaving aside the question of the *essence* of memorial.

9 In the Hebrew Bible, the verb to remember (*zakar*) in its various forms appears 221 times, and the noun *zikkaron* (memorial sign), twenty-two times (Brevard S. Childs, *Memory and Tradition in Israel*, Studies in Biblical Theology 37 [London: SCM Press, 1962], 9). It is this term *zikkaron* that the Greek Septuagint translates as "anamnesis," the term we find used in the Eucharistic passage from 1 Corinthians. It is also worth noting that the word *yad* is also translated as "memorial" in certain contexts (e.g., 2 Sam 18:18; Isa 56:5), and some readers will be aware that Israel's official Holocaust memorial is called Yad Vashem ("a memorial and a name," from Isa 56:5). However, this appears to be used specifically in reference to a memorial location or monument of some kind, so we will not focus on this term.

10 Childs, *Memory and Tradition*, 51.

11 Another example might be that of the Sukkot ritual (Lev 23:32–33). They were commanded to dwell in sukkah for seven days in order that they might know a historical fact that they already knew. As Dru Johnson points out to us, the Sukkot ritual may be a more obvious example of participation and reenactment than the Seder. But one reason we choose to focus on Seder here is because of its parallels with the Eucharist (a meal instituted by Christ during the celebration of the Seder).

12 Gabrielle M. Spiegel, "Memory and History: Liturgical Time and Historical Time," *History and Theory* 41, no. 2 (2002): 149–62.

13 Childs, *Memory and Tradition*, 56.

14 Childs, *Memory and Tradition*, 53.

15 Though it is important that observation of the Shabbat goes beyond the Kabbalat Shabbat (the ritual marking the start of the Shabbat) and Havdalah (the ritual marking its conclusion) to the community's activity on the day itself. However, given that Childs focuses on

active remembrance, we think it reasonable to narrow our focus to specific ritual practices, particularly the Seder meal.

16 The importance of actualization is made clear in contemporary Rabbinic discussions of remembrance. There are two mitzvoth (commandments) regarding remembrance of the Exodus. *Zechiras yetziat Mitzrayim*, remembering the Exodus, is the mitzvah of daily remembrance of the events of the Exodus. *Sippur yetziat Mitzrayim*, the recounting of the Exodus, refers to the practice of telling the story of the Exodus through the Seder meal on the festival of Passover. There are a number of rabbinic discussions on the ways in which these two commandments should be distinguished, and these differences can be organized into three main themes. The first distinction is the social dimension of the remembrance. *Zechira* is a solitary activity, part of the daily routines of prayers and blessings conducted in the life of the religious Jew. Most rabbis would see it as satisfied through recalling the thought or through inaudibly speaking of it. In contrast, *Sippur* is necessarily a communal activity. The recounting is built around a meal (*seder*) shared with others. This Seder meal is conducted in a didactic, dialogic form (therefore necessitating audible speech). It is structured around questions asked by the children to the adults, who are to educate the children about the different elements of the meal. The second theme is that of authority. *Zechira* is "merely a rabbinic obligation" (Yonason Sacks, "The Mitzvah of Sippur Yetzias Mitzrayim," *Pesach To-Go*, Nissan 5770 [March 2010], archived June 30, 2022, https://web.archive.org/web/20220630143642/https://www.yutorah.org/togo/pesach/articles/Pesach_To-Go_-_5770_Rabbi_Sacks.pdf). In contrast, *Sippur* "bears the stringency of a Biblical imperative," stemming directly from the mitzvoth found in Torah passages such as Exodus 10:2 and 13:8. The final distinction is the narrative form of the remembrance. *Sippur* is a recounting of the Exodus story through the liturgical script of the *Haggadah*, the telling. *Zechira* has no such requirements. In the words of Rav Michael Susman,

> To fulfil the obligation of *Zechira*, simply recalling the event is sufficient. On the other hand, the mitzvah of *Sippur* demands a level of elucidation and detail which can never be exhausted. . . . By telling the story we are not only drawn into the narrative and encouraged to see it as our own, but we are forced to respond to it. (Michael Susman, "Zechira and Sippur," *Online Torah*, March 22, 2017, https://en.harova.org/online_torah_books/zechira-and-sippur/)

17 Yosef Hayim Yerushalmi, *Zakhor: Jewish History and Jewish Memory* (Seattle: University of Washington Press, 1989), 44–45.

18 N. T. Wright, *The Day the Revolution Began* (London: SPCK, 2016), 185–86; emphasis original.

19 Church of England, *1662 Book of Common Prayer.* The title of this part is "The Order for the Administration of the Lord's Supper."

20 Remembrance in the Christian community must also go beyond the practice of the Eucharist—as Volf describes, "to remember in a reconciling way, I need to do more than participate in celebrations of Holy Communion crafted to foster reconciliation. Everyday practices must reflect what the community celebrates . . . My participation in a community of those who celebrate right remembering and struggle to practice it will make my own right remembering both intellectually plausible and practically possible" (*End of Memory*, 128).

21 Gordon D. Fee, *The First Epistle to the Corinthians* (Grand Rapids: Eerdmans, 1987), 466.

22 Richard B. Hays, *First Corinthians*, Interpretation (Louisville: Westminster John Knox), 196.

23 Axel Seemann, "Reminiscing Together: Joint Experiences, Epistemic Groups, and Sense of Self," *Synthese* 196, no. 12 (2019): 4813–28.

24 Alan Baddeley, "What Is Autobiographical Memory?" in *Theoretical Perspectives on Autobiographical Memory*, ed. Martin A. Conway et al. (Dordrecht: Springer, 2013), 14.

25 See, for comparison, Wright, *Day the Revolution Began*, 185–86.

26 Endel Tulving, "Episodic and Semantic Memory," in *Organization of Memory*, ed. Endel Tulving and Wayne Donaldson (New York: Academic Press, 1972), 381–403.

27 On the "WWW" criterion, see Thomas Suddendorf and Janie Busby, "Mental Time Travel in Animals?" *Trends in Cognitive Sciences* 7, no. 9 (2003): 391–96.

28 Endel Tulving, "Episodic Memory: From Mind to Brain," *Annual Review of Psychology* 53 (2002): 1–25.

29 See Michaelian, *Mental Time Travel*; Thomas Suddendorf et al., "Mental Time Travel and the Shaping of the Human Mind," *Philosophical Transactions of the Royal Society B: Biological Sciences* 364, no. 1521 (2009): 1317–24.

30 Tulving, "Episodic Memory."

31 Stanley B. Klein and Shaun Nichols, "Memory and the Sense of Personal Identity," *Mind* 121, no. 483 (2012): 677–702.

32 Cara Laney and Elizabeth F. Loftus, "Truth in Emotional Memories," in *Emotion and the Law: Psychological Perspectives*, ed. Brian H. Bornstein and Richard L. Wiener (New York: Springer, 2009), 157–83. For example, when memories are encoded, agents

selectively attend to the relevant details of the scene. During storage, the most salient parts of the memory are preserved. When retrieved, agents recall the most salient aspects of the memory, or those most relevant to the present context. This flexibility leaves human memory highly susceptible to error. The work of Loftus and colleagues has demonstrated the fallibility of human memory and challenges of obtaining accurate eyewitness testimony (Elizabeth F. Loftus, *Eyewitness Testimony*, 2nd ed. [Cambridge, Mass.: Harvard University Press, 1996]). Humans forget and distort memories consistently, and we are confronted with memories we would rather forget (Daniel L. Schacter, "The Seven Sins of Memory: Insights from Psychology and Cognitive Neuroscience," *American Psychologist* 54, no. 3 [1999]: 182–203). When recalling past events, we are influenced by the form of the questions we are asked about these events (Philip S. Dale et al., "The Influence of the Form of the Question on the Eyewitness Testimony of Preschool Children," *Journal of Psycholinguistic Research* 7, no. 4 [1978]: 269–77). New, misleading information interferes with recall of accurate memories (D. A. Bekerian and J. M. Bowers, "Eyewitness Testimony: Were We Misled?" *Journal of Experimental Psychology: Learning, Memory, and Cognition* 9, no. 1 [1983]: 139). In fact, humans can be tricked into believing they have memories of events that are in fact completely fabricated (Elizabeth F. Loftus, "Planting Misinformation in the Human Mind: A 30-Year Investigation of the Malleability of Memory," *Learning & Memory* 12, no. 4 [2005]: 361–66).

33 It is important to note there are alternative analyses of the functional role of episodic memory (e.g., Johannes B. Mahr and Gergeley Csibra, "Why Do We Remember? The Communicative Function of Episodic Memory," *Behavioral and Brain Sciences* 41 [2018], https://doi.org/10.1017/S0140525X17000012). It suffices for our present discussion to identify one important functional role of episodic memory, regardless of the evolutionary contexts that gave rise to this ability.

34 D. H. Ingvar, "'Memory of the Future': An Essay on the Temporal Organization of Conscious Awareness," *Human Neurobiology* 4, no. 3 (1985): 127–36; Daniel L. Schacter et al., "The Future of Memory: Remembering, Imagining, and the Brain," *Neuron* 76, no. 4 (2012): 677–94; Thomas Suddendorf and Michael C. Corballis, "The Evolution of Foresight: What Is Mental Time Travel, and Is It Unique to Humans?" *Behavioral and Brain Sciences* 30, no. 3 (2007): 299–313; Karl K. Szpunar, "Episodic Future Thought: An Emerging Concept," *Perspectives on Psychological Science* 5, no. 2 (2010): 142–62.

35 For discussions of neural evidence, see discussions by Denis Perrin and Kourken Michaelian, "Memory as Mental Time Travel," in *The Routledge Handbook of Philosophy of Memory*, ed. Sven Bernecker and Kourken Michaelian (Milton Keynes: Routledge, 2017), 228–39; Schacter et al., "The Future of Memory."

36 Daniel L. Schacter and Kevin P. Madore, "Remembering the Past and Imagining the Future: Identifying and Enhancing the Contribution of Episodic Memory," *Memory Studies* 9, no. 3 (2016): 245–55.

37 Karl K. Szpunar and Kathleen B. McDermott, "Episodic Future Thought and Its Relation to Remembering: Evidence from Ratings of Subjective Experience," *Consciousness and Cognition* 17, no. 1 (2008): 330–34.

38 Demis Hassabis and Eleanor A. Maguire, "Deconstructing Episodic Memory with Construction," *Trends in Cognitive Sciences* 11, no. 7 (2007): 299–306.

39 Daniel L. Schacter and Donna Rose Addis, "The Cognitive Neuroscience of Constructive Memory: Remembering the Past and Imagining the Future," *Philosophical Transactions of the Royal Society B: Biological Sciences* 362, no. 1481 (2007): 773–86; Szpunar and McDermott, "Episodic Future Thought."

40 Szpunar and McDermott, "Episodic Future Thought."

41 Klein and Nichols, "Memory."

42 Szpunar, "Episodic Future Thought."

43 Schacter and Addis, "Cognitive Neuroscience of Constructive Memory."

44 Robyn Fivush and Natalie Merrill, "An Ecological Systems Approach to Family Narratives," *Memory Studies* 9, no. 3 (2016): 305–14.

45 Yerushalmi, *Zakhor.*

46 Szpunar and McDermott, "Episodic Future Thought."

47 With thanks to Eve Ridgeway for this point.

48 Wright, *Day the Revolution Began*, 185–86.

49 Clinton Merck et al., "Collective Mental Time Travel: Creating a Shared Future Through Our Shared Past," *Memory Studies* 9, no. 3 (2016): 284–94.

50 As above, the preferred term in the literature is "Collective MTT." Since we already use "collective" in a different sense, we continue to use "group" here.

51 William Hirst and David Manier, "Towards a Psychology of Collective Memory," *Memory* 16, no. 3 (2008): 183–200.

52 Michaelian and Sutton, "Collective Mental Time Travel."

53 E.g., Tollefsen et al., "Alignment," 49–64.

54 Piotr M. Szpunar and Karl K. Szpunar, "Collective Future Thought: Concept, Function, and Implications for Collective Memory Studies," *Memory Studies* 9, no. 4 (2016), 376–89.

55 Michaelian and Sutton, "Collective Mental Time Travel."

56 This has obvious connections to the way we have conceived of joint and collective gratitude in the previous section, as well as the distinction between affect and decision.

57 Julian Bacharach, "Is There Such a Thing as Joint Attention to the Past?" *Topoi* 43, no. 2 (2024): 323–35; Felipe De Brigard, "Memory, Attention, and Joint Reminiscing," in *New Directions in the Philosophy of Memory*, ed. Kourken Michaelian et al. (New York: Routledge, 2018), 200–220; Christoph Hoerl and Teresa McCormack, "Joint Reminiscing as Joint Attention to the Past," in *Joint Attention: Communication and Other Minds; Issues in Philosophy and Psychology*, ed. Naomi Eilan, 260–86; Seemann, "Reminiscing Together."

58 Carpenter and Liebal, "Joint Attention." To make this contrast clearer, take the example given in chapter 2: I can stand next to a stranger at the train station while we both look at the train timetables. Though we are attending to the same target, we are not doing so *together* (in the strictest possible sense) until we share some kind of mutual recognition that makes our common target of attention truly shared.

59 O'Madagain and Tomasello, "Joint Attention to Mental Content."

60 Gallotti et al., "Alignment in Social Interactions."

61 Seemann, "Reminiscing Together."

62 Shteynberg, "Collective Perspective," 93–97.

63 See chapter 1; Vygotsky, *Mind in Society*; Heinz Werner and Bernard Kaplan, *Symbol Formation: An Organismic-Developmental Approach to Language and Expression of Thought* (New York: Wiley, 1963).

64 Dan P. McAdams, "The Psychology of Life Stories," *Review of General Psychology* 5, no. 2 (2001): 100–122.

65 Schacter and Madore, "Remembering the Past."

66 Klein and Nichols, "Memory."

67 Fivush and Merrill, "Ecological Systems Approach"; Elaine Reese and Kate Farrant, "Social Origins of Reminiscing," in *Autobiographical Memory and the Construction of a Narrative Self: Developmental and Cultural Perspectives*, ed. Robyn Fivush and Catherine A. Haden (Sussex: Psychology Press, 2003), 29–48.

68 Reese and Farrant, "Social Origins of Reminiscing"; Seemann, "Reminiscing Together."

69 Bruner, *Acts of Meaning*; Barbara Rogoff, *Apprenticeship in Thinking: Cognitive Development in Social Context* (Oxford: Oxford University Press, 1990); Vygotsky, *Mind in Society.*

70 The emphasis on mothers has been a consequence of the relative ease of recruiting maternal participants. Some work with fathers has been conducted (e.g., Robyn Fivush and Wibaad Zaman, "Gender, Subjective Perspective, and Autobiographical Consciousness," in *The Wiley Handbook on the Development of Children's Memory*, ed. Patricia J. Bauer and Robyn Fivush [Chichester: John Wiley & Sons, 2013], 586–604).

71 Robyn Fivush and Catherine A. Haden, eds., *Autobiographical Memory and the Construction of a Narrative Self: Developmental and Cultural Perspectives* (Sussex: Psychology Press, 2003); Robyn Fivush et al., "Elaborating on Elaborations: Role of Maternal Reminiscing Style in Cognitive and Socioemotional Development," *Child Development* 77, no. 6 (2006): 1568–88; Katherine Nelson and Robyn Fivush, "The Emergence of Autobiographical Memory: A Social Cultural Developmental Theory," *Psychological Review* 111, no. 2 (2004): 486; Karen Salmon and Elaine Reese, "Talking (Or Not Talking) About the Past: The Influence of Parent-Child Conversation About Negative Experiences on Children's Memories," *Applied Cognitive Psychology* 29, no. 6 (2015): 791–801.

72 Kate Farrant and Elaine Reese, "Maternal Style and Children's Participation in Reminiscing: Stepping Stones in Children's Autobiographical Memory Development," *Journal of Cognition and Development* 1, no. 2 (2000): 193–225; Reese and Farrant, "Social Origins of Reminiscing."

73 Emily S. Cleveland and Elaine Reese, "Maternal Structure and Autonomy Support in Conversations About the Past: Contributions to Children's Autobiographical Memory," *Developmental Psychology* 41, no. 2 (2005): 376.

74 Reese and Farrant, "Social Origins of Reminiscing."

75 Elaine Reese et al., "Origins of Mother-Child Reminiscing Style," *Development and Psychopathology* 31, no. 2 (2019): 631–42.

76 Robyn Fivush, "Maternal Reminiscing Style and Children's Developing Understanding of Self and Emotion," *Clinical Social Work Journal* 35, no. 1 (2007): 37–46.

77 Robyn Fivush, "Remembering and Reminiscing: How Individual Lives Are Constructed in Family Narratives," *Memory Studies* 1, no. 1 (2008): 49–58.

78 Theodore E. A. Waters and Robyn Fivush, "Relations Between Narrative Coherence, Identity, and Psychological Well-Being in Emerging Adulthood," *Journal of Personality* 83, no. 4 (2015): 441–51.

79 Tilmann Habermas and Susan Bluck, "Getting a Life: The Emergence of the Life Story in Adolescence," *Psychological Bulletin* 126, no. 5 (2000): 748.

80 Fivush, "Remembering and Reminiscing."

81 Jennifer G. Bohanek et al., "Family Narrative Interaction and Children's Sense of Self," *Family Process* 45, no. 1 (2006): 39–54.

82 Bohanek et al., "Family Narrative."

83 Kelly A. Marin et al., "Positive Effects of Talking About the Negative: Family Narratives of Negative Experiences and Preadolescents' Perceived Competence," *Journal of Research on Adolescence* 18, no. 3 (2008): 573–93.

84 Dimitris Bolis and Leonhard Schilbach, "'I Interact Therefore I Am': The Self as a Historical Product of Dialectical Attunement," *Topoi* 39, no. 3 (2020): 521–34; Kate C. McLean and Moin Syed, "Personal, Master, and Alternative Narratives: An Integrative Framework for Understanding Identity Development in Context," *Human Development* 58, no. 6 (2015): 318–49.

85 Fivush and Merrill, "Ecological Systems Approach."

86 Fivush, "Remembering and Reminiscing."

87 Lawrence G. Calhoun and Richard G. Tedeschi, "The Foundations of Posttraumatic Growth: An Expanded Framework," in *Handbook of Posttraumatic Growth: Research and Practice*, ed. Lawrence G. Calhoun and Richard G. Tedeschi (Abingdon-on-Thames: Routledge, 2014), 17–38, https://doi.org/10.4324/9781315805597.

88 Jan Assmann, "Communicative and Cultural Memory," in *Cultural Memory Studies: An International and Interdisciplinary Handbook*, ed. Astrid Erll and Ansgar Nünning (New York: de Gruyter, 2008), 109–18.

89 As Eve Ridgeway has helpfully pointed out to us, our account of jointness in rites of remembrance does not address in detail the spatial copresence of the ritual. Our reason for this lack of focus is that we think the account of spatial copresence outlined previously in the book applies rather straightforwardly to the Eucharist and Seder. The temporal distance is a distinctive feature of these practices that requires a more detailed account. So, to avoid repetition, we have largely given an account of temporal jointness here.

90 Torrance, *Worship*, 75.

6 BAPTISM AND THE BOUNDARIES OF JOINTNESS

1 We are grateful to a group of church children's workers whom we met with as part of a Knowledge Exchange workshop in St Andrews in 2021. Their reflections on church practice and the inclusion of children helped inform the content of this chapter.

2 See Church of England, "Millions Join Worship Online as Churches Bring Services into the Home in Pandemic Year," March 16, 2021, https://www.churchofengland.org/news-and-media/news-releases/millions-join-worship-online-churches-bring-services-home-pandemic.

3 E.g., Roy F. Baumeister and Mark R. Leary, "The Need to Belong: Desire for Interpersonal Attachments as a Fundamental Human Motivation," *Psychological Bulletin* 117, no. 3 (1995): 497–529.

4 E.g., David Buttelmann and Robert Böhm, "The Ontogeny of the Motivation that Underlies In-Group Bias," *Psychological Science* 25, no. 4 (2014): 921–27; Yarrow Dunham et al., "Consequences of 'Minimal' Group Affiliations in Children," *Child Development* 82, no. 3 (2011): 793–811.

5 E.g., Brian Brock, *Wondrously Wounded: Theology, Disability, and the Body of Christ*, Studies in Theology, Religion, and Disability (Waco: Baylor University Press, 2019); Miroslav Volf, *After Our Likeness: The Church as the Image of the Trinity* (Grand Rapids: Eerdmans, 1998).

6 N. T. Wright, *Paul and the Faithfulness of God* (Minneapolis, Minn.: Fortress Press, 2013), 421–23.

7 Scot McKnight, *It Takes a Church to Baptize: What the Bible Says about Infant Baptism* (Grand Rapids: Brazos, 2018).

8 McKnight, *It Takes a Church*, 22.

9 Louis Weil, *A Theology of Worship*, The New Church's Teaching Series 12 (Lanham, Md.: Cowley, 2001), 19.

10 Benjamin T. Conner, *Amplifying Our Witness: Giving Voice to Adolescents with Developmental Disabilities* (Grand Rapids: Eerdmans, 2012), 91.

11 John Calvin, *Institutes of the Christian Religion*, ed. John T. McNeill, trans. Ford Lewis Battles (London: Westminster 1960), 1332, IV 10.

12 From a Baptist perspective, the practice of dedication serves to mark infants as an important part of the community, even if it has differing theological significance to baptism.

13 Margaret Gilbert, *Joint Commitment: How We Make the Social World* (Oxford: Oxford University Press, 2013), 174.

14 Gilbert, *Joint Commitment*, 174.

15 Cockayne, *Explorations in Analytic Ecclesiology*, 82.

16 These examples are based on examples given by the members of our focus group hosted in St Andrews.

17 Author's own example.

18 Brandon M. Woo et al., "Human Morality Is Based on an Early-Emerging Moral Core," *Annual Review of Developmental Psychology* 4 (2022): 41–61.

19 We note this evidence is primarily from Western contexts. An ongoing, large-scale replication effort is also currently in progress (Kelsey Lucca et al., "Infants' Social Evaluation of Helpers and Hinderers: A Large-Scale, Multi-Lab, Coordinated Replication Study," preprint, *PsyArXiv*, June 28, 2021, https://doi.org/10.31234/osf.io/qhxkm).
20 Hamlin et al., "Social Evaluation."
21 J. Kiley Hamlin et al., "How Infants and Toddlers React to Antisocial Others," *Proceedings of the National Academy of Sciences* 108, no. 50 (2011): 19931–36.
22 Buttelmann and Böhm, "Ontogeny of the Motivation," 921–27; Dunham et al., "Consequences," 793–811.
23 Jerome W. Berryman, *The Spiritual Guidance of Children: Montessori, Godly Play, and the Future* (Harrisburg, Pa.: Morehouse, 2013), 8.
24 Sofia Cavalletti, *Religious Potential of the Child: Experiencing Scripture and Liturgy with Young Children*, 2nd ed., trans. Patricia M. Coulter and Julie M. Coulter (New York: Liturgy Training Publications, 1993).
25 Faith G. Pawl, "Minding Children in the Study of Liturgy," *TheoLogica* 4, no. 1 (2020): 6–29.
26 Pawl, "Minding Children," 9–10.
27 Pawl, "Minding Children," 23.
28 Cavalletti, *Religious Potential*, 37.
29 Developmental psychologists who are interested in the role of ritual in shaping children's learning have highlighted that rituals play an important role in children's social development. They define rituals specifically as socially stipulated group conventions whose purported effects are not achieved by a physical mechanism—meaning, the purpose of the action is the action itself, not the outcome (Watson-Jones and Legare, "Social Functions of Group Rituals," 42). Children participating in such group actions learn to identify fellow group members, maintain strong relationships with these members, and display commitment to the group (Mark Nielsen, "The Social Glue of Cumulative Culture and Ritual Behavior," *Child Development Perspectives* 12, no. 4 [2018]: 264–68; Watson-Jones and Legare, "Social Functions of Group Rituals"). According to these findings, and in keeping with Pawl's line of argument, children are very much being shaped by ritual actions before we might expect them to grasp complex theological concepts. However, this does not exhaust the question of quite how children are formed by rituals and religious liturgies in particular—this is a question for further consideration.

30 It is also important to note that we could see this line of argument extending naturally to, for example, the neurodiverse. If we define, say, an autistic person solely in terms of cognitive or motivational deficits relative to a neurotypical person, we fail to appreciate that they bring a different rather than lacking kind of experience. For more detailed discussions of this topic, see Kristen Bottema-Beutel et al., "Avoiding Ableist Language: Suggestions for Autism Researchers," *Autism in Adulthood* 3, no. 1 (2021): 18–29; Vikram K. Jaswal and Nameera Akhtar, "Being Versus Appearing Socially Uninterested: Challenging Assumptions About Social Motivation in Autism," *Behavioral and Brain Sciences* 42 (2019), https://doi.org/10.1017/S0140525X18001826; Steven K. Kapp et al., "Deficit, Difference, or Both? Autism and Neurodiversity," *Developmental Psychology* 49, no. 1 (2013): 59.

31 Pawl, "Minding Children," 26.

32 Gareth B. Matthews, "Philosophy and the Young Child," *Metaphilosophy* 10, no. 3–4 (1979): 368.

33 See the Messy Church website for more information: https://www.messychurch.org.uk/.

34 Johnson, *Knowledge by Ritual*, 238–39.

35 Siposova and Carpenter, "New Look at Joint Attention," 260–74.

36 Campbell, "Joint Attention and Common Knowledge," 289.

37 See, for example, United Nations Children's Fund, *Early Moments Matter for Every Child* (New York: UNICEF, September 2017), https://www.unicef.org/reports/early-moments-matter-every-child. Focusing on our UK context, a number of large projects with national reach have been established, including the BBC Tiny Happy People Project (https://www.bbc.co.uk/tiny-happy-people), the Talk to Your Baby campaign (https://literacytrust.org.uk/early-years/talk-your-baby-conference/), and the First 1001 Days movement (https://parentinfantfoundation.org.uk/1001-days/).

38 For example, infants in the womb become attuned to the sound of their mother's voice (Barbara S. Kisilevsky et al., "Effects of Experience on Fetal Voice Recognition," *Psychological Science* 14, no. 3 [2003]: 220–24; Vincent M. Reid and Kirsty Dunn, "The Fetal Origins of Human Psychological Development," *Current Directions in Psychological Science* 30, no. 2 [2021]: 144–50). Starting neonatally and increasing across their first year, infants preferentially attend to infant-directed speech (ManyBabies Consortium, "Quantifying Sources of Variability in Infancy Research Using the Infant-Directed-Speech Preference," *Advances in Methods and Practices in Psychological Science* 3, no. 1 [2020]: 24–52; Judith E. Pegg et al., "Preference for Infant-Directed over Adult-Directed

Speech: Evidence from 7-Week-Old Infants," *Infant Behavior and Development* 15, no. 3 [1992]: 325–45) and, between two to six months of age, start to engage in interactive exchanges with their caregivers (Colwyn Trevarthen and Kenneth J. Aitken, "Infant Intersubjectivity: Research, Theory, and Clinical Applications," *Journal of Child Psychology and Psychiatry* 42, no. 1 [2001]: 3–48; Tronick et al., "Infant's Response to Entrapment," 1–13). See Reid and Dunn, "Fetal Origins," for a review of research on neonatal development, and for reviews of infant intersubjectivity and joint attention in the first year, see Trevarthen and Aitken, "Infant Intersubjectivity"; Henrike Moll et al., "Sharing Experiences in Infancy: From Primary Intersubjectivity to Shared Intentionality," *Frontiers in Psychology* 12 (2021), https://doi.org/10.3389/fpsyg.2021.667679.

39 Calvin, *Institutes* 1332.IV.10.

CONCLUSION

1 Torrance, *Worship*, 20.

2 Though, see Bryan Chambliss, "Attending Together in Digital Environments."

3 The exception being the work of Shteynberg and colleagues, whom we have cited throughout.

4 Battich et al., "Coordinating Attention."

BIBLIOGRAPHY

Adams, Fred, and Rebecca Garrison. "The Mark of the Cognitive." *Minds and Machines* 23, no. 3 (2013): 339–52.

Adams, Frederick, and Kenneth Aizawa. *The Bounds of Cognition*. Oxford: Blackwell, 2008.

Adamson, Lauren B., and Janet E. Frick. "The Still Face: A History of a Shared Experimental Paradigm." *Infancy* 4, no. 4 (2003): 451–73.

Adolph, Karen E. "Psychophysical Assessment of Toddlers' Ability to Cope with Slopes." *Journal of Experimental Psychology: Human Perception and Performance* 21, no. 4 (1995): 734–50.

Adolph, Karen E., and Justine E. Hoch. "Motor Development: Embodied, Embedded, Enculturated, and Enabling." *Annual Review of Psychology* 70 (2019): 141–64.

Ainsworth, Mary D. Salter, Mary C. Blehar, Everett Waters, and Sally N. Wall. *Patterns of Attachment: A Psychological Study of the Strange Situation*. Hillsdale, N.J.: Lawrence Erlbaum, 1978.

Aizawa, Ken. "What Is This Cognition That Is Supposed to Be Embodied?" *Philosophical Psychology* 28, no. 6 (2015): 755–75.

Akhtar, Nameera, and Morton A. Gernsbacher. "On Privileging the Role of Gaze in Infant Social Cognition." *Child Development Perspectives* 2, no. 2 (2008): 59–65.

Algoe, Sara B. "Find, Remind, and Bind: The Functions of Gratitude in Everyday Relationships." *Social and Personality Psychology Compass* 6, no. 6 (2012): 455–69.

Algoe, Sara B., Jonathan Haidt, and Shelly L. Gable. "Beyond Reciprocity: Gratitude and Relationships in Everyday Life." *Emotion* 8, no. 3 (2008): 425–29.

Allen, Colin. "On (Not) Defining Cognition." *Synthese* 194, no. 11 (2017): 4233–49.

Allport, Gordon W. "The Historical Background of Social Psychology." In *The Handbook of Social Psychology*, 3rd ed., edited by Gardner Lindzey and E. Aronson. New York: Random House / Erlbaum, 1985.

Anderson, David I., Joseph J. Campos, David C. Witherington, et al. "The Role of Locomotion in Psychological Development." *Frontiers in Psychology* 4 (2013). https://doi.org/10.3389/fpsyg.2013.00440.

Assmann, Jan. "Communicative and Cultural Memory." In *Cultural Memory Studies: An International and Interdisciplinary Handbook*, edited by Astrid Erll and Ansgar Nünning. New York: de Gruyter, 2008.

Astington, Janet Wilde, and Jennifer M. Jenkins. "A Longitudinal Study of the Relation Between Language and Theory-of-Mind Development." *Developmental Psychology* 35, no. 5 (1999): 1311–20.

Bacharach, Julian. "Is There Such a Thing as Joint Attention to the Past?" *Topoi* 43, no. 2 (2024): 323–35.

Baddeley, Alan. "What Is Autobiographical Memory?" In *Theoretical Perspectives on Autobiographical Memory*, edited by Martin A. Conway, David C. Rubin, Hans Spinnler, and Willem A. Wagenaar. Dordrecht: Springer, 2013.

Baesler, E. James, and Kevin L. Ladd. "Exploring Prayer Contexts and Health Outcomes: From the Chair to the Pew." *Journal of Communication and Religion* 32, no. 2 (2009): 347–74.

Baillargeon, Renée, Elizabeth S. Spelke, and Stanley Wasserman. "Object Permanence in Five-Month-Old Infants." *Cognition* 20, no. 3 (1985): 191–208.

Bakeman, Roger, and Lauren B. Adamson. "Coordinating Attention to People and Objects in Mother-Infant and Peer-Infant Interaction." *Child Development* 55, no. 4 (1984): 1278–89.

Barbour, Ian G. *When Science Meets Religion: Enemies, Strangers, or Partners?* London: SPCK, 2000.

Barrett, Justin L. *TheoPsych: A Psychological Science Primer for Theologians*. Knoxville: Blueprint 1543, 2022.

Barrett, Lisa Feldman. "Are Emotions Natural Kinds?" *Perspectives on Psychological Science* 1, no. 1 (2006): 28–58.

Barwise, Jon. "The Situation in Logic." *CSLI Lecture Notes* 17 (1989).

Bastian, Brock, Jolanda Jetten, and Laura J. Ferris. "Pain as Social Glue: Shared Pain Increases Cooperation." *Psychological Science* 25, no. 11 (2014): 2079–85.

Bates, Elizabeth, Laura Benigni, Inge Bretherton, Luigia Camaioni, and Virginia Volterra. *The Emergence of Symbols: Cognition and Communication in Infancy*. New York: Academic Press, 1979.

Bateson, Mary Catherine. "Mother-Infant Exchanges: The Epigenesis of Conversational Interaction." *Annals of the New York Academy of Sciences* 263, no. 1 (1975): 101–13.

Battich, Lucas, Merle Fairhurst, and Ophelia Deroy. "Coordinating Attention Requires Coordinated Senses." *Psychonomic Bulletin & Review* 27, no. 6 (2020): 1126–38.

Baumeister, Roy F., and Mark R. Leary. "The Need to Belong: Desire for Interpersonal Attachments as a Fundamental Human Motivation." *Psychological Bulletin* 117, no. 3 (1995): 497–529.

Bekerian, D. A., and J. M. Bowers. "Eyewitness Testimony: Were We Misled?" *Journal of Experimental Psychology: Learning, Memory, and Cognition* 9, no. 1 (1983): 139–45.

Benson, Bruce Ellis. *Liturgy as a Way of Life: Embodying the Arts in Christian Worship.* The Church and Postmodern Culture. Grand Rapids: Baker Books, 2013.

Berryman, Jerome W. *The Spiritual Guidance of Children: Montessori, Godly Play, and the Future.* Harrisburg, Pa.: Morehouse, 2013.

Bertocci, Peter A., and Richard M. Millard. *Personality and the Good: Psychological and Ethical Perspectives.* New York: David McKay, 1963.

Boesch, Christophe, and Hedwige Boesch. "Tool Use and Tool Making in Wild Chimpanzees." *Folia Primatologica* 54, no. 1–2 (1990): 86–99.

Bohanek, Jennifer G., Kelly A. Marin, Robyn Fivush, and Marshall P. Duke. "Family Narrative Interaction and Children's Sense of Self." *Family Process* 45, no. 1 (2006): 39–54.

Bolis, Dimitris, and Leonhard Schilbach. "'I Interact Therefore I Am': The Self as a Historical Product of Dialectical Attunement." *Topoi* 39, no. 3 (2020): 521–34.

Bonhoeffer, Dietrich. *Life Together and Prayerbook of the Bible.* Vol. 5 of *Dietrich Bonhoeffer Works.* Minneapolis: 1517 Media, 2004.

Boothby, Erica J., Margaret S. Clark, and John A. Bargh. "Shared Experiences Are Amplified." *Psychological Science* 25, no. 12 (2014): 2209–16.

Boothby, Erica J., Leigh K. Smith, Margaret S. Clark, and John A. Bargh. "Psychological Distance Moderates the Amplification of Shared Experience." *Personality and Social Psychology Bulletin* 42, no. 10 (2016): 1431–44.

Botero, Maria. "Tactless Scientists: Ignoring Touch in the Study of Joint Attention." *Philosophical Psychology* 29, no. 8 (2016): 1200–14.

Bottema-Beutel, Kristen, Steven K. Kapp, Jessica Nina Lester, Noah J. Sasson, and Brittany N. Hand. "Avoiding Ableist Language: Suggestions for Autism Researchers." *Autism in Adulthood* 3, no. 1 (2021): 18–29.

Boyer, Pascal, and Brian Bergstrom. "Evolutionary Perspectives on Religion." *Annual Review of Anthropology* 37 (2008): 111–30.

Brandone, Amanda C. "Infants' Social and Motor Experience and the Emerging Understanding of Intentional Actions." *Developmental Psychology* 51, no. 4 (2015): 512–24.

Brandone, Amanda C., Wyntre Stout, and Kelsey Moty. "Intentional Action Processing Across the Transition to Crawling: Does the Experience of Self-Locomotion Impact Infants' Understanding of Intentional Actions?" *Infant Behavior and Development* 60 (2020). https://doi.org/10.1016/j.infbeh.2020.101470.

Bratman, Michael E. *Shared Agency: A Planning Theory of Acting Together.* Oxford: Oxford University Press, 2013.

Brock, Brian. *Wondrously Wounded: Theology, Disability, and the Body of Christ.* Studies in Religion, Theology, and Disability. Waco: Baylor University Press, 2019.

Brown, Warren S., and Brad D. Strawn. *The Physical Nature of Christian Life: Neuroscience, Psychology, and the Church.* Cambridge: Cambridge University Press, 2012.

Bruin, Leon de, Michiel van Elk, and Albert Newen. "Reconceptualizing Second-Person Interaction." *Frontiers in Human Neuroscience* 6 (2012). https://doi.org/10.3389/fnhum.2012.00151.

Brümmer, Vincent. *What Are We Doing When We Pray? On Prayer and the Nature of Faith.* London: Routledge, 2017.

Bruner, Jerome S. *Acts of Meaning.* Cambridge, Mass.: Harvard University Press, 1990.

Bryan, Gharad, Dean Karlan, and Scott Nelson. "Commitment Devices." *Annual Review of Economics* 2, no. 1 (2010): 671–98.

Buttelmann, David, and Robert Böhm. "The Ontogeny of the Motivation that Underlies In-Group Bias." *Psychological Science* 25, no. 4 (2014): 921–27.

Byrne, Richard W., Lucy A. Bates, and Cynthia J. Moss. "Elephant Cognition in Primate Perspective." *Comparative Cognition & Behavior Reviews* 4 (2009): 65–79.

Calhoun, Lawrence G., and Richard G. Tedeschi. "The Foundations of Posttraumatic Growth: An Expanded Framework." In *Handbook of Posttraumatic Growth: Research and Practice*, edited by Lawrence G. Calhoun and Richard G. Tedeschi. Abingdon-on-Thames: Routledge, 2014. https://doi.org/10.4324/9781315805597.

Call, Josep, Brian Hare, Malinda Carpenter, and Michael Tomasello. "'Unwilling' Versus 'Unable': Chimpanzees' Understanding of Human Intentional Action." *Developmental Science* 7, no. 4 (2004): 488–98.

Calvin, John. *Institutes of the Christian Religion*. Edited by John T. McNeill. Translated by Ford Lewis Battles. London: Westminster Press, 1960.

Campbell, John. "Joint Attention and Common Knowledge." In *Joint Attention: Communication and Other Minds; Issues in Philosophy and Psychology*, edited by Naomi Elian, Christoph Hoerl, Teresa McCormack, and Johannes Roessler. Oxford: Clarendon Press, 2005.

Campos, Joseph J., David I. Anderson, Marianne A. Barbu-Roth, Edward M. Hubbard, Matthew J. Hertenstein, and David Witherington. "Travel Broadens the Mind." *Infancy* 1, no. 2 (2000): 149–219.

Carpendale, Jeremy I. M., and Ailidh B. Carpendale. "The Development of Pointing: From Personal Directedness to Interpersonal Direction." *Human Development* 53, no. 3 (2010): 110–26.

Carpendale, Jeremy I. M., and Charlie Lewis. "Constructing an Understanding of Mind: The Development of Children's Social Understanding Within Social Interaction." *Behavioral and Brain Sciences* 27, no. 1 (2004): 79–151.

Carpenter, Malinda, and Kristin Liebal. "Joint Attention, Communication, and Knowing Together in Infancy." In *Joint Attention: New Developments in Psychology, Philosophy of Mind, and Social Neuroscience*, edited by Axel Seemann. Cambridge, Mass.: MIT Press, 2011.

Carpenter, Malinda, Katherine Nagell, and Michael Tomasello. "Social Cognition, Joint Attention, and Communicative Competence from 9 to 15 Months of Age." *Monographs of the Society for Research in Child Development* 63, no. 4 (1998): 1–143.

Carruthers, Peter. "Mindreading in Infancy." *Mind & Language* 28, no. 2 (2013): 141–72.

Cavalletti, Sofia. *Religious Potential of the Child: Experiencing Scripture and Liturgy with Young Children*. 2nd ed. Translated by Patricia M. Coulter and Julie M. Coulter. New York: Liturgy Training Publications, 1993.

Chambliss, Bryan. "Attending Together in Digital Environments." *Topoi* 43, no. 2 (2024): 311–22.

Charles, Sarah Jane, Valerie van Mulukom, Miguel Farias, et al. "Religious Rituals Increase Social Bonding and Pain Threshold." Preprint, *PsyArXiv*, January 31, 2020. https://doi.org/10.31234/osf.io/my4hs.

Chartrand, Tanya L., and Rick van Baaren. "Human Mimicry." In *Advances in Experimental Social Psychology*, vol. 41, edited by Mark P. Zanna. London: Academic Press, 2009.

Chartrand, Tanya L., and John A. Bargh. "The Chameleon Effect: The Perception-Behavior Link and Social Interaction." *Journal of Personality and Social Psychology* 76, no. 6 (1999): 893–910.

Childs, Brevard S. *Memory and Tradition in Israel*. Studies in Biblical Theology 37. London: SCM Press, 1962.

Childs, Luke. "How the Daily Office Is Different from a 'Quiet Time.'" *Anglican Compass*, November 19, 2018. https://anglicancompass.com/how-the-daily-office-is-different-from-a-quiet-time/.

Chittka, Lars. "Bee Cognition." *Current Biology* 27, no. 19 (2017): 1049–53.

Chun, Yohang. "Tongsung Kido (A Unique Korean Prayer)." *Upper New York Conference News*, May 10, 2017. http://www.unyumc.org/news/article/tongsung-kido-a-unique-korean-prayer.

Church of England. "Millions Join Worship Online as Churches Bring Services into the Home in Pandemic Year." March 16, 2021. https://www.churchofengland.org/news-and-media/news-releases/millions-join-worship-online-churches-bring-services-home-pandemic.

Church of England. *1662 Book of Common Prayer*. Cambridge: John Baskerville, 1762. https://www.churchofengland.org/sites/default/files/2019-10/the-book-of-common-prayer-1662.pdf.

Church of England. "Holy Communion Service." *Common Worship*. 2000. https://www.churchofengland.org/prayer-and-worship/worship-texts-and-resources/common-worship/holy-communion-service.

Chwe, Michael Suk-Young. *Rational Ritual: Culture, Coordination, and Common Knowledge*. Princeton, N.J.: Princeton University Press, 2001.

Citron, Aryeh. "Minyan: The Prayer Quorum." *Chabad*, accessed November 7, 2024. https://www.chabad.org/library/article_cdo/aid/1176648/jewish/Minyan-The-Prayer-Quorum.htm.

Clark, Herbert H. *Using Language*. Cambridge: Cambridge University Press, 1996.

Cleveland, Emily S., and Elaine Reese. "Maternal Structure and Autonomy Support in Conversations About the Past: Contributions to Children's Autobiographical Memory." *Developmental Psychology* 41, no. 2 (2005): 376–88.

Coakley, Sarah. "Beyond Belief." In *The Vocation of Theology Today: A Festschrift for David Ford*, edited by Tom Greggs, Rachel Muers, and Simeon Zahl. Eugene, Ore.: Wipf and Stock, 2013.

Cockayne, Joshua. *Explorations in Analytic Ecclesiology: That They May Be One*. Oxford: Oxford University Press, 2023.

Cockayne, Joshua, and David Efird. "Common Worship." *Faith and Philosophy: Journal of the Society of Christian Philosophers* 35, no. 3 (2018): 299–325.

Cockayne, Joshua, David Efird, Gordon Haynes, et al. "Experiencing the Real Presence of Christ in the Eucharist." *Journal of Analytic Theology* 5 (2017): 175–96.

Cockayne, Joshua, and Gideon Salter. "Feasts of Memory: Collective Remembering, Liturgical Time Travel and the Actualisation of the Past." *Modern Theology* 37, no. 2 (2021): 275–95.

Cockayne, Joshua, and Gideon Salter. "Group Gratitude: A Taxonomy." Preprint, *Journal of Value Inquiry*, January 12, 2023. https://doi.org/10.1007/s10790-022-09924-3.

Cockayne, Joshua, and Gideon Salter. "Liturgical Anthropology: A Developmental Perspective." *TheoLogica* 6, no. 1 (2022): 72–106.

Cockayne, Joshua, and Gideon Salter. "Liturgical Gratitude to God." *Religions* 13, no. 9 (2022). https://doi.org/10.3390/rel13090795

Cockayne, Joshua, and Gideon Salter. "Praying Together: Corporate Prayer and Shared Situations." *Zygon* 54, no. 3 (2019): 702–30.

Collins, Stephanie. *Group Duties: Their Existence and Their Implications for Individuals*. Oxford: Oxford University Press, 2019.

Conner, Benjamin T. *Amplifying Our Witness: Giving Voice to Adolescents with Developmental Disabilities*. Grand Rapids: Eerdmans, 2012.

Coupe, Nia, Sarah Peters, Sarah Rhodes, and Sarah Cotterill. "The Effect of Commitment-Making on Weight Loss and Behavior Change in Adults with Obesity/Overweight: A Systematic Review." *BMC Public Health* 19, no. 1 (2019): 1–16.

Csibra, Gergely. "Recognizing Communicative Intentions in Infancy." *Mind & Language* 25, no. 2 (2010): 141–68.

Csibra, Gergely. "Teleological and Referential Understanding of Action in Infancy." *Philosophical Transactions of the Royal Society of London. Series B: Biological Sciences* 358, no. 1431 (2003): 447–58.

Cummins, Denise Dellarosa. "Dominance Hierarchies and the Evolution of Human Reasoning." *Minds and Machines* 6, no. 4 (1996): 463–80.

Cuneo, Terence. *Ritualized Faith: Essays on the Philosophy of Liturgy*. Oxford: Oxford University Press, 2016.

Dale, Philip S., Elizabeth F. Loftus, and Linda Rathbun. "The Influence of the Form of the Question on the Eyewitness Testimony of Preschool Children." *Journal of Psycholinguistic Research* 7, no. 4 (1978): 269–77.

Davies, Martin. "Knowledge (Explicit, Implicit and Tacit): Philosophical Aspects." In *International Encyclopedia of the Social and Behavioral Sciences*, 2nd ed., edited by James D. Wright, vol. 13. Elsevier, 2015.

Davis, Jacqueline, Jonathan Redshaw, Thomas Suddendorf, et al. "Does Neonatal Imitation Exist? Insights from a Meta-Analysis of 336 Effect Sizes." *Perspectives on Psychological Science* 16, no. 6 (2021): 1373–97.

Davison, Andrew. "Science and Specificity: Interdisciplinary Teaching Between Theology, Religion, and the Natural Sciences." *Zygon* 57, no. 1 (2022): 233–43.

De Brigard, Felipe. "Memory, Attention, and Joint Reminiscing." In *New Directions in the Philosophy of Memory*, edited by Kourken Michaelian, Dorothea Debus, and Denis Perrin. New York: Routledge, 2018.

Delafield-Butt, Jonathan T., and Colwyn Trevarthen. "The Ontogenesis of Narrative: From Moving to Meaning." *Frontiers in Psychology* 6 (2015). https://doi.org/10.3389/fpsyg.2015.01157.

Dennett, Daniel C. "Beliefs About Beliefs (Commentary on Premack, et al.)." *Behavioral and Brain Sciences* 1 (1978): 568–70.

Di Fabio, Annamaria, Letizia Palazzeschi, and Ornella Bucci. "Gratitude in Organizations: A Contribution for Healthy Organizational Contexts." *Frontiers in Psychology* 8 (2017). https://doi.org/10.3389/fpsyg.2017.02025.

Doyle, C. Andrew. *Embodied Liturgy: Virtual Reality and Liturgical Theology in Conversation*. New York: Church Publishing, 2021.

Duncan, Seth, and Lisa Feldman Barrett. "Affect Is a Form of Cognition: A Neurobiological Analysis." *Cognition and Emotion* 21, no. 6 (2007): 1184–211.

Dunham, Yarrow, Andrew Scott Baron, and Susan Carey. "Consequences of 'Minimal' Group Affiliations in Children." *Child Development* 82, no. 3 (2011): 793–811.

Dunnington, Kent. "Being Grateful and Feeling Grateful: Reconsidering the Phenomenology of Gratitude to God." *Journal of Positive Psychology* 19, no. 1 (2024): 1–10.

Dunst, Carl J., and Danielle Z. Kassow. "Caregiver Sensitivity, Contingent Social Responsiveness, and Secure Infant Attachment." *Journal of Early and Intensive Behavior Intervention* 5, no. 1 (2008): 40–56.

Eastman, Susan Grove. *Paul and the Person: Reframing Paul's Anthropology*. Grand Rapids: Eerdmans, 2017.

Echterhoff, Gerald, E. Tory Higgins, and John M. Levine. "Shared Reality: Experiencing Commonality with Others' Inner States About the World." *Perspectives on Psychological Science* 4, no. 5 (2009): 496–521.

Ehli, Samantha, Julia Wolf, Albert Newen, Silvia Schneider, and Babett Voigt. "Determining the Function of Social Referencing: The Role of Familiarity and Situational Threat." *Frontiers in Psychology* 11, (2020). https://doi.org/10.3389/fpsyg.2020.538228.

Eilan, Naomi, ed. *Joint Attention: Communication and Other Minds; Issues in Philosophy and Psychology*. Oxford: Oxford University Press, 2005.

Emery, Nathan J., and Nicola S. Clayton. "The Mentality of Crows: Convergent Evolution of Intelligence in Corvids and Apes." *Science* 306, no. 5703 (2004): 1903–7.

Emmons, Robert A. "Gratitude, Subjective Well-Being, and the Brain." In *The Science of Subjective Well-Being*, edited by Michael Eid and Randy J. Larsen. New York: Guilford, 2008.

Emmons, Robert A. *Gratitude Works! A 21-Day Program for Creating Emotional Prosperity*. Hoboken, N.J.: John Wiley & Sons, 2013.

Emmons, Robert A. *Thanks! How the New Science of Gratitude Can Make You Happier*. Boston: Houghton Mifflin Harcourt, 2007.

Emmons, Robert A., and Cheryl A. Crumpler. "Gratitude as a Human Strength: Appraising the Evidence." *Journal of Social and Clinical Psychology* 19, no. 1 (2000): 56–69.

Emmons, Robert A., and Robert Stern. "Gratitude as a Psychotherapeutic Intervention." *Journal of Clinical Psychology* 69, no. 8 (2013): 846–55.

Evans, Jonathan, and David E. Over. *Rationality and Reasoning*. Hove: Psychology Press, 1996.

Fabian, Johannes. *Talk About Prayer: An Ethnographic Commentary*. London: Palgrave Macmillan, 2015.

Fantasia, Valentina, Alessandra Fasulo, Alan Costall, and Beatriz López. "Changing the Game: Exploring Infants' Participation in Early Play Routines." *Frontiers in Psychology* 5 (2014). https://doi.org/10.3389/fpsyg.2014.00522.

Farmer, Herbert H. *The World and God: A Study in Prayer, Providence, and Miracle in Christian Experience*. London: Nisbet & Co Ltd., 1942.

Farrant, Kate, and Elaine Reese. "Maternal Style and Children's Participation in Reminiscing: Stepping Stones in Children's Autobiographical Memory Development." *Journal of Cognition and Development* 1, no. 2 (2000): 193–225.

Fee, Gordon D. *The First Epistle to the Corinthians*. Grand Rapids: Eerdmans, 1987.

Fehr, Ryan, Ashley Fulmer, Eli Awtrey, and Jared A. Miller. "The Grateful Workplace: A Multilevel Model of Gratitude in Organizations." *Academy of Management Review* 42, no. 2 (2017): 361–81.

Fischer, Ronald, Rohan Callander, Paul Reddish, and Joseph Bulbulbia. "How Do Rituals Affect Cooperation?" *Human Nature* 24, no. 2 (2013): 115–25.

Fivush, Robyn. "Maternal Reminiscing Style and Children's Developing Understanding of Self and Emotion." *Clinical Social Work Journal* 35, no. 1 (2007): 37–46.

Fivush, Robyn. "Remembering and Reminiscing: How Individual Lives Are Constructed in Family Narratives." *Memory Studies* 1, no. 1 (2008): 49–58.

Fivush, Robyn, and Catherine A. Haden, eds. *Autobiographical Memory and the Construction of a Narrative Self: Developmental and Cultural Perspectives*. Sussex: Psychology Press, 2003.

Fivush, Robyn, Catherine A. Haden, and Elaine Reese. "Elaborating on Elaborations: Role of Maternal Reminiscing Style in Cognitive and Socioemotional Development." *Child Development* 77, no. 6 (2006): 1568–88.

Fivush, Robyn, and Natalie Merrill. "An Ecological Systems Approach to Family Narratives." *Memory Studies* 9, no. 3 (2016): 305–14.

Fivush, Robyn, and Widaad Zaman. "Gender, Subjective Perspective, and Autobiographical Consciousness." In *The Wiley Handbook on the Development of Children's Memory*, edited by Patricia J. Bauer and Robyn Fivush. Chichester: John Wiley & Sons, 2013.

Flanagan, Eamon. "Prayer and Sacred Spaces." Website of St. Peter's Church, Phibsborough, accessed November 7, 2024. https://www.stpetersphibsboro.ie/prayer-and-sacred-places/.

Froh, Jeffrey J., William J. Sefick, and Robert A. Emmons. "Counting Blessings in Early Adolescents: An Experimental Study of Gratitude and Subjective Well-Being." *Journal of School Psychology* 46, no. 2 (2008): 213–33.

Gallotti, M., M. T. Fairhurst, and C. D. Frith. "Alignment in Social Interactions." *Consciousness and Cognition* 48 (2017): 253–61.

Gilbert, Margaret. *Joint Commitment: How We Make the Social World.* Oxford: Oxford University Press, 2013.

Gilbert, Margaret. "Mutual Recognition, Common Knowledge, and Joint Attention." In *Hommage à Wlodek: Philosophical Papers Dedicated to Wlodek Rabinowicz*, edited by T. Rønnow-Rasmussen, B. Petersson, J. Josefsson, and D. Egonsson. Department of Philosophy, Lund University, 2007. https://www.fil.lu.se/hommageawlodek/site/papper/GilbertMargaret.pdf.

Gilbert, Margaret. "Obligation and Joint Commitment." *Utilitas* 11, no. 2 (1999): 143–63.

Giordan, Giuseppe. "Toward a Sociology of Prayer." In *Religion, Spirituality, and Everyday Practice*, edited by Giuseppe Giordan and William H. Swatos Jr. New York: Springer, 2011.

Giordan, Giuseppe, and Linda Woodhead, eds. *A Sociology of Prayer.* London: Routledge, 2015.

Gómez, Juan-Carlos. "Second Person Intentional Relations and the Evolution of Social Understanding." *Behavioral and Brain Sciences* 19, no. 1 (1996): 129–30.

Gómez, Juan-Carlos, Verena Kersken, Derek Ball, and Amanda Seed. "Knowing Without Knowing: Implicit Cognition and the Minds of Infants and Animals [Saber sin saber: La cognición implícita y las mentes de niños pequeños y animales]." *Studies in Psychology* 38, no. 1 (2017): 37–62.

Gräfenhain, Maria, Tanya Behne, Malinda Carpenter, and Michael Tomasello. "Young Children's Understanding of Joint Commitments." *Developmental Psychology* 45, no. 5 (2009): 1430–43.

Gray, Jeremy R. "Integration of Emotion and Cognitive Control." *Current Directions in Psychological Science* 13, no. 2 (2004): 46–48.

Green, Adam. "Reading the Mind of God (Without Hebrew Lessons): Alston, Shared Attention, and Mystical Experience." *Religious Studies* 45, no. 4 (2009): 455–70.

Green, Adam, and Keith A. Quan. "More than Inspired Propositions: Shared Attention and the Religious Text." *Faith and Philosophy: Journal of the Society of Christian Philosophers* 29, no. 4 (2012): 416–30.

Gulliford, Liz, Blaire Morgan, and Kristján Kristjánsson. "Recent Work on the Concept of Gratitude in Philosophy and Psychology." *Journal of Value Inquiry* 47, no. 3 (2013): 285–317.

Gunby, Chris. "Advantages of Meta Quest 3, Quest 2, and Quest Pro for Corporate Training." *Virtual Speech*, September 27, 2023. https://virtualspeech.com/blog/advantages-oculus-training.

Habermas, Tilmann, and Susan Bluck. "Getting a Life: The Emergence of the Life Story in Adolescence." *Psychological Bulletin* 126, no. 5 (2000): 748–69.

Hamlin, J. Kiley, Karen Wynn, and Paul Bloom. "Social Evaluation by Preverbal Infants." *Nature* 450, no. 7169 (2007): 557–59.

Hamlin, J. Kiley, Karen Wynn, Paul Bloom, and Neha Mahajan. "How Infants and Toddlers React to Antisocial Others." *Proceedings of the National Academy of Sciences* 108, no. 50 (2011): 19931–36.

Hardin, Curtis D., and E. Tory Higgins. "Shared Reality: How Social Verification Makes the Subjective Objective." In *The Interpersonal Context*, vol. 3 of *Handbook of Motivation and Cognition*, edited by Richard M. Sorrentino and E. Tory Higgins. New York: Guilford, 1996.

Hare, Brian, Josep Call, and Michael Tomasello. "Do Chimpanzees Know What Conspecifics Know?" *Animal Behaviour* 61, no. 1 (2001): 139–51.

Harrison, Peter, ed. *The Cambridge Companion to Science and Religion.* Cambridge: Cambridge University Press, 2010.

Hassabis, Demis, and Eleanor A. Maguire. "Deconstructing Episodic Memory with Construction." *Trends in Cognitive Sciences* 11, no. 7 (2007): 299–306.

Hauerwas, Stanley. *In Good Company: The Church as Polis*. South Bend, Ind.: University of Notre Dame Press, 1995.

Hay, David, and Rebecca Nye. *The Spirit of the Child*. Rev. ed. London: Jessica Kingsley, 2006.

Hays, Richard B. *First Corinthians*. Interpretation. Louisville: Westminster John Knox.

Heyes, Cecilia M., and Chris D. Frith. "The Cultural Evolution of Mind Reading." *Science* 344, no. 6190 (2014): 1–6.

Hirst, William, and David Manier. "Towards a Psychology of Collective Memory." *Memory* 16, no. 3 (2008): 183–200.

Hobson, R. Peter. "What Puts the Jointness into Joint Attention?" In *Joint Attention: Communication and Other Minds; Issues in Philosophy and Psychology*, edited by Naomi Eilan. Oxford: Oxford University Press, 2005.

Hobson, Peter, and Jessica Hobson. "Joint Attention or Joint Engagement? Insights from Autism." In *Joint Attention: New Developments in Psychology, Philosophy of Mind, and Social Neuroscience*, edited by Axel Seemann. Cambridge, Mass.: MIT Press, 2011.

Hoemann, Katie, and Lisa Feldman Barrett. "Concepts Dissolve Artificial Boundaries in the Study of Emotion and Cognition, Uniting Body, Brain, and Mind." *Cognition and Emotion* 33, no. 1 (2019): 67–76.

Hoerl, Christoph, and Teresa McCormack. "Joint Reminiscing as Joint Attention to the Past." In *Joint Attention: Communication and Other Minds; Issues in Philosophy and Psychology*, edited by Naomi Eilan. Oxford: Oxford University Press, 2005.

Hofsten, Claes von, Peter Vishton, Elizabeth S. Spelke, Qi Feng, and Kerstin Rosander. "Predictive Action in Infancy: Tracking and Reaching for Moving Objects." *Cognition* 67, no. 3 (1998): 255–85.

Howard-Snyder, Daniel, and Frances Howard-Snyder. "The Puzzle of Petitionary Prayer." *European Journal for Philosophy of Religion* 2, no. 2 (2010): 43–68.

Huebner, Bryce. "Socially Embedded Cognition." *Cognitive Systems Research* 25–26 (2012–2013): 13–18.

Humphrey, Caroline, and James Laidlaw. *The Archetypal Actions of Ritual: A Theory of Ritual Illustrated by the Jain Rite of Worship.* New York: Oxford University Press, 1994.

Hurtado, Larry. *One God, One Lord: Early Christian Devotion and Ancient Jewish Monotheism.* 3rd ed. London: Bloomsbury, 2015.

Hutto, Daniel D. *Folk Psychological Narratives: The Sociocultural Basis of Understanding Reasons.* Cambridge, Mass.: MIT Press, 2008.

Ingvar, D. H. "'Memory of the Future': An Essay on the Temporal Organization of Conscious Awareness." *Human Neurobiology* 4, no. 3 (1985): 127–36.

Jaswal, Vikram K., and Nameera Akhtar. "Being Versus Appearing Socially Uninterested: Challenging Assumptions About Social Motivation in Autism." *Behavioral and Brain Sciences* 42 (2019). https://doi.org/10.1017/S0140525X18001826.

Jeeves, Malcolm A., and Thomas E. Ludwig. *Psychological Science and Christian Faith: Insights and Enrichments from Constructive Dialogue.* West Conshohocken, Pa.: Templeton Foundation Press, 2018.

Johnson, Dru. *Knowledge by Ritual: A Biblical Prolegomenon to Sacramental Theology.* Winona Lake, Ind.: Eisenbrauns, 2016.

Johnson, Mark H., Michael I. Posner, and Mary K. Rothbart. "Components of Visual Orienting in Early Infancy: Contingency Learning, Anticipatory Looking, and Disengaging." *Journal of Cognitive Neuroscience* 3, no. 4 (1991): 335–44.

Jones, Susan S., and Hye-Won Hong. "Onset of Voluntary Communication: Smiling Looks to Mother." *Infancy* 2, no. 3 (2001): 353–70.

Kaemingk, Matthew, and Cory B. Willson. *Work and Worship: Reconnecting Our Labor and Liturgy.* Grand Rapids: Baker Academic, 2020.

Kahneman, Daniel. *Thinking, Fast and Slow.* London: Macmillan, 2011.

Kapitány, Rohan, Christopher Kavanagh, and Harvey Whitehouse. "Ritual Morphospace Revisited: The Form, Function and Factor Structure of Ritual Practice." *Philosophical Transactions of the Royal Society B* 375, no. 1805 (2020). https://doi.org/10.1098/rstb.2019.0436.

Kapitány, Rohan, and Mark Nielsen. "The Ritual Stance and the Precaution System: The Role of Goal-Demotion and Opacity in Ritual and Everyday Actions." *Religion, Brain & Behavior* 7, no. 1 (2017): 27–42.

Kapp, Steven K., Kristen Gillespie-Lynch, Lauren E. Sherman, and Ted Hutman. "Deficit, Difference, or Both? Autism and Neurodiversity." *Developmental Psychology* 49, no. 1 (2013): 59–71.

Karau, Steven J., and Aric J. Wilhau. "Social Loafing and Motivation Gains in Groups: An Integrative Review." In *Individual Motivation Within Groups*, edited by Steven J. Karau. London: Academic Press, 2020.

Karau, Steven J., and Kipling D. Williams. "Social Loafing: A Meta-Analytic Review and Theoretical Integration." *Journal of Personality and Social Psychology* 65, no. 4 (1993): 681–706.

Karmiloff-Smith, Annette. *Beyond Modularity: A Developmental Perspective on Cognitive Science*. Cambridge, Mass.: MIT Press, 1992.

Kavanagh, Christopher M., Rohan Kapitány, Idhamsyah Eka Putra, and Harvey Whitehouse. "Exploring the Pathways Between Transformative Group Experiences and Identity Fusion." *Frontiers in Psychology* 11 (2020). https://doi.org/10.3389/fpsyg.2020.01172.

Kern, Andrea, and Henrike Moll. "On the Transformative Character of Collective Intentionality and the Uniqueness of the Human." *Philosophical Psychology* 30, no. 3 (2017): 319–37.

Kidder, Annemarie S. *Making Confession, Hearing Confession: A History of the Cure of Souls*. Collegeville, Minn.: Liturgical Press, 2010.

Kidwell, Mardi, and Don H. Zimmerman. "Joint Attention as Action." *Journal of Pragmatics* 39, no. 3 (2007): 592–611.

Kierkegaard, Søren. *Upbuilding Discourses in Various Spirits*. Edited and translated by Howard V. Hong and Edna H. Hong. Kierkegaard's Writings 15. Princeton, N.J.: Princeton University Press, 2009.

Kim, In Kyeong, and Elizabeth S. Spelke. "Infants' Sensitivity to Effects of Gravity on Visible Object Motion." *Journal of Experimental Psychology: Human Perception and Performance* 18, no. 2 (1992): 385–93.

King, Derek S. *The Church and the Problem of Divine Hiddenness: Mirrors of God*. Abingdon-on-Thames: Routledge, 2022.

Kisilevsky, Barbara S., Sylvia M. J. Hains, Kang Lee, et al. "Effects of Experience on Fetal Voice Recognition." *Psychological Science* 14, no. 3 (2003): 220–24.

Klein, Stanley B., and Shaun Nichols. "Memory and the Sense of Personal Identity." *Mind* 121, no. 483 (2012): 677–702.

Knoblich, Günther, Stephen Butterfill, and Natalie Sebanz. "Psychological Research on Joint Action: Theory and Data." In *The Psychology of Learning and Motivation*, vol. 54, edited by Brian H. Ross. San Diego: Elsevier Academic, 2011.

Köymen, Bahar, and Michael Tomasello. "The Early Ontogeny of Reason Giving." *Child Development Perspectives* 14, no. 4 (2020): 215–20.

Krupenye, Christopher, Fumihiro Kano, Satoshi Hirata, Josep Call, and Michael Tomasello. "Great Apes Anticipate that Other Individuals Will Act According to False Beliefs." *Science* 354, no. 6308 (2016): 110–14.

Laland, Kevin, and Amanda Seed. "Understanding Human Cognitive Uniqueness." *Annual Review of Psychology* 72 (2021): 689–716.

Laney, Cara, and Elizabeth F. Loftus. "Truth in Emotional Memories." In *Emotion and the Law: Psychological Perspectives*, edited by Brian H. Bornstein and Richard L. Wiener. New York: Springer, 2009.

Leavens, David A., Jo Sansone, Anna Burfield, Sian Lightfoot, Stefanie O'Hara, and Brenda K. Todd. "Putting the 'Joy' in Joint Attention: Affective-Gestural Synchrony by Parents Who Point for Their Babies." *Frontiers in Psychology* 5 (2014). https://doi.org/10.3389/fpsyg.2014.00879.

Legare, Cristine H., and Mark Nielsen. "Ritual Explained: Interdisciplinary Answers to Tinbergen's Four Questions." *Philosophical Transactions of the Royal Society B* 375, no. 1805 (2020). https://doi.org/10.1098/rstb.2019.0419.

León, Felipe, Thomas Szanto, and Dan Zahavi. "Emotional Sharing and the Extended Mind." *Synthese* 196, no. 12 (2019): 4847–67.

Lewis, David K. *Convention: A Philosophical Study*. Cambridge, Mass.: Harvard University Press, 1969.

Liden, Robert C., Sandy J. Wayne, Renata A. Jaworski, and Nathan Bennet. "Social Loafing: A Field Investigation." *Journal of Management* 30, no. 2 (2004): 285–304.

List, Christian, and Philip Pettit. *Group Agency: The Possibility, Design, and Status of Corporate Agents*. Oxford: Oxford University Press, 2011.

Liszkowski, Ulf, Malinda Carpenter, and Michael Tomasello. "Pointing Out New News, Old News, and Absent Referents at 12 Months of Age." *Developmental Science* 10, no. 2 (2007): F1–F7.

Liszkowski, Ulf, Marie Schäfer, Malinda Carpenter, and Michael Tomasello. "Prelinguistic Infants, but Not Chimpanzees, Communicate About Absent Entities." *Psychological Science* 20, no. 5 (2009): 654–60.

Loftus, Elizabeth F. *Eyewitness Testimony*. 2nd ed. Cambridge, Mass.: Harvard University Press, 1996.

Loftus, Elizabeth F. "Planting Misinformation in the Human Mind: A 30-Year Investigation of the Malleability of Memory." *Learning & Memory* 12, no. 4 (2005): 361–66.

Lokhorst, Anne Marike, Carol Werner, Henk Staats, Eric van Dijk, and Jeff L. Gale. "Commitment and Behavior Change: A Meta-Analysis and Critical Review of Commitment-Making Strategies in Environmental Research." *Environment and Behavior* 45, no. 1 (2013): 3–34.

Lucca, Kelsey, Arthur Capelier-Mourguy, Krista Byers-Heinlein, et al. "Infants' Social Evaluation of Helpers and Hinderers: A Large-Scale, Multi-Lab, Coordinated Replication Study." Preprint, *PsyArXiv*, June 28, 2021. http://doi.org/10.31234/osf.io/qhxkm.

Luhrmann, Tanya M. *When God Talks Back: Understanding the American Evangelical Relationship with God*. New York: Vintage, 2012.

Mahler, Margaret S., Fred Pine, and Anni Bergman. *The Psychological Birth of the Human Infant: Symbiosis and Individuation*. New York: Basic Books, 1975.

Mahr, Johannes B., and Gergely Csibra. "Why Do We Remember? The Communicative Function of Episodic Memory." *Behavioral and Brain Sciences* 41 (2018). https://doi.org/10.1017/S0140525X17000012.

Manthorpe, Jill, Steve Iliffe, Patricia Gillen, et al. "Clapping for Carers in the Covid-19 Crisis: Carers' Reflections in a UK Survey." *Health & Social Care in the Community* 30, no. 4 (2022): 1442–49.

ManyBabies Consortium. "Quantifying Sources of Variability in Infancy Research Using the Infant-Directed-Speech Preference." *Advances in Methods and Practices in Psychological Science* 3, no. 1 (2020): 24–52.

Marin, Kelly A., Jennifer G. Bohanek, and Robyn Fivush. "Positive Effects of Talking About the Negative: Family Narratives of Negative Experiences and Preadolescents' Perceived Competence." *Journal of Research on Adolescence* 18, no. 3 (2008): 573–93.

Marino, Lori, Richard C. Connor, R. Ewan Fordyce, et al. "Cetaceans Have Complex Brains for Complex Cognition." *PLoS Biology* 5, no. 5 (2007). https://doi.org/10.1371/journal.pbio.0050139.

Matthews, Gareth B. "Philosophy and the Young Child." *Metaphilosophy* 10, nos. 3–4 (1979): 354–68.

McAdams, Dan P. "The Psychology of Life Stories." *Review of General Psychology* 5, no. 2 (2001): 100–122.

McCullough, Michael E., Shelley D. Kilpatrick, Robert A. Emmons, and David B. Larson. "Is Gratitude a Moral Affect?" *Psychological Bulletin* 127, no. 2 (2001): 249–66.

McGrath, Alister E. "Response: Science and Religion—The State of the Art." *Zygon* 57, no. 1 (2022): 267–86.

McKnight, Scot. *It Takes a Church to Baptize: What the Bible Says about Infant Baptism*. Grand Rapids: Brazos, 2018.

McLean, Kate C., and Moin Syed. "Personal, Master, and Alternative Narratives: An Integrative Framework for Understanding Identity Development in Context." *Human Development* 58, no. 6 (2015): 318–49.

McNeill, William H. *Keeping Together in Time: Dance and Drill in Human History*. Cambridge, Mass.: Harvard University Press, 1997.

Meins, Elizabeth. *Security of Attachment and the Social Development of Cognition*. Sussex: Psychology Press, 1997.

Meltzoff, Andrew N. "Imitation and Other Minds: The 'Like Me' Hypothesis." In *Perspectives on Imitation: From Neuroscience to Social Science*, edited by Susan Hurley and Nick Chater, vol. 2. Cambridge, Mass.: MIT Press, 2005.

Meltzoff, Andrew N., Lynne Murray, Elizabeth Simpson, et al. "Re-Examination of Oostenbroek et al. (2016): Evidence for Neonatal Imitation of Tongue Protrusion." *Developmental Science* 21, no. 4 (2018). http://doi.org/10.1111/desc.12609.

Mercier, Hugo, and Dan Sperber. *The Enigma of Reason*. Cambridge, Mass.: Harvard University Press, 2017.

Mercier, Hugo, and Dan Sperber. "Why Do Humans Reason? Arguments for an Argumentative Theory." *Behavioral and Brain Sciences* 34, no. 2 (2011): 57–74.

Merck, Clinton, Meymune N. Topcu, and William Hirst. "Collective Mental Time Travel: Creating a Shared Future Through Our Shared Past." *Memory Studies* 9, no. 3 (2016): 284–94.

Michael, John, Natalie Sebanz, and Günther Knoblich. "Observing Joint Action: Coordination Creates Commitment." *Cognition* 157 (2016): 106–13.

Michaelian, Kourken. *Mental Time Travel: Episodic Memory and Our Knowledge of the Personal Past*. Cambridge, Mass.: MIT Press, 2016.

Michaelian, Kourken, and John Sutton. "Collective Mental Time Travel: Remembering the Past and Imagining the Future Together." *Synthese* 196, no. 12 (2019): 4933–60.

Milward, Sophie J., and Malinda Carpenter. "Joint Action and Joint Attention: Drawing Parallels Between the Literatures." *Social and Personality Psychology Compass* 12, no. 4 (2018). https://doi.org/10.1111/spc3.12377.

Mitchell, Margaret M. *Paul and the Rhetoric of Reconciliation: An Exegetical Investigation of the Language and Composition of 1 Corinthians.* Louisville: Westminster John Knox, 1993.

Moll, Henrike, and Andy Meltzoff. "Perspective Taking and Its Foundation in Joint Attention." In *Perception, Causation, and Objectivity: Issues in Philosophy and Psychology*, edited by Johannes Roessler, Hemdat Lerman, and Naomi Eilan. Oxford: Oxford University Press, 2011.

Moll, Henrike, Andrew N. Meltzoff, Katharina Merzsch, and Michael Tomasello. "Taking Versus Confronting Visual Perspectives in Preschool Children." *Developmental Psychology* 49, no. 4 (2013): 646–54.

Moll, Henrike, Ellyn Pueschel, Qianhui Ni, and Alexandra Little. "Sharing Experiences in Infancy: From Primary Intersubjectivity to Shared Intentionality." *Frontiers in Psychology* 12 (2021). https://doi.org/10.3389/fpsyg.2021.667679.

Moore, Chris, and John Barresi. "The Role of Second-Person Information in the Development of Social Understanding." *Frontiers in Psychology* 8 (2017). https://doi.org/10.3389/fpsyg.2017.01667.

Mundy, Peter, and Lisa Newell. "Attention, Joint Attention, and Social Cognition." *Current Directions in Psychological Science* 16, no. 5 (2007): 269–74.

Nagy, Emese, Karen Pilling, Victoria Blake, and Hajnalka Orvos. "Positive Evidence for Neonatal Imitation: A General Response, Adaptive Engagement." *Developmental Science* 23, no. 2 (2020). https://doi.org/10.1111/desc.12894.

Nelson, Katherine, and Robyn Fivush. "The Emergence of Autobiographical Memory: A Social Cultural Developmental Theory." *Psychological Review* 111, no. 2 (2004): 486–511.

Nielsen, Mark. "The Social Glue of Cumulative Culture and Ritual Behavior." *Child Development Perspectives* 12, no. 4 (2018): 264–68.

Nora, Pierre. "Between Memory and History: Les Lieux de Mémoire." *Representations* 26 (1989): 7–24.

Norton, Michael I., and Francesca Gino. "Rituals Alleviate Grieving for Loved Ones, Lovers, and Lotteries." *Journal of Experimental Psychology: General* 143, no. 1 (2014): 266–72.

O'Dowd, Ryan P. "Memory on the Boundary: Epistemology in Deuteronomy." In *The Bible and Epistemology: Biblical Soundings on the Knowledge of God*, edited by Mary Healy and Robin Parry. Milton Keynes: Paternoster, 2007.

O'Madagain, Cathal, and Michael Tomasello. "Joint Attention to Mental Content and the Social Origin of Reasoning." *Synthese* 198, no. 5 (2021): 4057–78.

Orwell, George. *1984*. New York: Signet Classics, 1981.

Over, Harriet, Adam Eggleston, and Richard Cook. "Ritual and the Origins of First Impressions." *Philosophical Transactions of the Royal Society B* 375, no. 1805 (2020). https://doi.org/10.1098/rstb.2019.0435.

Parker, Priya. *The Art of Gathering: How We Meet and Why It Matters*. London: Penguin, 2020.

Pawl, Faith G. "Minding Children in the Study of Liturgy." *TheoLogica* 4, no. 1 (2020): 6–29.

Pegg, Judith E., Janet F. Werker, and Peter J. McLeod. "Preference for Infant-Directed over Adult-Directed Speech: Evidence from 7-Week-Old Infants." *Infant Behavior and Development* 15, no. 3 (1992): 325–45.

Perkin, John. "How Quakers Worship." *Quakers in Britain*, accessed November 7, 2024. https://www.quaker.org.uk/about-quakers/our-faith/how-quakers-worship.

Perrin, Denis, and Kourken Michaelian. "Memory as Mental Time Travel." In *The Routledge Handbook of Philosophy of Memory*, edited by Sven Bernecker and Kourken Michaelian. Milton Keynes: Routledge, 2017.

Perry, John, and Joanna Leidenhag. "What Is Science-Engaged Theology?" *Modern Theology* 37, no. 2 (2021): 245–53.

Pessoa, Luiz. "On the Relationship Between Emotion and Cognition." *Nature Reviews Neuroscience* 9, no. 2 (2008): 148–58.

Piaget, Jean. *The Origins of Intelligence in Children*. Translated by Margaret Cook. London: W. W. Norton, 1952.

Racine, Timothy P., and Jeremy I. M. Carpendale. "The Role of Shared Practice in Joint Attention." *British Journal of Developmental Psychology* 25, no. 1 (2007): 3–25.

Ramstead, Maxwell J. D., Samuel P. L. Veissière, and Laurence J. Kirmayer. "Cultural Affordances: Scaffolding Local Worlds Through Shared Intentionality and Regimes of Attention." *Frontiers in Psychology* 7 (2016). https://doi.org/10.3389/fpsyg.2016.01090.

Reddy, Vasudevi. *How Infants Know Minds*. Cambridge, Mass.: Harvard University Press, 2008.

Reddy, Vasudevi, Gabriela Markova, and Sebastian Wallot. "Anticipatory Adjustments to Being Picked Up in Infancy." *PLOS ONE* 8, no. 6 (2013). https://doi.org/10.1371/journal.pone.0065289.

Reese, Elaine, and Kate Farrant. "Social Origins of Reminiscing." In *Autobiographical Memory and the Construction of a Narrative Self: Developmental and Cultural Perspectives*, edited by Robyn Fivush and Catherine A. Haden. Sussex: Psychology Press, 2003.

Reese, Elaine, Elizabeth Meins, Charles Fernyhough, and Luna Centifanti. "Origins of Mother-Child Reminiscing Style." *Development and Psychopathology* 31, no. 2 (2019): 631–42.

Reeves, Jim. "We Thank Thee." Track 1 on *We Thank Thee*. RCA Victor LSP-2552. Released 1962.

Reid, Vincent M., and Kirsty Dunn. "The Fetal Origins of Human Psychological Development." *Current Directions in Psychological Science* 30, no. 2 (2021): 144–50.

Reid, Vincent M., Kirsty Dunn, Robert J. Young, Johnson Amu, Tim Donovan, and Nadja Reissland. "The Human Fetus Preferentially Engages with Face-Like Visual Stimuli." *Current Biology* 27, no. 12 (2017): 1825–28. https://doi.org/10.1016/j.cub.2017.05.044.

Richardson, Michael J., Kerry L. Marsh, Robert W. Isenhower, Justin R. L. Goodman, and R. C. Schmidt. "Rocking Together: Dynamics of Intentional and Unintentional Interpersonal Coordination." *Human Movement Science* 26, no. 6 (2007): 867–91.

Risko, Evan F., and Alan Kingstone. "Eyes Wide Shut: Implied Social Presence, Eye Tracking and Attention." *Attention, Perception, & Psychophysics* 73 (2011): 291–96.

Rochat, Philippe, Jane G. Querido, and Tricia Striano. "Emerging Sensitivity to the Timing and Structure of Protoconversation in Early Infancy." *Developmental Psychology* 35, no. 4 (1999): 950–57.

Rogers, Todd, Katherine L. Milkman, and Kevin G. Volpp. "Commitment Devices: Using Initiatives to Change Behavior." *JAMA* 311, no. 20 (2014): 2065–66.

Rogoff, Barbara. *Apprenticeship in Thinking: Cognitive Development in Social Context*. Oxford: Oxford University Press, 1990.

Rogoff, Barbara, Jacqueline Baker-Sennett, Pilar Lacasa, and Denise Goldsmith. "Development Through Participation in Sociocultural Activity." *New Directions for Child and Adolescent Development* 67 (Spring 1995): 45–65.

Rosmarin, David H., Steven Pirutinsky, Adam B. Cohen, Yardana Galler, and Elizabeth J. Krumrei. "Grateful to God or Just Plain Grateful? A Comparison of Religious and General Gratitude." *Journal of Positive Psychology* 6, no. 5 (2011): 389–96.

Rossmanith, Nicole, and Vasudevi Reddy. "Structure and Openness in the Development of Self in Infancy." *Journal of Consciousness Studies* 23, no. 1–2 (2016): 237–57.

Russell, James A., and Lisa Feldman Barrett. "Core Affect, Prototypical Emotional Episodes, and Other Things Called Emotion: Dissecting the Elephant." *Journal of Personality and Social Psychology* 76, no. 5 (1999): 805–19.

Sacks, Yonason. "The Mitzvah of Sippur Yetzias Mitzrayim," *Pesach To-Go*, Nissan 5770 (March 2010). Archived June 30, 2020. https://web.archive.org/web/20220630143642/https://www.yutorah.org/togo/pesach/articles/Pesach_To-Go_-_5770_Rabbi_Sacks.pdf.

Salmon, Karen, and Elaine Reese. "Talking (Or Not Talking) About the Past: The Influence of Parent-Child Conversation About Negative Experiences on Children's Memories." *Applied Cognitive Psychology* 29, no. 6 (2015): 791–801.

Salter, Gideon, and Richard Breheny. "Removing Shared Information Improves 3- and 4-Year-Olds' Performance on a Change-of-Location Explicit False Belief Task." *Journal of Experimental Child Psychology* 187 (2019). https://doi.org/10.1016/j.jecp.2019.104665.

Scaife, M., and J. S. Bruner. "The Capacity for Joint Visual Attention in the Infant." *Nature* 253, no. 5489 (1975): 265–66.

Schacter, Daniel L. "The Seven Sins of Memory: Insights from Psychology and Cognitive Neuroscience." *American Psychologist* 54, no. 3 (1999): 182–203.

Schacter, Daniel L., and Donna Rose Addis. "The Cognitive Neuroscience of Constructive Memory: Remembering the Past and Imagining the Future." *Philosophical Transactions of the Royal Society B: Biological Sciences* 362, no. 1481 (2007): 773–86.

Schacter, Daniel L., Donna Rose Addis, Demis Hassabis, Victoria C. Martin, R. Nathan Spreng, and Karl K. Szpunar. "The Future of Memory: Remembering, Imagining, and the Brain." *Neuron* 76, no. 4 (2012): 677–94.

Schacter, Daniel L., and Kevin P. Madore. "Remembering the Past and Imagining the Future: Identifying and Enhancing the Contribution of Episodic Memory." *Memory Studies* 9, no. 3 (2016): 245–55.

Schilbach, Leonhard, Bert Timmermans, Vasudevi Reddy, et al. "Toward a Second-Person Neuroscience." *Behavioral and Brain Sciences* 36, no. 4 (2013): 393–414.

Schmeichel, Brandon J., and David Tang. "Individual Differences in Executive Functioning and Their Relationship to Emotional Processes and Responses." *Current Directions in Psychological Science* 24, no. 2 (2015): 93–98.

Schmidt, Richard C., and Michael J. Richardson. "Dynamics of Interpersonal Coordination." In *Coordination: Neural, Behavioral and*

Social Dynamics, edited by Armin Fuchs and Victor K. Jirsa. Berlin: Springer, 2008.

Searle, John R. "Collective Intentions and Actions." In *Consciousness and Language*, edited by John R. Searle. Cambridge: Cambridge University Press, 2002.

Searle, John R. *Making the Social World: The Structure of Human Civilization*. Oxford: Oxford University Press, 2010.

Sebanz, Natalie, Harold Bekkering, and Günther Knoblich. "Joint Action: Bodies and Minds Moving Together." *Trends in Cognitive Sciences* 10, no. 2 (2006): 70–76.

Sebanz, Natalie, Günther Knoblich, and W. Prinz, "Representing Others' Actions: Just Like One's Own?" *Cognition* 88, no. 3 (2003): B11–B21.

Seemann, Axel, ed. *Joint Attention: New Developments in Psychology, Philosophy of Mind, and Social Neuroscience*. Cambridge, Mass.: MIT Press, 2011.

Seemann, Axel. "Joint Attention: Toward a Relational Account," In *Joint Attention: New Developments in Psychology, Philosophy of Mind, and Social Neuroscience*, edited by Axel Seeman. Cambridge, Mass.: MIT Press, 2011.

Seemann, Axel. "Reminiscing Together: Joint Experiences, Epistemic Groups, and Sense of Self." *Synthese* 196, no. 12 (2019): 4813–28.

Seglenieks, Chris. *Johannine Belief and Graeco-Roman Devotion: Reshaping Devotion for John's Graeco-Roman Audience*. WUNT 2/528. Tübingen: Mohr Siebeck, 2020.

Shin, Yoo. *Pentecostalism, Postmodernism, and Reformed Epistemology: James K. A. Smith and the Contours of a Postmodern Christian Epistemology*. Lanham, Md.: Lexington / Fortress Academic, 2021.

Shteynberg, Garriy. "A Collective Perspective: Shared Attention and the Mind." *Current Opinion in Psychology* 23 (October 2018): 93–97.

Shteynberg, Garriy. "Shared Attention." *Perspectives on Psychological Science* 10, no. 5 (2015): 579–90.

Shteynberg, Garriy, and Adam D. Galinsky. "Implicit Coordination: Sharing Goals with Similar Others Intensifies Goal Pursuit." *Journal of Experimental Social Psychology* 47, no. 6 (2011): 1291–94.

Shteynberg, Garriy, Jacob B. Hirsh, Evan P. Apfelbaum, Jeff T. Larsen, Adam D. Galinsky, and Neal J. Roese. "Feeling More Together: Group Attention Intensifies Emotion." *Emotion* 14, no. 6 (2014): 1102–14.

Shteynberg, Garriy, Jacob B. Hirsh, R. Alexander Bentley, and Jon Garthoff. "Shared Worlds and Shared Minds: A Theory of Collective Learning and a Psychology of Common Knowledge." *Psychological Review* 127, no. 5 (2020): 918–31.

Siposova, Barbara, and Malinda Carpenter. "A New Look at Joint Attention and Common Knowledge." *Cognition* 189 (2019): 260–74.

Siposova, Barbara, Michael Tomasello, and Malinda Carpenter. "Communicative Eye Contact Signals a Commitment to Cooperate for Young Children." *Cognition* 179 (2018): 192–201.

Smith, James K. A. *Desiring the Kingdom: Worship, Worldview, and Cultural Formation*. Vol. 1 of *Cultural Liturgies*. Grand Rapids: Baker Academic, 2009.

Smith, James K. A. Review of *Ritualized Faith: Essays on the Philosophy of Liturgy* by Terence Cuneo. *Scottish Journal of Theology* 71, no. 1 (2018): 118–19. https://doi.org/10.1017/S0036930617000126.

Sorce, James F., Robert N. Emde, Joseph J. Campos, and Mary D. Klinnert. "Maternal Emotional Signaling: Its Effect on the Visual Cliff Behavior of 1-Year-Olds." *Developmental Psychology* 21, no. 1 (1985): 195–200.

Spagnola, Mary, and Barbara H. Fiese. "Family Routines and Rituals: A Context for Development in the Lives ofYoung Children." *Infants & Young Children* 20, no. 4 (2007): 284–99.

Sperber, Dan, and Dierdre Wilson. *Relevance: Communication and Cognition*. 2nd ed. Malden, Mass.: Blackwell, 1995.

Spiegel, Gabrielle M. "Memory and History: Liturgical Time and Historical Time." *History and Theory* 41, no. 2 (2002): 149–62.

Spilka, Bernard, and Kevin L. Ladd. *The Psychology of Prayer: A Scientific Approach*. New York: Guilford, 2012.

Stanley, Jason. *Know How*. Oxford: Oxford University Press, 2011.

Strawn, Brad D., and Warren S. Brown. *Enhancing Christian Life: How Extended Cognition Augments Religious Community*. Lisle, Ill.: InterVarsity, 2020.

Stump, Eleonore. "Omnipresence, Indwelling, and the Second-Personal." *European Journal for Philosophy of Religion* 5, no. 4 (2013): 29–53.

Stump, Eleonore. "Petitionary Prayer." *American Philosophical Quarterly* 16, no. 2 (1979): 81–91.

Suddendorf, Thomas, Donna Rose Addis, and Michael C. Corballis. "Mental Time Travel and the Shaping of the Human Mind." *Philosophical Transactions of the Royal Society B: Biological Sciences* 364, no. 1521 (2009): 1317–24.

Suddendorf, Thomas, and Janie Busby. "Mental Time Travel in Animals?" *Trends in Cognitive Sciences* 7, no. 9 (2003): 391–96.

Suddendorf, Thomas, and Michael C. Corballis. "The Evolution of Foresight: What Is Mental Time Travel, and Is It Unique to Humans?" *Behavioral and Brain Sciences* 30, no. 3 (2007): 299–313.

Susman, Michael. "Zechira and Sippur." *Online Torah*, March 22, 2017. https://en.harova.org/online_torah_books/zechira-and-sippur/.

Szpunar, Karl K. "Episodic Future Thought: An Emerging Concept." *Perspectives on Psychological Science* 5, no. 2 (2010): 142–62.

Szpunar, Karl K., and Kathleen B. McDermott. "Episodic Future Thought and Its Relation to Remembering: Evidence from Ratings of Subjective Experience." *Consciousness and Cognition* 17, no. 1 (2008): 330–34.

Szpunar, Piotr M., and Karl K. Szpunar. "Collective Future Thought: Concept, Function, and Implications for Collective Memory Studies." *Memory Studies* 9, no. 4 (2016): 376–89.

Taylor, Charles. *Human Agency and Language*. Vol. 1. Cambridge: Cambridge University Press, 1985.

Taylor, W. David O. *A Body of Praise: Understanding the Role of Our Physical Bodies in Worship*. Grand Rapids: Baker, 2023.

Thompson, Deanna A. *The Virtual Body of Christ in a Suffering World*. Nashville: Abingdon, 2016.

Todorov, Tzvetan. "The Abuses of Memory." *Common Knowledge* 5 (1996): 6–26.

Tollefsen, Deborah Perron. *Groups as Agents*. Hoboken, N.J.: John Wiley & Sons, 2015.

Tollefsen, Deborah, Rick Dale, and Alexandra Paxton. "Alignment, Transactive Memory, and Collective Cognitive Systems." *Review of Philosophy and Psychology* 4, no. 1 (2013): 49–64.

Tomasello, Michael. *Becoming Human: A Theory of Ontogeny*. Cambridge, Mass.: Harvard University Press, 2019.

Tomasello, Michael. *The Cultural Origins of Human Cognition*. Cambridge, Mass.: Harvard University Press, 1999.

Tomasello, Michael, "Joint Attention as Social Cognition." In *Joint Attention: Its Origins and Role in Development*, edited by Chris Moore, Philip J. Dunham, and Phil Dunham. Sussex: Psychology Press, 1995.

Tomasello, Michael. "The Moral Psychology of Obligation." *Behavioral and Brain Sciences* 43 (2020). http://doi.org/10.1017/S0140525X19001742.

Tomasello, Michael. *A Natural History of Human Thinking*. Cambridge, Mass.: Harvard University Press, 2014.

Tomasello, Michael, Malinda Carpenter, Josep Call, Tanya Behne, and Henrike Moll. "Understanding and Sharing Intentions: The Origins of Cultural Cognition." *Behavioral and Brain Sciences* 28, no. 5 (2005): 675–735.

Torrance, James B. *Worship, Community, and the Triune God of Grace*. Milton Keynes: Paternoster, 1996.

Tracy, Jessica L., and Daniel Randles. "Four Models of Basic Emotions: A Review of Ekman and Cordaro, Izard, Levenson, and Panksepp and Watt." *Emotion Review* 3, no. 4 (2011): 397–405.

Trevarthen, Colwyn, and Kenneth J. Aitken. "Infant Intersubjectivity: Research, Theory, and Clinical Applications." *Journal of Child Psychology and Psychiatry* 42, no. 1 (2001): 3–48.

Tribble, Evelyn B., and Nicholas Keene. *Cognitive Ecologies and the History of Remembering: Religion, Education and Memory in Early Modern England*. New York: Palgrave Macmillan, 2011.

Tronick, Edward, Heidelise Als, Lauren Adamson, Susan Wise, and T. Berry Brazelton. "The Infant's Response to Entrapment Between Contradictory Messages in Face-to-Face Interaction." *Journal of the American Academy of Child Psychiatry* 17, no. 1 (1978): 1–13.

Tsang, Jo-Ann. "(Un)Special Favors: Gratitude for Group-Based Benefits." *Journal of Positive Psychology* 16, no. 1 (2021): 27–37.

Tulving, Endel. "Episodic and Semantic Memory." In *Organization of Memory*, edited by Endel Tulving and Wayne Donaldson. New York: Academic Press, 1972.

Tulving, Endel. "Episodic Memory: From Mind to Brain." *Annual Review of Psychology* 53 (2002): 1–25.

Tuomela, Raimo. *Social Ontology: Collective Intentionality and Group Agents*. Oxford: Oxford University Press, 2013.

Ulanov, Ann Belford, and Barry Ulanov. *Primary Speech: A Psychology of Prayer*. Louisville, Ky.: Westminster John Knox, 1982.

Underhill, Evelyn. *Worship*. London: Mayflower, 1936.

United Nations Children's Fund. *Early Moments Matter for Every Child*. UNICEF, September 2017. https://www.unicef.org/reports/early-moments-matter-every-child.

Užgiris, Ina C. "Two Functions of Imitation During Infancy." *International Journal of Behavioral Development* 4, no. 1 (1981): 1–12.

Varela, Francisco J., Evan Thompson, and Eleanor Rosch. *The Embodied Mind: Cognitive Science and Human Experience*. Rev. ed. Cambridge, Mass.: MIT Press, 2017.

Vasil, Jared, and Michael Tomasello. "Effects of 'We'-Framing on Young Children's Commitment, Sharing, and Helping." *Journal of Experimental Child Psychology* 214 (2022). https://doi.org/10.1016/j.jecp.2021.105278.

Veissière, Samuel P., Axel Constant, Maxwell J. D. Ramstead, Karl J. Friston, and Laurence J. Kirmayer. "Thinking Through Other Minds: A Variational Approach to Cognition and Culture." *Behavioral and Brain Sciences* 43 (2020). https://doi.org/10.1017/S0140525X19001213.

Venezia, Meaghan, Daniel S. Messinger, Danielle Thorp, and Peter Mundy. "The Development of Anticipatory Smiling." *Infancy* 6, no. 3 (2004): 397–406.

Volf, Miroslav. *After Our Likeness: The Church as the Image of the Trinity*. Grand Rapids: Eerdmans, 1998.

Volf, Miroslav. *The End of Memory: Remembering Rightly in a Violent World*. Grand Rapids: Eerdmans, 2006.

Vygotsky, Lev S. *Mind in Society: The Development of Higher Psychological Processes*. Edited by Michael Cole, Vera John-Steiner, Sylvia Scribner, and Ellen Souberman. Cambridge, Mass.: Harvard University Press, 1978.

Walton, Gregory M., Geoffrey L. Cohen, David Cwir, and Steven J. Spencer. "Mere Belonging: The Power of Social Connections." *Journal of Personality and Social Psychology* 102, no. 3 (2012): 513–32.

Waters, Theodore E. A., and Robyn Fivush. "Relations Between Narrative Coherence, Identity, and Psychological Well-Being in Emerging Adulthood." *Journal of Personality* 83, no. 4 (2015): 441–51.

Watkins, Philip C. "Gratitude and Subjective Well-Being." In *The Psychology of Gratitude*, edited by Robert A. Emmons and Michael E. McCullough. Oxford: Oxford University Press, 2004.

Watson-Jones, Rachel E., and Christine H. Legare. "The Social Functions of Group Rituals." *Current Directions in Psychological Science* 25, no.1 (2016): 42–46.

Watts, Fraser. *Psychology, Religion, and Spirituality: Concepts and Applications*. Cambridge: Cambridge University Press, 2017.

Weil, Louis. *A Theology of Worship*. The New Church's Teaching Series 12. Lanham, Md.: Cowley, 2001.

Wen, Nicole J., Aiyana K. Willard, Michaela Caughy, and Cristine H. Legare. "Watch Me, Watch You: Ritual Participation Increases In-Group Displays and Out-Group Monitoring in Children." *Philosophical Transactions of the Royal Society B* 375, no.1805 (2020). https://doi.org/10.1098/rstb.2019.0437.

Werner, Heinz, and Bernard Kaplan. *Symbol Formation: An Organismic-Developmental Approach to Language and Expression of Thought*. New York: Wiley, 1963.

Whitehouse, Harvey, and Jonathan A. Lanman. "The Ties That Bind Us: Ritual, Fusion, and Identification." *Current Anthropology* 55, no. 6 (2014): 674–95.

Whiten, Andrew, Victoria Horner, and Frans B. M. de Waal. "Conformity to Cultural Norms of Tool Use in Chimpanzees." *Nature* 437, no. 7059 (2005): 737–40.

Wimmer, Heinz, and Josef Perner. "Beliefs About Beliefs: Representation and Constraining Function of Wrong Beliefs in Young Children's Understanding of Deception." *Cognition* 13, no. 1 (1983): 103–28.

Witvliet, John D. "The Mysterious Mingling of Divine and Human Agency in Liturgical Participation." In *What Is Jesus Doing? God's Activity in the Life and Work of the Church*, edited by Edwin Chr. van Driel. Downers Grove, Ill.: InterVarsity, 2020.

Wolterstorff, Nicholas. *Acting Liturgically: Philosophical Reflections on Religious Practice*. Oxford: Oxford University Press, 2018.

Wolterstorff, Nicholas. *The God We Worship: An Exploration of Liturgical Theology*. Grand Rapids: Eerdmans, 2015.

Wolterstorff, Nicholas. "Knowing God Liturgically." *Journal of Analytic Theology* 4 (2016): 1–16.

Woo, Brandon M., Enda Tan, and J. Kiley Hamlin. "Human Morality Is Based on an Early-Emerging Moral Core." *Annual Review of Developmental Psychology* 4 (2022): 41–61.

Woodworth, Robert S. "Individual and Group Behaviour." *American Journal of Sociology* 44, no. 6 (1939): 823–28.

World Health Organization. "COVID-19 Pandemic Triggers 25% Increase in Prevalence of Anxiety and Depression Worldwide." March 2, 2022. https://www.who.int/news/item/02-03-2022-covid-19-pandemic-triggers-25-increase-in-prevalence-of-anxiety-and-depression-worldwide.

Worthington, Everett L., Jr. *Forgiveness and Reconciliation: Theory and Application*. London: Routledge, 2013.

Wright, N. T. *The Day the Revolution Began*. London: SPCK, 2016.

Wright, N. T. *Paul and the Faithfulness of God*. Minneapolis: Fortress, 2013.

Wright, W. S. T. "Confession in the Church of England." *Theology* 37, no. 220 (1938): 212–19.

Yerushalmi, Yosef Hayim. *Zakhor: Jewish History and Jewish Memory*. Seattle: University of Washington Press, 1989.

Zahavi, Dan. "You, Me, and We: The Sharing of Emotional Experiences." *Journal of Consciousness Studies* 22, no. 1–2 (2015): 84–101.

Zahavi, Dan, and Philippe Rochat. "Empathy ≠ Sharing: Perspectives from Phenomenology and Developmental Psychology." *Consciousness and Cognition* 36 (2015): 543–53.

Zahavi, Dan, and Glenda Satne. "Varieties of Shared Intentionality: Tomasello and Classical Phenomenology." In *Beyond the Analytic-Continental Divide: Pluralist Philosophy in the Twenty-First Century*, edited by Jeffrey A. Bell, Andrew Cutrofello, and Paul M. Livingston. London: Routledge, 2016.

Zahl, Simeon. "Beyond the Critique of Soteriological Individualism: Relationality and Social Cognition." *Modern Theology* 37, no. 2 (2021): 336–61.

INDEX

www.ingramcontent.com/pod-product-compliance
Lightning Source LLC
Chambersburg PA
CBHW022156050725
29021CB00002B/5